RAFI AHMAD KIDWAI

The True Nationalist

Indian Freedom Fighters Series-42

Rafi Ahmad Kidwai

The True Nationalist

S.R. BAKSHI

Anmol Publications

New Delhi (India)

ANMOL PUBLICATIONS
4378/4B, Ansari Road
Daryaganj, New Delhi-110 002

Rafi Ahmad Kidwai : The True Nationalist

ISBN 81-7041-606-X

PRINTED IN INDIA

Published by J.L. Kumar for Anmol Publications, New Delhi
and Printed at Renu Printers, Maujpur, Delhi-53.

Preface

Rafi Ahmad Kidwai's role in our freedom struggle is most significant. At a fairly young age, he came into contact with the Nehru family and Mahatma Gandhi. He was a fine organiser and superb administrator. He gained popularity among the masses on account of his social behaviour. Indeed he always aspired to help the poor and the needy. As a Congress leader in U.P. and Food and Agriculture Minister in the central cabinet, his contribution was most significant.

The chapters deal with his early career, his political ideology, his role in the freedom movement and the rich legacy he left for the people of our sub-continent. I have also given a glossary and the bibliography at the end of the Chapters.

I have consulted the material in the Nehru Memorial Museum and Library, Sapru House Library and Indian Council of Historical Research Library, New Delhi. I feel beholden to the authorities of these institutions for helping me during my researches.

S.R. Bakshi

Contents

1

Early Career

Rafi Ahmad Kidwai was born on 18 February 1894 in a small village, Masauli, in the district of Barabanki of U.P. His father, Imtiaz Ali, was manager of the Court of Wards and enjoyed the reputation of being efficient and honest official in his department. Rafi passed his High School examination in 1913 from the Government High School of Barabanki and went for undergraduate Courses to the M.A.O. College at Aligarh. During his college days, he showed been interest in games. He showed much interest in the writings of Tolstoy, Scott, Dostoievsky and Dickens. He graduated in 1919 and two years later when he was to appear for the Bachelor of Laws examination, he left the college and joined the Gandhian movement. His father was unhappy about Rafi's decision. As a result of his political activities, Rafi Ahmad was arrested at Barabanki and sentenced to ten months' hard labour. His brother, Shafig Ahmad, got one year.

Rafi Ahmad was married in 1918 when he was an undergraduate student. His wife came from a neighbouring village. She lived in purdah. She gave birth to a son who died at the age of seven. The son's death was a great shock to her and Rafi Ahmad. Begum Rafi Ahmed spent most of her time counting beads, saying prayers, fasting and reciting the Quran.

When Rafi Ahmad was released, he visited Anand Bhavan

to seek the blessings of Pandit Motilal Nehru. At this point of time, Jawaharlal Nehru, Jayaprakash Narayan, Rammanohar Lohia, Dr. Ashraf and a few others had emerged as leaders of the youths in our sub-continent. Motilal Nehru was impressed by the sincerity of Rafi Ahmad and since that day, Anand Bhawan became a second home to Rafi Ahmad, and he became very active member of the Indian National Congress. His patriotic fervour soon made him a popular worker among the economically weaker sections of our society.

In politics, the two Nehrus, father and son, differed widely. Motilal was a giant among intellectuals and created a record as a lawyer at the Allahabad High Court Bar. His knowledge of law and constitution had destined him for parliamentary life. He was aristocratic and lived luxuriously. Motilal was fond of good food and good life. Some of his colleagues believed that he did not overcome his love for liquor till the end.

Motilal was a friend and admirer of Gandhiji, but he did not believe in a life of austerity and simplicity. He would wear spotless khadi clothes but spinning was a ritual and not an article of faith with him. Gandhiji's threefold constructive programme of khadi, Hindu-Muslim unity and prohibition, would leave him cold, and before Gandhiji came out of the Yarvada jail, Motilal had started organising the Swaraj Party to fight freedom's battle inside the legislature. In 1928, Motilal produced a monumental report demanding Dominion Status, all Dominions being "autonomous communities within the British Empire, equal in status, in no way subordinate one to another in any aspect of their domestic or external affairs, though united by a common allegiance to the Crown, and freely associated as members of the British Commonwealth of Nations." Motilal played a colourful role in the Central Legislative Assembly as the leader of the Swaraj Party till he resigned in 1930 in response to the boycott resolution of the Lahore Congress.

Jawaharlal was a radical socialist with leanings towards Marxism. He believed in mass action. Jawaharlal was deeply impressed by Gandhiji; for some time he gave up meat diet and lived on vegetarian food. He was well versed in Marxist doctrines and the history of the Russian Revolution. Between the social structures of Russia and India there were remarkable similarities—preponderance of agriculture, an oppressed and discontented peasantry, a small industrial proletariat and an urge for liberation. Gandhiji's constructive programme fell short of Jawaharlal's revolutionary ideas. While his faithful adherents—Rajagopalachari, Vallabhbhai and Rajendra Prasad—were busy sustaining Gandhiji's politics through constructive activities and Motilal was organising the Swaraj Party, Jawaharlal went on a pilgrimage to Moscow where he seems to have discovered the panacea for India's ills. He returned in a mood of ecstacy and wrote applauding the Soviet system.

Jawaharlal's faith in non-violence was never complete like Gandhiji's. With the slackening tempo of political activities in the mid twenties his faith was further diluted. Peasants as a rule lack in solidarity and if they have to fight a revolution, they would need a hard core of militant workers. In Russia, the core was provided by terrorists and trained cadres of Bolsheviks. Congressmen of the Gandhian school were not the men for it and Jawaharlal, with the support of Rafi Ahmad, began to build a militant cadre. Reports reached Gandhiji who felt that Jawaharalal was going too fast, and wrote: "Your plunging into the 'Republican Army' was a hasty step. But I do not mind these acts of yours so much, as I mind your encouraging mischief-makers and hooligans. I do not know whether you still believe in an un-adulterated non-violence. But even if you have altered your views, you could not think that unlicensed and unbridled violence is going to deliver the country." Gandhiji's admonition acted as a damper on Nehru.

Like the two Nehrus, Rafi Ahmad had no attraction for Gandhiji's constructive programme. He had full faith in Motilal and Jawaharlal. He joined the Swaraj Party and campaigned for it in the 1923 General Elections. In 1926 he stood on the Swarajist ticket from the Lucknow-Faizabad. Divisions Mohammedan Rural Constituency and won. He was sworn-in and became the Chief Whip of the Swaraj Party. Rafi did good lobbying; but as a debator he made no mark in the Assembly. He asked just a few questions and did no more.

Rafi entered into a lasting partnership with Jawaharlal. He became complementary to him. Jawaharlal was superb at thinking, Rafi excelled in action. Jawaharlal would plan and Rafi would act. The two worked among the peasantry in Allahabad and the neighbouring districts—Partapgarh, Rae Bareli, Sultanpur, Fatehpur—to prepare for revolutionary action. The peasants became militant. When the great depression of the thirties came, they were unable to meet the landowners' demand. The landowners oppressed them and beat and ejected them. All through Jawaharlal and Rafi Ahmad espoused their cause and finally plunged the country into a major struggle.'

Rafi Ahmad Kidwai had a simple life. His dress consisted of a loose-fitting *achkan* and white *pyjama*. He could never be caught bareheaded. He would don a white khadi cap in summer and a fur cap in winter and remove it only late in the night when retiring. His was the smallest family : husband and wife. His house was open to numerous friends, brothers, cousins, nephews, nieces and their children. He was a man of few words. He wrote sparingly. He seldom wrote letters to friends or relatives. He would deal many problems on telephone. He worked silently and did not believe in gaining publicity for his socio-economic and political work. He was a warm-hearted person who even supported his opponents in several ways. He helped widows and other people who came to him for financial support.

Rafi Ahmad did not believe in amassing wealth rather he distributed it among the poor and the needy. It is said that several persons took advantage of his magnaninity and approached him for financial assistance. When Rafi Ahmad died he left no financial assets behind, rather he was to owe about one lakh of rupees to his friends. His honesty and sincerity earned much fame for him.

Rafi loved to spring surprises on his colleagues. Once he took out from his pocket two currency notes bearing the same number and quickly thrust them into the hands of the then Finance Minister, John Matthai. They were forged. On another occasion, when the import of costly watches was banned, he presented a gold watch to John Matthai, adding that it was smuggled. He had a passion for teasing Kailash Nath Katju and never lost an opportunity to play a joke on him.

Once it happened that a young man, who was staying as a guest with Rafi, stole his fountain-pen. Rafi was clever enough to spot the thief, but instead of questioning him, before retiring on the following night, he left his wrist watch on the table in the office room which had a communicating door with the young man's bedroom. Another person might have used the device as a trap to catch the culprit, but that was not Rafi's way. How could the young man forego the temptation? He pocketed the watch and walked out of Rafi's room before the glare of the sunrise could expose him. Rafi's personal assistant called the police and reported the theft.

Rafi was then the Minister of Police in U.P., and what could be a greater disgrace for the police than that this theft should go untraced? They caught the young man while he was selling the watch. The case was put up for trial before a magistrate and the charge was proved. As the magistrate was about to pronounce the sentence, he was handed a letter in Rafi's own hand-writing, saying that he had made a present of the watch to the accused. The police were fooled and humiliated, but what could they do? I was told later that the young man did not benefit from Rafi's generosity, but persisted in his evil ways. He collected money in Rafi's name and misused it.

Jawaharlal has related an interesting story of how Rafi once corrected the censor. In the early thirties Congressmen's correspondence was heavily censored. Jawaharlal and others felt greatly annoyed at this. The censor was impersonal, unseen and unknown, insulated against attacks or criticism. Rafi was also greatly irritated because delays in the delivery of letters upset his engagements. All over the world censorship is unpleasant : in India it was hateful. The Indian censor was clumsy. On the letter he would leave signs which told one that an unwanted eye had probed through personal secrets and love matters. On many an occasion letters were delayed or lost. Refi wanted to tell the censor to do his job a little more efficiently, but to whom was he to write ? The censor was probably some C.I.D. officer whose existence and work were never acknowledged openly. Rafi solved the difficulty. He addressed a letter to himself knowing that it would pass through the hands of the censor. The censor took note of the contents, and there was some improvement. It was an ingenious device.

Rafi was open and accessible to everybody—known and unknown—but once he made up his mind to avoid a person, he could do it most ingeniously. One of his colleagues—a lady member of Parliament—was far too insistent on a private talk with him. Rafi wanted to avoid her. She kept watch and one day learnt that Rafi was going alone in a car to Ambala the following day before dawn. The lady arrived at Rafi's residence well before time and felt confident that she had beaten Rafi Ahmad. Rafi was too much of a gentleman to be overtly rude. He kept her engaged over a cup of tea and delayed the departure. Meanwhile, Algurai Shastri had been asked on the telephone to come. When the lady opened the door and stepped into the car, inside she found Algurai Shastri, who had the reputation of being the drum-beater of the Congress. If anyone told him a secret, before the cock crowed next, the story would be the common property of the town.

Rafi Ahmad was one of the founder-directors of the *National Herald*, the prominent Congress daily of Lucknow. For sometime it became difficult to run the paper on account of financial difficulties. Even its founders began to leave the management. But Rafi Ahmad saw to it that finances should be supplied to the newspaper for its smooth functioning.

He indeed was very considerate with his subordinates who functioned under him in any capacity. He always showed sympathy for them and endeavoured to support them in every possible way. On account of his excellent behaviour, he was loved and respected by one and all.

In domestic environments he lived a simple life. Indeed he was a true Gandhian who followed the Mahatma throughout the long-drawn political struggle in our sub-continent. Whenever there was a call for sacrifice, Kidwai offered his services spontaneously.

Rafi was obliging and generous in the extreme. Whenever he did anything for somebody, he took good care to avoid leaving behind the feeling that he had done a favour. A person unknown to Rafi Ahmad had built a new house in Muzaffarnagar and wanted electric connection of his old house to be shifted to the new one. The old connection was snapped quickly enough but the new one did not arrive. New connections those days were banned on account of the shortage of power. When all his efforts had failed, the owner approached a local Congressman, who dropped a postcard to Rafi Ahmad, the Communications Minister at Delhi. Next day a telegram arrived inviting both the owner and the writer to come to Delhi. When the Congressman apologised to Rafi Ahmad for bothering him with such a trivial matter, Rafi replied, "On my part I am thinking what a shame it is that you have had to come all the way for such a trifle."

A down and out Brahmin boy, who had been disowned by his father, buttonholed Rafi Ahmad outside the Council Chamber, when he was the Home Minister of U.P. The boy had been jailed for wire-cutting in the Quit India Movement of 1942, but he was now completely forgotten and forsaken, with no one to help him. He wanted an appointment as a constable, but Rafi secured him a Sub-Inspector's *jhabba.*

Rafi was one of the founder-directors of the *National Herald*, the Congress daily of Lucknow. Newspapers are exhaustingly expensive when they are run to further political ideals and not commercially. One after another its founders dropped out, but to the end of his life, Rafi stuck to the *National Herald*, showing no signs of declining interest. He continued to supply the finances.

The story of the appointment of the *National Herald's* first editor is related by Rama Rao himself. "Are you sure you can edit a daily newspaper?" asked Rafi of Rama Rao. "About the only thing I know is to produce a newspaper. I am afraid I know nothing else," replied Rama Rao. Rafi could feel that Rama Rao had half resented the question. "If that is so, you may join any day you can," said Rafi. Rama Rao became the editor and boss of the paper. Rafi had the habit of sizing up the man, and once satisfied he would leave everything to him.

Rufus Francis Mudie, an able civilian, who rose to high political offices in Delhi in pre-Independence India, and after Partition became Governor of West Punjab in Pakistan had come in close contact with Rafi Ahmad Kidwai as his departmental secretary for Revenue in the first Congress Ministry of U.P. After the Congress had gone out of office, D.P. Mukherjee, a professor of Lucknow University, whose services had been temporarily borrowed by the Information Department, happened to meet Francis Mudie. "Who is the most intelligent politician of our times?" asked Mudie. Mukherjee named Lloyd George, Clemenceau and a few others. "No, come nearer home," suggested Mudie. Mukherjee mentioned Gandhi, Jinnah, and others. "No, come nearer still," insisted Mudie and added, "He is close by—Rafi. He is a great politician, the greatest I know." Those who have known Mudie will realize what those words mean.

Rafi was one of the most selfless persons I have come across. He had no love for money or worldly belongings. He had something of Robin Hood in him—fleece the rich and feed the poor. His methods were, however, gentle and persuasive. He had a large circle of admirers from whom he would collect huge sums of money. What he collected was immediately passed on to others. His funds would flow out faster than they came in. When he died, he left debts amounting to well over a lakh of rupees and a dilapidated ancestral house, gone into disrepair from continuous want of maintenance. Rafi believed that money was always white, never black. It could never be tainted. If used to good purpose, badly earned money became good.

Rafi's bedroom was something of a museum, full of all kinds of trinkets and wares, an assortment of watches, fountain-pens, shawls, cigar and cigarette cases, lighters, electrical goods, which friends returning from tours abroad would bring him as presents. He had no personal use for most of there and would distribute them freely among friends.

Rafi was never known to have disappointed political workers, widows, and sickly and indigent persons. If he had no ready money, he would instantly borrow from a friend or acquaintance or overdraw on his-bank account. For him, there was no distinction between a friend or a foe in distress. In the far distant villages of Bengal and South India, I have heard stories of how Rafi's generosity came to save the life of a few fathers about to commit suicide, because they had no money to pay the dowry for the marriage of their grown-up daughters. Rafi has been dead for nearly a decade, but his memory is more fresh in the minds of people than of others equally high in politics, who died after him.

Rafi Ahmad was a living, moving and acting human enigma. A systematic analysis of his frequently amazing actions, whether in terms of ideals or of character or of political strategy, beats my capacity of narration. He was an individual having no parallel. In the ideal of man he had little interest. He accepted man as he is with all his virtues and foibles. He hated sermonising. He never exploited the difficulties of any man and when his enemies were in trouble, he went all out to help them. Rafi was full of inconsistencies and contradictions. He defied all categorisation. I have related above a few anecdotes of his life, some of which apparently are not too flattering, to present a profile of the complex personality of Rafi Ahmad Kidwai.

Rafi Ahmad was greatly influenced by Bal Gangadhar Tilak and Mrs. Annie Besant, who had made much Contribution in the freedom movement in the first two decades of the twentieth century. With the foundation of the Home Rule Movement, both these leaders influenced the people of India, the youths and peasants in all the regions. Their speeches on public fora were well-attended and they attracted the people with their charismatic personality.

With the commencement of the global war, a new era started, on the political scene when Gandhi emerged as a leader of the Indian National Congress. The sudden and untimely deaths of Gopal Krishna Gokhale and Pheroze Shah Mehta gave a serious set-back to the freedom struggle. The bureaucracy of the Raj was much engaged in several intricacies of the war and Congress, at this point of time, showed its desire to cooperate with the Raj with the hope that there could be better terms for negotiations when the war was over.

The statement of E.S. Montagu, the Secretary of State in August 1917 was somewhat assuring and one could surmise that the tables could be smooth after the span of one-and-a-half year. Meanwhile the Champaran Satyagraha launched by Gandhi in 1917 gave him the sense of satisfaction and strengthened his political 'game' by which he felt much honoured and respected leader.

2

Indian Politics

The year 1919 developed a few problems for our leaders as well as the nation. The Rowlatt Bills proved very callous in contents and the loss to the human limbs was immense with its applicability resulting into the ghastly and bloody at the Jallianwala Bagh, Amritsar. Not only the people of Punjab or India felt much shocked at the results of this tragedy dent several regions of Asia and Europe were critical of the doings of the Raj.

At this point of time three political issues were taken by the Congress leadership is Punjab wrongs, khilafat and Swaraj. The problem was discussed at the special session held at Calcutta in September 1920 and the programme for Non-cooperation was finalised at the Nagpur session of the Congress. A call for boycott of various kinds was given by Gandhi and people were asked to participate in the Non-Cooperation Movement *en masse*.

The reception to the call of Gandhi was remarkable on political stage of our sub-continent. The participation of the people in the movement, 1921-22 was a glaring phenomenon and the category of such people represented upper middle class, middle class and lower middle class including teachers, lawyers, doctors, peasantry, labour, students and women. They came out of their hearths and homes spontaneously and engaged themselves in any kind of financial and physical exercise.

It was a non-violent movement, men and women resorting to picketing wine, ganja, opium and toddy shops, propagating swadeshi, boycotting schools, colleges and councils, resorting to resignations from government services, and last but not the least joining newly-opened Vidyapiths in Punjab, Gujarat, Bihar and elsewhere. Several students joined these national institutions as a protest against the policy of the British Raj.

This kind of model lasted practically during the year 1921 when thousands of satyagrahis were put behind the bars. There were convictions without trial. The living condition in the jails was horrible as the meals served were of low standard. The barrecks were dirty and a few dozens of persons were hurled at one place. No newspaper was allowed for them what to talk of other basic amenities.

Prominent leaders like Motilal Nehru, Lajpat Rai, C.R. Das, Jawaharlal Nehru, Rajendra Prasad and several others were in jails. Gandhi was not arrested as yet. In February 1922, there happened a tragedy at Chauri Chaura, near Gorakhpur, in the United Provinces. Violence erupted there and as a result thereof sixteen policemen were burnt to death. Gandhi took it a challenge and test for his non-violent cult. He was critical of the behaviour of Congress workers at Chauri Chaura and felt humiliated before the people of our sub-continent. He cried halt to the Non-Cooperation Movement and explained in clear language that under these circumstances when the fundamental principles of his creed were being violated, it was no longer possible to continue the movement. There was much hue and cry against Gandhi's decision. Motilal Nehru, C.R. Das, Lajpat Rai, Jawaharlal Nehru and several others were critical of Gandhi's decision. Lajpat Rai gave a long statement against Gandhi's decision. Indeed the leaders of the Congress were divided in their opinions.

The success of the Non-Cooperation Movement in Barabanki could be attributed to the sincere efforts of Rafi Ahmad

Kidwai who spearheaded the non-violent movement in the Gandhian style. At Rae Bareli and Fyzabad, the gained its intensity on account of the participation of thousands of kisans, indeed greatly patronised by young Nehru at that point of time.

Their economic grievances has greatly upset their social status and they now wanted to see proper remedy for it. The economic pressure on the landless labour and the peasantry engaged on land had become unbearable. So far so they needed mobilisation, a word of promise by which they could have the consolation for their future as well as the future of their wards. The lead in this direction was given by young Rafi Ahmad Kidwai who moved from village to village in order to mobilise the illiterare peasantry. As a consequence thereof about seventy thousand kisans launched the movement to show agrarian unrest against the revenue-policy of the Raj. At one point of time the movement went out of control and let to riots at Fyzabad. The police resorted to firing which resulted in several casualties. Besides there were riots at Aligarh also. The excited and infuriated mole launched an attack on the tehsil treasury and the police resorted to firing to disperse the mob. The government took stern action against the agitators and got them arrested and convicted. The Congress and the Khilafat were declared as illegal organisation and the top leaders and thousands of volunteers were put behind the bars. Rafi Ahmed Kidwai was also lodged in jail and, in fact, his political career began with his participation in the first Non-cooperation Movement, 1920-22. In fact the successful non-violent non-cooperation at Barabanki could be attributed to the patriotic efforts of Rafi Ahmad and his several comrades who showed faith and respect for him. During these days, Rafi Ahmad's younger brother, Shafi, showed a kind of resentment against the functioning of the Raj and resigned his post of Assistant Registrar, cooperative societies and joined the Non-Cooperation Movement.

Their father was in difficulty on account of political behaviour of his sons who had launched an anti-Raj stance under no less no a leader than Mahatma Gandhi. The government indeed got annoyed with Imtiaz Ali and at some level he was put into a haphazard position. He was called to Barabanki by the European Magistrate to explain his conduct and was asked to put restraint on his sons. An honest and upright official as he was, he could not check the political style of his sons Even the Governor and the Commissioner wanted to remove him from service, but they at last realised the sincerity of Imtiaz Ali and did not take any kind of action against him.

In the Lucknow jail, where Rafi Ahmed was lodged, the condition of living and meals was deplorable. There was scarcity of water and political prisoners—several in number—used one tap for taking bath. Rafi Ahmad felt sky to take bath in the open and for several days could not do so. Besides he never made any demand for pan, cigarette or any special edible. Thus he kept his life in a disciplined way.

Like several other political prisoners, Rafi Ahmad was released on the eve of the suspension of the Non-Cooperation Movement. His sincerity and patriotic zeal soon paid him dividends which greatly enhanced his social status. He was picked up by Pandit Motilal Nehru as his Personal Secretary. He felt much honoured at this appointment and from this day onward, he was considered as a respectable member of the Nehru family. In fact Rafi Ahmad showed much respect for every member of the Nehru family. After the death of Motilal Nehru his relationship with Jawaharlal Nehru remained very cordial. And this is the reason that he soon became political leader in U.P. and was brought to centre on the eve of independence. He, however, held several political positions in the Congress organisation.

After the Non-cooperation Movement, Rafi Ahmad Kidwai was assigned the task of mobilising the political programme of the Congress in U.P. He began to tour several regions of the province and met educated and uneducated people. He spoke them at many public fora and enlogised the services of the Nehru family. He also met peasants working in the fields, labourers in commercial concerns, students and teachers in schools and colleges, lawyers in courts and other people whom he apprised of the socio-economic and political programme of the Indian National Congress. He even addressed meetings of women and apprised them of their sacred duty to the nation besides their domestic functions. So in 1920s Rafi Ahmad became a popular and respectable leader in the province on account of his helpful behaviour in every walk of life.

"Nehru gave vent to his feelings on political issues like Non-Cooperation Movement, non-voilence communal problem, peasantry and Domimion Status: 'I spent three days in the villages, came back to Allahabad, and then went again. During these brief visits we wandered about a great deal from village to village, feeding with the peasants, living with them in their mud huts, talking to them for long hours, and often addressing meetings, big and small. We had originally gone in a light car and the peasants were so keen that hundreds of them, working overnight, built temporary roads across the fields so that our car could go right into the interior. Often the car got stuck and was bodily lifted out by scores of willing hands. But we had to leave the car eventually and to do most of our journeying by foot. Everywhere we went we were accompanied by policemen, C.I.D. men, and a Deputy Collector from Lucknow. I am afraid we gaven them a bad time with our continuous marching across fields and they were quite tired out and fed up with us and the *kisans*. The Deputy Collector was a somewhat effeminate youth from Lucknow and he had turned up in patent leather pumps! He begged us sometimes to restrain our ardour and I think he ultimately dropped out, being unable to keep up with us.

It was the hottest time of the year, June, just before the monsoon. The sun scorched and blinded. I was quite unused to going out in the sun and ever since my return from England I had gone to the hills for part of every summer. And now I was wandering about all day in the open sun with not even a sun-hat, my head being wrapped in a small towel. So full was

I of other matters that I quite forgot about the heat and it was only on my return to Allahabad, when I noticed the rich tan I had developed, that I remembered what I had gone through. I was pleased with myself for I realised that I could stand the heat with the best of them and my fear of it was wholly unjustified. I have found that I can bear both extreme heat and great cold without much discomfort, and this has stood me in good stead in my work as well as in my periods in prison. This was no doubt due to my general physical fitness and my habit of taking exercise, a lesson I learnt from my father, who was a bit of a an athlete and, almost to the end of his days, continued his daily exercise. His head became covered with silvery hair, his face was deeply furrowed and looked old and weary with thought, but the rest of his body, to within a year or two of his death, seemed to be twenty years younger.

Even before my visit to Partabgarh in June 1920, I had often passed through villages, stopped there and talked to the peasants. I had seen them in their scores of thousands on the banks of the Ganges during the big *melas* and we had taken our Home Rule propaganda to them. But somehow I had not fully realised what they were and what they meant to India. Like most of us, I took them for granted. This realisation came to me during these Partabgarh visits and ever since then my mental picture of India always contains this naked, hungry mass. Perhaps there was some kind of electricity in the air, perhaps I was in a receptive frame of mind and the pictures I saw and the impressions I gathered were indelibly impressed on my mind.

These peasants took away the shyness from me and taught me to speak in public. Till then I hardly spoke at a public gathering; I was frightened at the prospect, especially if the speaking was to be done in Hindustani, as it almost always was. But I could not possibly avoid addressing these peasant gatherings, and how could I be shy of these poor unsophisticated people? I did not know the arts of oratory and so I spoke to them, man to man, and told them what I had in my mind and in my heart. Whether the gathering consisted of a few persons or of ten thousand or more I stuck to my conversational and rather personal method of speaking, and I found that, whatever might be lacking in it, I could at least go on. I was fluent enough. Perhaps many of them could not understand a great deal of what I said. My language or my thought was not simple enough for them. Many did not hear me when the gathering was very large for my voice did not carry far. But all this did not matter much to them when once they had given their confidence and faith to a person.

I went back to Mussoorie to my mother and wife but my mind was full of the *kisans* and I was eager to be back. As soon as I returned I resumed my visits to the villages and watched the agrarian movement grow in strength. The down-trodden *kisan* began to gain a new confidence in himself and walked straighter with head up. His fear of the landlords' agents and the police lessened, and when there was an eject-ment from a holding no other *kisan* would make an offer for that land. Physical violence on the part of the zamindars' servants and illegal exactions became infrequent, and when-ever an instance occurred, it was immediately reported and an attempt at an inquiry was held. This checked the zamindars' agents as well as the police, The taluqadars were frightened and were on the defensive and the provincial government promised an amendment of the Oudh Tenancy Law.

The taluqadars and the big zamindars, the lords of the land, the "natural leaders of the people", as they are proud of calling themselves, had been the spoilt children of the British Government, but that Government had succeeded, by the special education and upbringing it provided or failed to provide for them, in reducing them, as a class, to a state of complete intellectual impotence. They did nothing at all for their tenantry, such as landlords in other countries have to some little extent often done, and became complete parasites on the land and the people. Their chief activity lay in endeavouring to placate the local officials, without whose favour they could not exist for long, and demanding ceaselessly a protection of their special interests and privileges.

The word 'zamindar' is rather deceptive, and one is apt to think that all zamindars are big landlords. In the *ryotwari* provinces in means the peasant proprietor. Even in the typical zamindari provinces, it includes in its fold the relatively few big landlords, thousands of middle landowners, and hundreds of thousands of persons who live in extreme poverty and are no better than tenants. In the United Provinces, so far as I can remember, there are a million and a half persons classed as zamindars. Probably over ninety per cent of these are almost on the same level as the poorest tenants, and another nine per cent are only moderately well off. The biggish landowners are not more than five thousand in the whole province, and of this number, about one-tenth might be considered the really big zamindars and taluqadars. In some instances the bigger tenants are better off than the destitute petty landowners. Both these poor landowners and the middle landlords, though often intellectually backward, are as a whole a fine body of men and women, and, with proper education and training, can be made into excellent citizens. They have taken a considerable part in the nationalist movement. Not so the taluqadars and the big zamindars, barring a few notable exceptions. They have not even the virtues of an aristocracy. As a class they are physically and intellectually degenerate and have outlived their day; they will continue only so long as an external power like the British Government props them up.

Right through the year 1921 I continued my visits to the rural areas, but my field of activity grew till it comprised the whole of the United Provinces. Non-co-operation had begun in earnest and its message had reached the remotest village. A host of Congress workers in each district went about the rural areas with the new message to which they often added, rather vaguely, a removal of *kisan* grievances. Swaraj was an all-embracing word to cover everything. Yet the two movements—non-co-operation and the agrarian—were quite separate, though they overlapped and influenced each other greatly in our province. As a result of Congress preaching, litigation went down with a rush and villages established their *punchayats* to deal with their disputes. Especially powerful was the influence of the Congress in favour of peace, for the new creed of non-violence was stressed wherever the Congress worker went. This may not have been fully appreciated or understood but it did prevent the peasantry from taking to violence.

This was no small result. Agrarian upheavals are notoriously violent, leading to *jacqueries*, and the peasants of part of Oudh in those days were desperate and at white heat. A spark would have lighted a flame. Yet they remained amazingly peaceful. The only instance of physical violence on a teluqadar that I remember was when a peasant went up to him as he was sitting in his own house, surrounded by his friends, and slapped him on the face on the ground that he was immoral and inconsiderate to his own wife!

There was violence of another kind later which led to conflicts with the Government. But this conflict was bound to come, for the Government could not tolerate this growing power of a united peasantry. The *kisans* took to travelling in railway trains in large numbers without tickets, especially when they had to attend their periodical big mass meetings which sometimes consisted of sixty or seventy thousand persons. It was difficult to move them and, unheard of thing, they openly defied the railway authorities, telling them that the old days were gone. At whose instigation they took to the free mass travelling I do not know. We had not suggested it to them. We suddendly heard that they were doing it. Stricter railway control prevented this later.

In the autumn of 1920 (when I was away in Calcutta attending the special session of the Congress) a few *kisan* leaders were arrested for some petty offence. They were to be tried in Partabgarh town but on the day of the trial a huge concourse of peasants filled the court compound and lined the route to the gaol where the accused leaders were kept. The magistrate's nerve gave way and he postponed the trial to the next day. But the crowd grew and almost surrounded the gaol. The *kisans* can easily carry on for a few days on a handful of parched gram. Ultimately the *kisan* leaders were discharged, perhaps after a formal trial inside the goal. I forget how this came about but for the *kisans* this was a great triumph and they began to think that they could always have their way by weight of numbers alone. To the Government this position was intolerable and soon after a similar occasion arose and this time it ended differently.

It was at the beginning of January 1921. I had just returned to Allahabad from the Nagpur Congress when I received a telegram from Rae Bareli asking me to go there immediately as trouble was expected. I left the next day. I discovered that some leading *kisans* had been arrested some days back and had been lodged in the local gaol. Remembering their success at Partabgarh and the tactics they had then adopted, the peasants marched to Rae Bareli town for a mass demonstration. But this time the Government was not going to permit it and additional police and military had been collected to stop the *kisans.* Just outside the town on the other side of a little river, the main body of the *kisans* was stopped. Many of them, however, streamed in from other directions. On arrival at the station I learnt of this situation and immediately I proceeded straight to the river where the military were said to face the peasants. On the way I received a hurriedly written note from the District Magistrate asking me to go back. I wrote my reply on the back of it enquiring under what law and what section he was asking me to go back and till I heard from him I proposed to go on. As I reached the river sounds of firing could be heard from the other side. I was stopped at the bridge by the military and as I waited there I was suddenly surrounded by large numbers of frightened *kisans* who had been hiding in the fields on this side of the river. So I held a meeting of about a couple of thousand peasants on the spot and tried to remove their fear and lessen their excitement. It was rather an unusual situation with firing going on their brethren within a stone's throw across a little stream and the military in evidence everywhere. But the meeting was quite successful and took away the edge from the *kisans*' fear. The District Magistrate then returned from the firing line and, at his request, I accompanied him to his house. There he kept me, under some pretext or other, for over two hours, evidently wanting to keep me away from the *kisans* and my colleagues in the city.

We found later that many men had been killed in the firing. The *kisans* had refused to disperse or to go back but otherwise they had been perfectly peaceful. I am quite sure that if I or some one else they trusted had been there and had asked them to do so they would have dispersed. They refused to take their orders from men they did not trust. Some one actually suggested to the Magistrate to wait for me a little but he refused. He could not permit an agitator to succeed where he had failed. That is not the way of foreign governments depending on prestige.

Firing on *kisans* took place on two occasions in Rae Bareli district about that time and then began, what was much worse, a reign of terror for every prominent *kisan* worker or member of a *panchayat*. Government had decided to crush the movement. Hand-spinning on the *charkha* was then spreading among the peasantry at the instance of the Congress. A *charkha* therefore became the symbol of sedition and its owner got into trouble, the *charkha* itself being often burnt. Thus the Government tried to crush by hundreds of arrests and other methods both the agrarian and the Congress movements in the rural areas of Rae Bareli and Partabgarh. Most of the principal workers were common to the two movements.

A little later, in the year 1921, Fyzabad district had its dose of widespread repression. The trouble started there in a peculiar way. The peasants of some villages went and looted the property of a taluqadar. It transpired subsequently that they had been incited to do so by the servants of another zamindar who had some kind of feud with the taluqadar. The poor ignorant peasants were actually told that it was the wish of Mahatma Gandhi that they should loot and they willingly agreed to carry out this behest, shouting "Mahatma Gandhi ki jai" in the process.

I was very angry when I heard of this and within a day or two of the occurrence I was on the spot, somewhere near Akbarpur in Fyzabad district. On arrival I called a meeting for the same day and within a few hours five or six thousand persons had collected from numerous villages within a radius of ten miles. I spoke harshly to them for the shame they had brought on themselves and our cause and said that the guilty persons must confess publicly. (I was full in those days of what I conceived to be the spirit of Gandhiji's Satyagraha). I called upon those who had participated in the looting to raise their hands, and strange to say, there, in the presence of numerous police officials, about two dozen hands went up. That meant certain trouble for them.

When I spoke to many of them privately later and heard their artless story of how they had been misled, I felt very sorry for them and I began to regret having exposed these foolish and simple folk to long terms of imprisonment. But the people who suffered were not just two or three dozen. The chance was too good to be lost and full advantage was taken of the occasion to crush the agrarian movement in that district. Over a thousand arrests were made, and the district gaol was overcrowded, and the trial went on for the best part of a year. Many died In prison during the trial. Many others received long sentences and in later years, when I went to prison, I came across some of them, boys and young men, spending their youth in prison.

The Indian *kisans* have little staying power, little energy to resist for long. Famines and epidemics come and slay them in their millions. It was surprising that they had shown for a whole year great powers of resistance against the combined pressure of government and landlord. But they began to weary a little and the determined attack of the Government on their movement ultimately broke its spirit for the time being. But it continued still in a lower key. There were not such vast demonstrations as before, but most villages contained old workers who had not been terrorised and who carried on the work in a small way. All this, it must be remembered, was prior to the gaol-going which the Congress started at the end of 1921. Even in this the *kisans* took a considerable part, in spite of all they had suffered during the previous year.

Frightened by the agrarian movement, the Government had hurried on with tenancy legislation. This promised some improvement in the lot of the *kisan* but the measure was toned down when it was found that the movement was already under control. The principal change it affected was to give a life tenancy to the *kisan* in Oudh. This sounded attractive to him but, as he has found out subsequently, his lot is in no way better.

Agrarian troubles continued to crop up in Oudh but on a smaller scale. The world depression which began in 1929, however, again created a great crisis owing to the fall in prices.

I have dealt with the oudh agrarian upheaval in some little detail because it lifted the veil and disclosed a fundamental aspect of the Indian problem to me to which nationalists had paid hardly any attention. Agrarian troubles are frequently taking place in various parts of India, symptoms of a deep-seated unrest, and the *kisan* agitation in certain parts of Oudh in 1920 and 1921 was but one of them, thought it was, in its own way, a remarkable and a revealing one. In its origin it was entirely unconnected with politics or politicians, and right through its course the influence of outsiders and politicians was of the slightest. From an all-India point of view, however, it was a local affair and very little attention was paid to it. Even the newspapers of the United Provinces largely ignored it. For their editors and the majority of their town-dwelling readers, the doings of mobs of semi-naked peasants had no real political or other significance.

The Punjab and the Khilafat wrongs were the topics of the day, and non-co-operations, which was to attempt to bring about a righting of these wrongs, was the all-absorbing subject. The larger issue of national freedom or Swaraj was for the moment not stressed. Gandhiji disliked vague and big objectives, he always preferred concentrating on something specific and definite. Nevertheless, Swaraj was very much in the air and in people's thoughts, and frequent reference was made to it in innumerable gatherings and conferences.

In the autumn of 1920 a special session of the Congress met at Calcutta to consider what steps should be taken and, in particular, to decide about non-co-operation. Lala Lajpat Rai, freshly back from the United States after a long absence from home, was the President. He disliked the new-fangled proposal of non-co-operation and opposed it. He was usually considered an Extremist in Indian politics, but his general outlook was definitely constitutional and moderate. Force of circumstances and not choice or convictions had made him an ally of Lokamanya Tilak and other Extremists in the early days of the century. But he had a social and economic outlook, strengthened by his long residence abroad, and this gave him a broader vision than that of most Indian leaders.

Wilfrid Scawen Blunt in his "Diaries" describes an interview he had (about 1909) with Gokhale and Lalaji. He is very hard on both, considering them far too cautious and afraid of facing realities. And yet Lalaji faced them far more than most Indian leaders. Blunt's impressions make us realise how low was the temper of our politics and our leaders at that time, and how an able and experienced foreigner was struck by them. But a decade had made a great difference to that temper.

Lala Lajpat Rai was not alone in his opposition; he had a great and impressive company with him. Indeed, almost the entire Old Guard of the Congress opposed Gandhiji's resolution of non-co-operation. Mr. C. R. Das led the opposition, not because he disapproved of the spirit behind the resolution, for he was prepared to go as far or even father, but chiefly because he objected to the boycott of the new legislatures.

Of the prominent leaders of the older generation my father was the only one to take his stand by Gandhiji at that time. It was no easy matter for him to do so. He sensed and was much influenced by the objections that had led most of his old colleagues to oppose. He hesitated, as they did, to take a novel step towards an unknown region, where it was hardly possible to keep one's old bearings. Yet he was inevitably drawn to some form of effective action, and the proposal did embody definite action, though not exactly on the lines of his thought. It took him a long time to make up his mind. He had long talks with Gandhiji and Mr. C. R. Das. Mr. Das and he were thrown a great deal together just then as they were both appearing, on opposite sides, in a big *mofussil* case. They looked at the problem from much the same point of view and there was very little difference between them even as regards the conclusion. Yet that little difference was just enough to keep them on either side of the main resolution as the Special Congress. Three months later they met again at the Nagpur Congress, and from then onwards they pulled together, ever coming nearer to each other.

I saw very little of father in those days before the Calcutta Special Congress. But whenever I met him, I noticed how he was continually grappling with this problem. Quite apart from the national aspect of the question there was the personal aspect. Non-co-operation meant his withdrawing from his legal practice; it meant a total break with his past life and a new fashioning of it—not an easy matter when one is on the eve of one's sixtieth birthday. It was a break from old political colleagues, from his profession, from the social life to which he had grown accustomed, and a giving up of many an expensive habit which he had grown into. For the financial aspect of the question was not an unimportant one, and it was obvious that he would have to reduce his standard of living if his income from his profession vanished.

But his reason, his strong sense of self-respect, and his pride, all led him step by step to throw in his lot wholeheartedly with the new movement. The accumulated anger with which a series of events, cluminating in the Punjab tragedy and its aftermath, filled him; the sense of utter wrong-doing and injustice, the bitterness of national humiliation, had to find some way out. But he was not to be swept away by a wave of enthusiasm. It was only when his reason, backed by the trained mind of a lawyer, had weighed all the pros and cons that he took the final decision and joined Gandhiji in his campaign.

He was attracted by Gandhiji as a man, and that no doubt was a factor which influenced him. Nothing could have made him a close associate of a person he disliked, for he was always strong in his likes and dislikes. But it was a strange combination—the saint, the stoic, the man of religion, one who went through life rejecting what it offers in the way of sensation and physical pleasure, and one who had been a bit of an epicure, who accepted life and welcomed and enjoyed its many sensations, and cared little for what may come in the hereafter. In the language of psychoanalysis it was a meeting of an introvert with an extrovert. Yet there were common bonds, common interests, which drew the two together and kept up, even when, in later years, their politics diverged, a close friendship between them.

Walter Pater, in one of his books, mentions how the saint and the epicure, starting from opposed points, travelling different paths, one with a religious temper, the other opposed to it, and yet both with an outlook which, in its stress and earnestness, is very unlike any lower development of temper, often understand each other better than either would understand the mere man of the world—and sometimes they actually touch.

This Special Session at Calcutta began the Gandhi era in Congress politics which has lasted since then, except for a period in the twenties when he kept in the background and allowed the Swaraj Party, under the leadership of Deshbandhu C. R. Das and my father, to fill the picture. The whole look of the Congress changed; European clothes vanished and soon only khadi was to be seen; a new class of delegate, chiefly drawn from the lower middle classes became the type of Congressman; the language used became increasingly Hindustani, or sometimes the language of the province where the session was held, as many of the delegates did not understand English, and there was also a growing prejudice against using a foreign language in our national work; and a new life and enthusiasm and earnestness became evident in Congress gatherings.

After the Congress was over Gandhiji paid a visit to the veteran editor of the *Amrit Bazaar Patrika*, Syt Motilal Ghose, who was lying on his death-bed, I accompanied him. Motilal Babu blessed Gandhiji and his movement, and he added that, as for himself, he was going away to other regions, and wherever these might be, he had one great satisfaction—he would be somewhere where the British Empire did not exist. At last he would be beyond the reach of this Empire!

On our way back from the Calcutta Special Congress I accompanied Gandhiji to Santiniketan on a visit to Rabindra Nath Tagore and his most lovable elder brother 'Boro Dada.' We spent some days there, and I remember C. F. Andrews giving me some books which interested and influenced me greatly. They dealt with the economic aspects of imperialism in Africa. One of these books—Morell's *Black Man's Burden*—moved me greatly.

About this time or a little later, C. F. Andrews wrote a pamphlet advocating independence for India. I think it was called *Independence—the Immediate Need.* This was a brilliant essay based on some of Seeley's writings on India, and it seemed to me not only to make out an unanswerable case for independence but also to mirror the inmost recesses of our hearts. The deep urge that moved us and our half-formed desires seemed to take clear shape in his simple and earnest language. There was no economic background or socialism in what he had written; it was nationalism pure and simple, the feeling of the humiliation of India and a fierce desire to be rid of it and to put an end to our continuing degradation. It was wonderful that C. F. Andrews, a foreigner and one belonging to the dominant race in India, should echo that cry of our inmost being. Non-co-operation was essentially, as Seeley had said long ago, "the notion that it was shameful to assist the foreigner in maintaining his domination". And Andrews had written that "the only way of self-recovery was through some vital upheaval from within. The explosive force needed for such an upheaval must be generated within the soul of India itself. It could not come through loans and gifts and grants and concessions and proclamations from without. It must come from within. . . .Therefore, it was with the intense joy of mental and spiritual deliverance from an intolerable burden, that I watched the actual outbreak of such an inner explosive force, as that which actually occurred when Mahatma Gandhi spoke to the heart of India the *mantram*—'Be free! Be slaves no more!' and the heart of India responded. In a sudden movement her fetters began to be loosened, and the pathway of freedom was opened."

The next three months witnessed the advancing tide of non-co-operation all over the country. The appeal for a boycott of the elections to the new legislatures was remarkably successful. It did not and could not prevent everybody from going to these councils and thus keep the seats vacant. Even a handful of voters could elect or there might be an unopposed election. But the great majority of voters abstained from voting, and all who cared for the vehementy expressed sense of the country refrained from standing as candidates. Sir Valentine Chirol happened to be in Allahabad on the election day, and he made a round of the polling booths. He returned amazed at the efficiency of the boycott. At one rural polling station, about fifteen miles from Allahabad city, he found that not a single voter had appeared. He gives an account of his experiences in one of his books on India.

The wisdom of this boycott had been questioned by Mr. C. R. Das and others at the Calcutta session, but they stood by the Congress decision. The elections being over, this point of difference was removed, and the next full session of the Congress at Nagpur in December 1920 saw a reunion of many of the old Congress leaders on the plank of non-co-operation. The very success of the movement had convinced many a doubter and waverer.

A few old leaders, however, dropped out of the Congress after Calcutta, and among these a popular and well-known figure was that of Mr. M. A. Jinnah. Sarojini Naidu had called him the "Ambassador of Hindu-Muslim unity", and he had been largely responsible in the past for bringing the Moslem League nearer to the Congress. But the new developments in the Congress—non-co-operation and the new constitution which made it more of a popular and mass organization—were thoroughly disapproved of by him. He disagreed on political grounds, but it was not politics in the main that kept him away. There were still many people in the Congress who were politically even less advanced than he was. But temperamentally he did not fit in at all with the new Congress. He felt completely out of his element in the khadi-clad crowd demanding speeches in Hindustani. The enthusiasm of the people outside struck him as mob-hysteria. There was as much difference between him and the Indian masses as between Savile Row and Bond Street and the Indian village with its mud-huts. He suggested once privately that only matriculates should be taken into the Congress. I do not know if he was serious in making this remarkable suggestion, but it was in harmony with his general outlook. So he drifted away from the Congress and became a rather solitary figure in Indian politics. Later, unhappily, the old Ambassador of Unity associated himself with the most reactionary elements in Muslim communalism.

The Moderates or Liberals had. of course, nothing to do with the Congress. They not only kept away from it; they merged themselves in the Government, became ministers and high officials under the new scheme, and helped in fighting non-co-operation and the Congress. They had obtained almost what they desired, some reforms had been granted, and so there was no need for them to agitate. While the country was seething with excitement and becoming more and more revolutionary, they became frankly counter-revolutionary, a part of the Government itself. They were completely cut off from the people and developed a habit, which has persisted since, of looking at problems from the official point of view. They ceased to be a party in any real sense and became a small number of individuals dotted about in a few big cities. Mr. Srinivasa Sastri became an Imperial Envoy, visiting, at the instance of the British Government, various British dominions as well as the United States of America, and strongly criticising the Congress and his own countrymen for the struggle they were carrying on against that Government.

And yet the Liberals were far from happy. It is not a pleasant experience to be cut off from one's own people, to sense hostility even though one may not see it or hear it. A mass upheaval is not kind to the non-conformists, though Gandhiji's repeated warnings made non-co-operation far milder and gentler to its opponents than it otherwise would have been. But even so, the very atmosphere stifled those who opposed the movement, just as it invigorated and filled with life and energy those who supported it. Mass upheavals and real revolutionary movements always have this double effect: they encourage and bring out the personality of those who constitute the masses or side with them, and at the same time they suppress psychologically and stifle those who differ from them.

This was the reason why some people complained that non-co-operation was intolerant and tended to introduce a dead uniformity of opinion and action. There was truth in this complaint, but the truth lay in this, that non-co-operation was a mass movement, and it was led by a man of commanding personality who inspired devotion in India's millions. A more vital truth, however, lay in its effect on the masses. There was a tremendous feeling of release there, a throwing-off of a great burden, a new sense of freedom. The fear that had crushed them retired into the background, and they straightened their backs and raised their heads. Even in remote bazaars the common folk talked of the Congress and Swaraj (for the Nagpur Congress had finally made Swaraj the goal), and what had happened in the Punjab, and the Khilafat—but the word 'Khilafat' bore a strange meaning in most of the rural areas. People thought it came from *khilaf*, an Urdu word meaning 'against' or 'opposed to', and so they took it to mean : opposed to Government! They discussed, of course, especially their own particular economic grievances. Innumerable meetings and conferences added greatly to their political education.

Many of us who worked for the Congress programme lived in a kind of intoxication during the year 1921. We were full of excitement and optimism and a buoyant enthusiasm. We sensed the happiness of a person crusading for a cause. We were not troubled with doubts or hesitation; our path seemed to lie clear in front of us and we marched ahead, lifted up by the enthusiasm of others, and helping to push on others. We worked hard, harder than we had ever done before, for we knew that the conflict with the Government would come soon, and we wanted to do as much as possible before we were removed.

Above all, we had a sense of freedom and a pride in that freedom. The old feeling of oppression and frustration was completely gone. There was no more whispering, no roundabout legal phraseology to avoid getting into trouble with the authorities. We said what we felt and shouted it out from the house-tops. What did we care for the consequences? Prison? We looked forward to it; that would help our cause still further. The innumerable spies and secret-service men who used to surround us and follow us about became rather pitiable individuals as there was nothing secret for them to discover. All our cards were always on the table.

We had not only a feeling of satisfaction at doing effective political work which was changing the face of India before our eyes and, as we believed, bringing Indian freedom very near, but also an agreeable sense of moral superiority over our opponents, both in regard to our goal and our methods. We were proud of our leader and of the unique method he had evolved, and often we indulged in fits of self-righteousness. In the midst of strife, and while we ourselves encouraged that strife, we had a sense of inner peace.

As our *moral* grew, that of the Government went down. They did not understand what was happening; it seemed that the old world they knew in India was toppling down. There was a new aggressive spirit abroad and self-reliance and fearlessness, and the great prop of British rule in India—prestige—was visibly wilting. Repression in a small way only strengthened the movement, and the Government hesitated for long before it would take action against the big leaders. It did not know what the consequences might be. Was the Indian Army reliable? Would the police carry out orders? As Lord Reading, the Viceroy, said in December 1921, they were "puzzled and perplexed".

An interesting circular was sent confidentially by the U.P. Government to its district officers in the summer of 1921. This circular, which was published later in a newspaper, stated with sorrow that the "initiative" was always with the "enemy", meaning the Congress, and this was an unfortunate state of affairs. Various methods were then suggested to regain the initiative, among them being the starting of those ludicrous bodies, the "Aman Sabhas". It was believed that this particular method of combating non-co-operation was adopted at the suggestion of the Liberal Ministers.

The nerves of many a British official began to give way. The strain was great. There was this ever-growing opposition and spirit of defiance which overshadowed official India like a vast monsoon cloud, and yet because of its peaceful methods it offered no handle, no grip, no opportunity for forcible suppression. The average Englishman did not believe in the *bonafides* of non-violence; he thought that all this was camouflage, a cloak to cover some vast secret design which would burst out in violent upheaval one day. Nurtured from childhood in the wide-spread belief that the East is a mysterious place, and in its bazaars and narrow lanes secret conspiracies are being continually hatched, the Englishman can seldom think straight on matters relating to these lands of supposed mystery. He never makes and attempt to understand that somewhat obvious and very unmysterious person the Easterner. He keeps well away from him, gets his ideas about him from tales abounding in spies and secret societies, and then allows his imagination to run riot. So it was in the Punjab early in April 1919 when a sudden fear overwhelmed the authorities and the English people generally, made them see danger everywhere, a widespread rising, a second mutiny with its frightful massacres, and, in a blind, instinctive attempt at self-preservation at any cost, led them to that frightfulness, of which Jallianwala and the Crawling Lane of Amritsar have become symbols and bywords.

The year 1921 was a year of great tension, and there was much to irritate and annoy and unnerve the official. What was actually happening was bad enough, but what was imagined was far worse. I remember an instance which illustrates this riot of the imagination. My sister Swarup's wedding, which was taking place at Allahabad, was fixed for the 10th May, 1921, the actual date having been calculated, as usual on such occasions, by a reference to the Samvat calendar, and an auspicious day chosen. Gandhiji and a number of leading Congressmen, including the Ali brothers, had been invited, and to suit their convenience, a meeting of the Congress Working Committee was fixed at Allahabad about that time. The local Congressmen wanted to profit by the presence of famous leaders from outside, and so they organised a district conference on a big scale, expecting a large number of peasants from the surrounding rural areas.

There was a great deal of bustle and excitement in Allahabad on account of these political gatherings. This had a remarkable effect on the nerves of some people. I learnt one day through a barrister friend that many English people were thoroughly upset and expected some sudden upheaval in the city. They distrusted their Indian servants, and carried about revolvers in their pockets. It was even said privately that the Allahabad Fort was kept in readiness for the English colony to retire there in case of need. I was much surprised and could not make out why any one should contemplate the possibility of a rising in the sleepy and peaceful city of Allahabad just when the very apostle of non-violence was going to visit us. Oh, it was said, May 10th (the day accidentally fixed for my sister's marriage) was the anniversary of the outbreak of the Mutiny at Meerut in 1857 and this was going to be celebrated!

Owing to the prominence given to the Khilafat movement in 1921 a large number of Moulvies and Muslim religious leaders took a prominent part in the political struggle. They gave a definite religious tinge to the movement, and Muslims generally were greatly influenced by it. Many a Westernised Muslim, who was not of a particularly religious turn of mind, began to grow a beard and otherwise conform to the tenets of Orthodoxy. The influence and prestige of the Moulvies, which had been gradually declining owing to new ideas and a progressive Westernisation, began to grow again and dominate Muslim community. The Ali brothers, themselves of a religious turn of mind, helped in this process, and so did Gandhiji, who paid the greatest regard to the Moulvies and the Maulanas.

Gandhiji, indeed, was continually laying stress on the religious and spiritual side of the movement. His religion was not dogmatic, but it did mean a definitely religious outlook on life, and the whole movement was strongly influenced by this and took on a revivalist character so far as the masses were concerned. The great majority of Congress workers naturally tried to model themselves after their leader and even repeated his language. And yet Gandhiji's leading colleagues in the

Working Committee—my father, Deshbandhu Das, Lala Lajpat Rai, and others—were not men of religion in the ordinary sense of the word, and they considered political problems on the political plane only. In their public utterances they did not bring in religion. But whatever they said had far less influence than the force of their personal example —had they not given up a great deal that the world values and taken to simpler ways of living? This in itself was taken as a sign of religion and helped in spreading the atmosphere of revivalism.

I used to be troubled sometimes at the growth of this religious element in our politics, both on the Hindu and the Muslim side. I did not like it at all. Much that Moulvies and Maulanas and Swamis and the like said in their public addresses seemed to me most unfortunate. Their history and sociology and economics appeared to me all wrong, and the religious twist that was given to everything prevented all clear thinking. Even some of Gandhiji's phrases sometimes jarred upon me—thus his frequent reference to *Rama Raj* as a golden age which was to return. But I was powerless to intervene, and I consoled myself with the thought that Gandhiji used the words because they were well known and understood by the masses. He had an amazing knack of reaching the heart of the people.

But I did not worry myself much over these matters. I was too full of my work and the progress of our movement to care for such trifles, as I thought at the time they were. A vast movement had all sorts and kinds of people in it, and so long as our main direction was correct, a few eddies and backwaters did not matter. As for Gandhiji himself, he was a very difficult person to understand, sometimes his language was almost incomprehensible to an average modern. But we felt that we knew him quite well enough to realise that he was a great and unique man and a glorious leader, and having put our faith in him we gave him an almost blank cheque, for the time being at least. Often we discussed his fads and peculiarities among ourselves and said, half-humorously, that when

Swaraj came these fads must not be encouraged.

Many of us, however, were too much under his influence in political and other matters to remain wholly immune even in the sphere of religion. Where a direct attack might not have succeeded, many an indirect approach went a long way to undermine the defences. The outward ways of religion did not appeal to me, and above all I disliked the exploitation of the people by the so-called men of religion, but still I toned down towards it. I came nearer to a religious frame of mind in 1921 than at any other time since my early boyhood. Even so I did not come very near.

What I admired was the moral and ethical side of our movement and of satyagraha. I did not give an absolute allegiance to the doctrine of non-violence or accept it for ever, but it attracted me more and more, and the belief grew upon me that, situated as we were in India and with our background and traditions, it was the right policy for us. The spiritualisation of politics, using the word not in its narrow religious sense, seemed to me a fine idea. A worthy end should have worthy means leading up to it. That seemed not only a good ethical doctrine but sound, practical politics, for the means that are not good often defeat the end in view and raise new problems and difficulties. And then it seemed so unbecoming, so degrading to the self-respect of an individual or a nation to submit to such means, to go through the mire. How can one escape being sullied by it? How can we march ahead swiftly and with dignity if we stoop or crawl?

Such were my thoughts then. And the non-co-operation movement offered me what I wanted—the goal of national freedom and (as I thought) the ending of the exploitation of the underdog, and the means which satisfied my moral sense and gave me a sense of personal freedom. So great was this personal satisfaction that even a possibility of failure did not count for much, for such failure could only be temporary. I did not understand or feel drawn to the metaphysical part of the Bhagavad Gita, but I liked to read the verses—recited every evening in Gandhiji's ashram prayers—which say what a man should be like: Calm of purpose, serene and unmoved, doing his job and not caring overmuch for the result of his action. Not being very calm or detached myself, I suppose, this ideal appealed to me all the more.

Nineteen Twenty-one was an extraordinany year for us. There was a strange mixture of nationalism and politics and religion and mysticism and fanaticism. Behind all this was agrarian trouble and, in the big cities, a rising working-class movement. Nationalism and a vague but intense country-wide idealism sought to bring together all these various, and sometimes mutually contradictory, discontents, and succeeded to a remarkable degree. And yet this nationalism itself was a composite force, and behind it could be distinguished a Hindu nationalism, a Muslim nationalism partly looking beyond the frontiers of India, and, what was more in consonance with the spirit of the times, an Indian nationalism. For the time being they overlapped and all pulled together. It was *Hindu-Musalman ki Jai* everywhere. It was remarkable how Gandhiji seemed to cast a spell on all classes and groups of people and drew them into one motley crowd struggling in one direction. He became, indeed (to use a phrase which has been applied to another leader), "a symbolic expression of the confused desires of the people".

Even more remarkable was the fact that these desires and passions were relatively free from hatred of the alien rulers against whom they were directed. Nationalism is essentially an anti-feeling, and it feeds and fattens on hatred and anger against other national groups, and especially against the foreign rulers of a subject country. There was certainly this hatred and anger in India in 1921 against the British but, in comparison with other countries similarly situated, it was extraordinarily little. Undoubtedly this was due to Gandhiji's insistence on the implications of non-violence. It was also due to the feeling of release and power that came to the whole country with the inauguration of the movement and the widespread belief in success in the near future. Why be angry and full of hate when we were doing so well and were likely to win through soon? We felt that we could afford to be generous.

We were not so generous in our bearts, though our actions were circumspect and proper, towards the handful of our own countrymen who took sides against us and opposed the national movement. It was not a question of hatred or anger, for they carried no weight whatever and we could ignore them. But deep within us was contempt for their weakness and opportunism and betrayal of national honour and self-respect.

So we went on, vaguely but intensely, the exhilaration of action holding us in its grip. But about our goal these was an entire absence of clear thinking. It seems surprising now, how completely we ignored the theoretical aspects, the philosophy of our movement as well as the definite objective that we should have. Of course we all grew eloquent about Swaraj, but each one of us probably interpreted the word in his or her own way. To most of the younger men it meant political independence, or something like it, and a democratic form of government, and we said so in our public utterances. Many of us also thought that inevitably this would result in a lessening of the burdens that crushed the workers and the peasantry. But it was obvious that to most of our leaders Swaraj meant something much less than independence. Gandhiji was delightfully vague on the subject, and he did not encourage clear thinking about it either. But he always spoke, vaguely but definitely, in terms of the under-dog, and this brought great comfort to many of us, although, at the same time, he was full of assurances to the top-dog also. Gandhiji's stress was never on the intellectual approach to a problem but on character and piety. He did succeed amazingly in giving backbone and character to the Indian people. There were many, however, who developed neither much backbone nor character, but who imagined that a limp body and a flabby look might be the outward semblance of piety.

It was this extraordinary stiffening-up of the masses that filled us with confidence. A demoralized, backward, and broken-up people suddenly straightened their backs and lifted their heads and took part in disciplined, joint action on a country-wide scale. This action itself, we felt, would give irresistable power to the masses. We ignored the necessity of thought behind the action; we forgot that without a concious ideology and objective the energy and enthusiasm of the masses must end largely in smoke. To some extent the revivalist element in our movement carried us on; a feeling that non-violence as conceived for political or economic movements or for righting wrongs was a new message which our people were destined to give to the world. We became victims to the curious illusion of all peoples and all nations that in some way they are a chosen race. Non-violence was the moral equivalent of war and of all violent struggle. It was not merely an ethical alternative, but it was effective also. Few of us, I think, accepted Gandhiji's old ideas about machinery and modern civilization. We thought that even he looked upon them as utopian and as largely inapplicable to modern conditions. Certainly most of us were not prepared to reject the achievements of modern civilization, although we may have felt that some variation to suit Indian conditions was possible. Personally, I have always felt attracted towards big machinery and fast travelling. Still there can be no doubt that Gandhiji's ideology influenced many people and made them critical of the machine and all its consequences. So, while some looked to the future, others looked back to the past. And, curiously, both felt that the joint action they were indulging in was worth while, and this made it easy to bear sacrifice and face self-denial.

I became wholly absorbed and wrapt in the movement, and large numbers of other people did likewise. I gave up all my other associations and contacts, old friends, books, even newspapers, except in so far as they dealt with the work in hand. I had kept up till then some reading of current books and had tried to follow the developments of world affairs. But there was no time for this now. In spite of the strength of my family bonds, I almost forgot my family, my wife, my daughter. It was only long afterwards that I realised what a burden and a trial I must have been to them in those days, and what amazing patience and tolerance my wife had shown towards me. I lived in offices and committee meetings and crowds. "Go to the villages" was the slogan, and we trudged many a mile across fields and visited distant villages and addressed peasant meetings. I experienced the thrill of mass-feeling, the power of influencing the mass. I began to understand a little the psychology of the crowd, the difference between the city masses and the peasantry, and I felt at home in the dust and discomfort, the pushing and jostling of large gatherings, though their want of discipline often irritated me. Since those days I have sometimes had to face hostile and angry crowds, worked up to a state when a spark would light a flame, and I found that that early experience and the confidence it begot in me stood me in good stead. Always I went straight to the crowd and trusted it, and so far I have always had courtesy and appreciation from it, even though there was no agreement. But crowds are fickle, and the future may have different experiences in store for me.

I took to the crowd and the crowd took to me, and yet I never lost myself in it; always I felt apart from it. From my separate mental perch I looked at it critically, and I never ceased to wonder how I, who was so different in every way from those thousands who surrounded me, different in habits, in desires, in mental and spiritual outlook, how I had managed to gain goodwill and a measure of confidence from these people. Was it because they took me for something other than I was ? Would they bear with me when they knew me better ? Was I gaining their goodwill under false pretences ? I tried to be frank and straightforward to them; I even spoke harshly to them sometimes and criticised many of their pet beliefs and customs, but still they put up with me. And yet I could not get rid of the idea that their affection was meant not for me as I was, but for some fanciful image of me that they had formed. How long could that false image endure ? And why should it be allowed to endure ? And when it fell down and they saw the reality, what then ?

I am vain enough in many ways, but there could be no question of vanity with these crowds of simple folk. There was no posing about them, no vulgarity, as in the case of many of us of the middle classes who consider ourselves their betters. They were dull certainly, uninteresting individually, but in the mass they produced a feeling of overwhelming pity and a sense of ever-impending tragedy.

Very different were our conferences where our chosen workers, including myself, performed on the platform. There was sufficient posing there and no lack of vulgarity in our flamboyant addresses. All of us must have been to some extent guilty of this, but some of the minor Khilafat leaders probably led the rest. It is not easy to behave naturally on a platform before a large audience, and few of us had previous experience of such publicity. So we tried to look as, we imagined, leaders should look, thoughtful and serious, with no trace of levity or frivolity. When we walked or talked or smiled we were conscious of thousands of eyes staring at us and we reacted accordingly. Our speeches were often very eloquent but, equally often, singularly pointless. It is difficult to see oneself as others see one. And so, unable to criticise myself, I took to watching carefully the ways of others, and I found considerable amusement in this occupation. And then the terrible thought would strike me that I might perhaps appear equally ludicrous to others.

Right through the year 1921 individual Congress workers were being arrested and sentenced, but there were no mass arrests. The Ali Brothers had received long sentences for inciting the Indian Army to disaffection. Their words, for which they had been sentenced, were repeated at hundreds of platforms by thousands of persons. I was threatened in the summer with proceedings for sedition because of some speeches I had delivered. No such step, however, was taken then. The end of the year brought matters to a head. The Prince of Wales was coming to India, and the Congress had proclaimed a boycott of all the functions in connection with his visit. Towards the end of November the Congress volunteers in

Bengal were declared illegal and this was followed by a similar declaration for the United Provinces. Deshbandhu Das gave a stirring message to Bengal : "I feel the handcuffs on my wrists and the weight of iron chains on my body. It is the agony of bondage. The whole of India is a vast prison. The work of the Congress must be carried on. What matters it whether I am taken or left ? What matters it whether I am dead or alive ?" In the U.P. we took up the challenge and not only announced that our volunteer organisation would continue to function, but published lists of names of volunteers in the daily newspapers. The first list was headed by my father's name. He was not a volunteer but, simply for the purpose of defying the Government order, he joined and gave his name. Early in December, a few days before the Prince came to our province, mass arrests began.

We knew that matters had at last come to a head; the inevitable conflict between the Congress and the Government was about to break out. Prison was still an unknown place, the idea of going there still a novelty. I was sitting rather late one day in the Congress office at Allahabad trying to clear up arrears of work. An excited clerk told me that the police had come with a search warrant and were surrounding the office building. I was, of course, a little excited also, for it was my first experience of the kind, but the desire to show off was strong, the wish to appear perfectly cool and collected, unaffected by the comings and goings of the police. So I asked a clerk to accompany the police officer in his search round the office rooms, and insisted on the rest of the staff carrying on their usual work and ignoring the police. A little later a friend and a colleague, who had been arrested just outside the office, came to me, accompanied by a policeman, to bid me good-bye. I was so full of the conceit that I must treat these novel occurrences as everyday happenings that I treated my colleague in a most unfeeling manner. Casually I asked him and the policeman to wait till I had finished the letter I was writing. Soon news came of other arrests in the city. I decided at last to go home and see what was happening there. I found the inevitable police searching part of the large house and learnt that they had come to arrest both father and me.

Nothing that we could have done would have fitted in so well with our programme of boycotting the Prince's visit. Wherever he was taken he was met with *hartals* and deserted streets. Allahabad, when he came, seemed to be a city of the dead; Calcutta, a few days later, suddenly put a temporary stop to all the activities of a great city. It was hard on the Prince of Wales; he was not to blame, and there was no feeling against him whatever. But the Government of India had tried to exploit his personality to prop up their decaying prestige.

There was an orgy of arrests and convictions, especially in the United Provinces and in Bengal. All the prominent Congress leaders and workers in shese provinces were arrested, and ordinary volunteers by the thousand went to prison. They were, at first, largely city men and there seemed to be an inexhaustible supply of volunteers for prison. The U.P. Provincial Congress Committee was arrested *en bloc* (55 members) as they were actually holding a committee meeting. Many people, who had so far taken no part in any Congress or political activity, were carried away by the wave of enthusiasm and insisted on being arrested. There were cases of Government clerks, returning from their offices in the evening, being swept away by this current and landing in gaol instead of their homes. Young men and boys would crowd inside the police lorries and refuse to come out. Every evening we could hear from inside the gaol, lorry after lorry arriving outside heralded by our slogans and shouts. The gaols were crowded and the gaol officials were at their wits' ends at this extraordinary phenomenon. It happened sometimes that a police lorry would bring, according to the warrant accompanying it, a certain number of prisoners—no names were or could be mentioned. Actually, a larger number than that mentioned would emerge from the lorry and the gaol officials did not know how to meet this novel situation. There was nothing in the *Jail Manual* about it.

Gradually the Government gave up the policy of indiscriminate arrests; only noted workers were picked out. Gradually also the first flush of enthusiasm of the people cooled down and, owing to the absence in prison of all the trusted workers, a feeling of indecision and helplessness spread. But the change was superficial only, and there was still thunder in the air and the atmosphere was tense and pregnant with revolutionary possibilities. During the months of December 1921 and January 1922 it is estimated that about thirty thousand persons were sentenced to imprisonment in connection with the non-co-operation movement. But though most of the prominent men and workers were in prison, the leader of the whole struggle, Mahatma Gandhi, was still out, issuing from day to day messages and directions which inspired the people, as well as checking many an undesirable activity. The Government had not touched him so far, for they feared the consequences, the reactions on the Indian Army and the police.

Suddenly, early in February 1922, the whole scene shifted, and we in prison learnt, to our amazement and consternation, that Gandhiji had stopped the aggressive aspects of our struggle, that he had suspended civil resistance. We read that this was because of what had happened near the village of Chauri Chaura where a mob of villagers had retaliated on some policemen by setting fire to the police-station and burning half a dozen or so policemen in it.

We were angry when we learnt of this stoppage of our struggle at a time when we seemed to be consolidating our position and advancing on all fronts. But our disappointment and anger in prison could do little good to any one, and civil resistance stopped and non-co-operation wilted away. After many months of strain and anxiety the Government breathed again, and for the first time had the opportunity of taking the initiative. A few weeks later they arrested Gandhiji and sentenced him for a long term of imprisonment.

The sudden suspension of our movement after the Chauri

Chaura incident was resented, I think, by almost all the prominent Congress leaders—other than Gandhiji of course. My father (who was in gaol at the time) was much upset by it. The younger people were naturally even more agitated. Our mounting hopes tumbled to the ground, and this mental reaction was to be expected. What troubled us even more were the reasons given for this suspension and the consequences that seemed to flow from them. Chauri Chaura may have been and was a deplorable occurrence and wholly opposed to the spirit of the non-violent movement; but were a remote village and a mob of excited peasants in an out-of-the-way place going to put an end, for some time at least, to our national struggle fot freedom? If this was the inevitable consequence of a sporadic act of violence, then surely there was something lacking in the philosophy and technique of a non-violent struggle. For it seemed to us to be impossible to guarantee against the occurrence of some such untoward incident. Must we train the three hundered and odd millions of India in the theory and practice of non-violent action before we could go forward? And, even so, how many of us could say that under extreme provocation from the police we would be able to remain perfectly peaceful? But even if we succeeded, what of the numerous *agents provocateurs*, stool pigeons, and the like who crept into our movement and indulged in violence themselves or induced others to do so? If this was the sole condition of its function, then the non-violent method of resistance would always fail.

We had accepted that method, the Congress had made that method its own, because of a belief in its effectiveness. Gadhiji had placed it before the country not only as the right method but as the most effective one for our purpose. In spite of its negative name it was a dynamic method, the very opposite of a meek submission to a tyrant's will. It was not a coward's refuge from action, but the brave man's defiance of evil and national subjection. But what was the use of the bravest and the strongest if a few odd persons—maybe even our opponents in the guise of friends—had the power to upset or end our movement by their rash behaviour?

Gandhiji had pleaded for the adoption of the way of non-violence, of peaceful non co-operation, with all the eloquence and persuasive power which he so abundantly possessed. His language had been simple and unadorned, his voice and appearance cool and clear and devoid of all emotion, but behind that outward covering of ice there was the heat of a blazing fire and concentrated passion, and the words he uttered winged their way to the innermost recesses of our minds and hearts, and created a strange ferment there. The way he pointed out was hard and difficult, but it was a brave path, and it seemed to lead to the promised land of freedom. Because of that promise we pledged our faith and marched ahead. In a famous article—"The Doctrine of the Sword"—he had written in 1920 :

"I do believe that when there is only a choice between cowardice and violence, I would advise violence . . . I would rather have India resort to arms in order to defend her honour than that she should in a cowardly manner become or remain a helpless victim to her own dishonour. But I believe that non-violence is infinitely superior to violence, forgiveness is more manly than punishment.

"Forgiveness adorns a soldier. But abstinence is forgiveness only when there is power to punish; it is meaningless when it pretends to proceed from a helpless creature. A mouse hardly forgives a cat when it allows itself to be torn to pieces by her . . . But I do not believe India to be helpless, I do not believe myself to be a helpless creature . . .

"Let me not be misunderstood. Strength does not come from physical capacity. It comes from an indomitable will . . . .

"I am not a visionary. I claim to be a practical idealist. The religion of non-violence is not meant merely for the Rishis and saints. It is meant for the common people as well. Non-violence is the law of our species as violence is the law of the brute. The spirit lies dormant in the brute and he knows no law but that of physical might. The dignity of man requires obedience to a higher law—to the strength of the spirit.

"I have therefore ventured to place before India the ancient law of self-sacrifice. For Satyagrah and its off-shoots, non-co-operation and civil resistance, are nothing but new names for the law of suffering. The Rishis who discovered the law of non-violence in the midst of violence, were greater geniuses than Newton. They were themselves greater warriors than Wellington. Having themselves known the use of arms, they realised their uselessness and taught a weary world that its salvation lay not through violence but through non-violence.

"Non-violence in its dynamic condition means conscious suffering. It does not mean meek submission to the will of the evil-doer, but it means the putting of one's whole soul against the will of the tyrant. Working under this law of our being, it is possible for a single individual to defy the whole might of an unjust empire to save his honour, his religion, his soul and lay the foundation for that empire's fall or regeneration.

"And so I am not pleading for India to practise non-violence because it is weak. I want her to practise non-violence being conscious of her strength and power. . . I want India to recognise that she has a soul that cannot perish, and that can rise triumphant above any physical weakness and defy the physical combination of a whole world. . . .

"I isolate this non-co-operation from Sinn Feinism, for, it is so conceived as to be incapable of being offered side by side with violence. But I invite even the school of violence to give this peaceful non-co-operation a trial. It will not fail through its inherent weakness. If may fail because of poverty of response. Then will be the time for real danger. The highsouled men, who are unable to suffer national humiliation any longer, will want to vent their wrath. They will take to violence. So far as I know, they must perish without delivering themselves or their country from the wrong. If India takes up the doctrine of the sword, she may gain momentary victory. Then

India will cease to be the pride of my heart. I am wedded to India because I owe my all to her. I believe absolutely that she has a mission for the world."

We were moved by these arguments, but for us and for the National Congress as a whole the non-violent method was not, and could not be, a religion or an unchallengeable creed or dogma. It could only be a policy and a method promising certain results, and by those results it would have to be finally judged. Individuals might make of it a religion or incontrovertible creed. But no political organisation, so long as it remained political, could do so.

Chauri Chaura and its consequences made us examine these implications of non-violence as a method, and we felt that, if Gandhiji's argument for the suspension of civil resistance was correct, our opponents would always have the power to create circumstances which would necessarily result in our abandoning the struggle. Was this the fault of the non-violent method itself or of Gandhiji's interpretation of it? After all, he was the author and originator of it, and who could be a better judge of what it was and what it was not? And without him where was our movement?

Many years later, just before the 1930 Civil Disobedience movement began, Gandhiji, much to our satisfaction, made this point clear. He stated that the movement should not be abandoned because of the occurrence of sporadic acts of violence. If the non-violent method of struggle could not function because of such almost inevitable happenings, then it was obvious that it was not an ideal method for all occasions, and this he was not prepared to admit. For him the method, being the right method, should suit all circumstances and should be able to function, at any rate in a restricted way, even in a hostile atmosphere. Whether this interpretation, which widened the scope of non-violent action, represented an evolution in his own mind or not I do not know.

As a matter of fact even the suspension of civil resistance in February 1922 was certainly not due to Chauri Chaura alone, although most people imagined so. That was only the last straw. Gandhiji has often acted almost by instinct; by long and close association with the masses he appears to have developed, as great popular leaders often do, a new sense which tells him how the mass feels, what it does and what it can do. He reacts to this instinctive feeling and fashions his action accordingly, and later, for the benefit of his surprised and resentful colleagues, tries to clothe his decision with reasons. This covering is often very inadequate, as it seemed after Chauri Chaura. At that time our movement, in spite of its apparent power and the widespread enthusiasm, was going to pieces. All organisation and discipline was disappearing; almost all our good men were in prison, and the masses had so far received little training to carry on by themselves. Any unknown man who wanted to do so could take charge of a Congress Committee and, as a matter of fact, large numbers of undesirable men, including *agents provocateurs*, came to the front and even controlled some local Congress and Khilafat organisations. There was no way of checking them.

This kind of thing is, of course, to some extent almost inevitable in such a struggle. The leaders must take the lead in going to prison, and trust to others to carry on. All that can be done is to train the masses in some simple kinds of activity and, even more so, to abstain from certain other kinds of activity. In 1930 we had already spent several years in giving some such training, and the Civil Disobedience movement then and in 1932 was a very powerful and organised affair. This was lacking in 1921 and 1922, and there was little behind the excitement and enthusiasm of the people. There is little doubt that if the movement had continued there would have been growing sporadic violence in many places. This would have been crushed by Government in a bloody manner and a reign of terror established which would have thoroughly demoralised the people.

These were probably the reasons and influences that worked in Gandhiji's mind, and granting his premises and the desirability of carrying on with the technique of non-violence,

From another and an entirely different view-point his decision might be considered wrong, but that view-point had nothing to do with the non-violent method. It was not possible to have it both ways. To invite a bloody suppression of the movement in that particular sporadic way and at that stage would not, of course, have put an end to the national movement, for such movements have a way of rising from their ashes. Temporary set-backs are often helpful in clarifying issues and in giving backbone; what matters is not a set-back or apparent defeat, but the principles and ideals. If these principles can be kept untarnished by the masses, then recovery comes soon. But what were our principles and objectives in 1921 and 1922? A vague Swaraj with no clear ideology behind it and a particular technique of non-violent struggle. The latter method would naturally have gone if the country had taken to sporadic violence on any big scale, and as to the former, there was little to hold on to. The people generally were not strong enough to carry on the struggle for long and, in spite of almost universal discontent with foreign rule and sympathy with the Congress, there was not enough backbone or organisation. They could not last. Even the crowds that went to prison did so on the spur of the moment, expecting the whole thing to be over very soon.

It may be, therefore, that the decision to suspend civil resistance in 1922 was a right one, though the manner of doing it left much to be desired and brought about a certain demoralisation.

It is possible, however, that this sudden bottling up of a great movement contributed to a tragic development in the country. The drift to sporadic and futile violence in the political struggle was stopped, but the suppressed violence had to find a way out, and in the following years this perhaps aggravated the communal trouble. The communalists of various denominations, mostly political reactionaries, had been forced to lie low because of the overwhelming mass support for the non-co-operation and civil disobedience movement. They his decision was right. He had to stop the rot and built anew.

emerged now from their retirement. Many others, secret service agents and people who sought to please the authorities by creating communal friction, also worked on the same theme. The Moplah rising and its extra-ordinarily cruel suppression—what a horrible thing was the baking to death of the Moplah prisoners in the closed railway vans !—had already given a handle to those who stirred the waters of communal discord. It is just possible that if civil resistance had not been stopped and the movement had been crushed by Government, there would have been less communal bitterness and less superfluous energy left for the subsequent communal riots.

Before civil resistance was called off an incident occurred which might have led to different results. The first wave of civil of resistance amazed and frightened the Government. It was then that Lord Reading, the Viceroy, said in a public speech that he was troubled and perplexed. The Prince of Wales was in India, and his presence added greatly to the Government's responsibility. An attempt was made by the Government in December 1921, soon after the mass arrests at the beginning of the month, to come to some understanding with the Congress. This was especially in view of the Prince's forthcoming visit to Calcutta. There were some informal talks between representatives of the Bengal Government and Deshbandhu Das, who was in gaol then. A proposal seems to have been made, that a small round table conference might take place between the Government and the Congress. This proposal appears to have fallen through because Gandhiji insisted that Maulana Mohamad Ali, who was then in prison in Karachi, should be present at this conference. Government would not agree to this.

Mr. C. R. Das did not approve of Gandhiji's attitude in this matter and, when he came out of prison later, he publicly criticised him and said that he had blundered. Most of us (we were in gaol) do not know the details of what took place then, and it is difficult to judge without all the facts. It seems, however, that little good could have come out of the conference at that stage. It was an effort on the part of Government to tide over somehow the period of the Prince's visit to Calcutta. The basic problems that faced us would have remained. Nine years later, when the nation and the Congress were far stronger, such a conference took place without any great results. But apart from this, it seems to me that Gandhiji's insistence on Mohamad Ali's presence was perfectly justified. Not only as a Congress leader but as the leader of the Khilafat movement—and the Khilafat question was then an important plank in the Congress programme—his presence was essential. No policy or manoeuvre can ever be a right one if it involves the forsaking of a colleague. The fact that Government were not prepared to release him from gaol itself shows that there was no likelihood of any results from a conference.

Both my father and I had been sentenced to six months' imprisonment on different charges and by different courts. The trials were farcical and, as was our custom, we took no part in them. It was easy enough, of course, to find enough material in our speeches or other activities for a conviction. But the actual choice was amusing. Father was tried as a member of an illegal organisation, the Congress Volunteers, and to prove this a form with his signature in Hindi was produced. The signature was certainly his, but, as it happened, he had hardly ever signed in Hindi before, and very few persons could recognise his Hindi signature. A tattered gentleman was then produced who swore to the signature. The man was quite illiterate, and he held the signature upside down when he examined it. My daughter, aged four at the time, had her first experience of the dock during father's trial, as he held her in his arms throughout.

My offence was distributing notices for a *hartal*. This was no offence under the law then, though I believe it is one now, for we are rapidly advancing towards Dominion Status. However, I was sentenced. Three months later I was informed in the prison, where I was with my father and others, that some revising authority had come to the conclusion that I was wrongly sentenced and I was to be discharged. I was surprised, as no one had taken any step on my behalf. The suspension of civil resistance had apparently galvanised the revising Judges into activity. I was sorry to go out, leaving my father behind.

I decided to go almost immediately to Gandhiji in Ahmedabad. Before I arrived there he had been arrested, and my interview with him took place in Sabarmati Prison. I was present at his trial. It was a memorable occasion, and those of us who were present are not likely ever to forget it. The judge, an Englishman, behaved with dignity and feeling. Gandhiji's statement to the court was a most moving one, and we came away, emotionally stirred, and with the impress of his vivid phrases and striking images in our mind.

I came back to Allahabad. I felt unhappy and lonely outside the prison when so many of my friends and colleagues were behind prison bars. I found that the Congress organisation was not functioning well and I tried to put it straight. In particular I interested myself in the boycott of foreign cloth. This item of our programme still continued in spite of the withdrawal of civil resistance. Nearly all the cloth merchants in Allahabad had pledged themselves not to import or purchase foreign cloth, and had formed an association for the purpose. The rules of this association laid down that any infringement would be punished by a fine. I found that several of the big dealers had broken their pledges and were importing foreign cloth. This was very unfair to those who stuck to their pledges. We remonstrated with little result, and the cloth dealers' association seemed to be powerless to take action. So we decided to picket the shops of the erring merchants. Even a hint of picketing was enough for our purpose. Fines were paid, pledges were taken afresh. The money from the fines went to the cloth merchants' association.

Two or three days later I was arrested, together with a number of colleagues who had taken part in the negotiations with the merchants. We were charged with criminal intimidation and extortion ! I was further charged with some other offences, including sedition. I did not defend myself, but I made a long statement in court. I was sentenced on at least three counts, including intimidation and extortion, but the sedition charge was not proceeded with, as it was probably considered that I had already got as much as I deserved. As far as I remember there were three sentences, two of which were for eighteen months and were concurrent. In all, I think, I was sentenced to a year and nine months. That was my second sentence. I went back to prison after about six weeks spent outside it.

I occupied myself with many activities and sought thereby to keep away from the problems that troubled me. But there was no escape from them, no getting away from the questions that were always being formed in my mind and to which I could find no satisfactory answer. Action now was partly an attempt to run away from myself; no longer was it a whole-hearted expression of the self as it had been in 1920 and 1921. I came out of the shell that had protected me then and looked round at the Indian scene as at well as the world outside. I found many changes that I had not so far noticed, new ideas, new conflicts, and instead of light I saw a growing confusion. My faith in Gandhiji's leadership remained, but I began to examine some parts of his programme more critically. But he was in prison and beyond our reach, and his advice could not be taken. Neither of the two Congress parties then functioning—the Council party and the No-changers—attracted me. The former was obviously veering towards reformism and constitutionalism, and these seemed to me to lead to a blind alley. The No-changers were supposed to be the ardent followers of the Mahatma, but like most disciples of the great, they prized the letter of the teaching more than the spirit. There was nothing dynamic about them, and in practice most of them were inoffensive and pious social reformers. But they had one advantage. They kept in touch with the peasant masses, while the Swarajists in the Councils were wholly occupied with parliamentary tactics.

Deshbandhu Das tried, soon after my discharge from prison,

to convert me to the Swarajist creed. I did not succumb to his advocacy, though I was by no means clear as to what I should do. It is curious and rather remarkable, but characteristic of him, that my father, who was at the time very keen on the Swaraj Party, never tried to press me or influence me in that direction. It was obvious that he would have been very pleased if I had joined him in his campaign, but with extraordinary consideration for me, he left me to myself so far as this subject was concerned.

During this period there grew up a close friendship between my father and Mr. C. R. Das. It was something much more than political *camaraderie*. There was a warmth and intimacy in it that I was not a little surprised to notice, since intimate friendships are perhaps rarely formed at advanced ages. My father had a host of acquaintances, and had the gift of laughing his way through them, but he was chary of friendship, and in later years he had grown rather cynical. And yet between him and Deshbandhu the barriers seemed to fall, and they took each other to heart. My father was nine years older, but was, physically, probably the stronger and the healthier of the two. Though both had the same background of legal training and success at the Bar, they differed in many ways. Mr. Das, in spite of being a lawyer, was a poet and had a poet's emotional outlook—I believe he has written fine poetry in Bengali. He was an orator, and he had a religious temperament. My father was more practical and prosaic; he was a great organiser, and he had little of religion in him. He had always been a fighter, ready to receive and give hard blows. Those whom he considered fools he suffered not at all, or at any rate not gladly; and opposition he could not tolerate. It seemed to him a challenge requiring the use of a broom. The two, my father and Deshbandhu, unlike in some ways as they were, fitted in and made a remarkable and effective combination for the leadership of a party, each in some measure supplying the other's deficiencies. And between the two of them there was absolute confidence, so much so that each had authorised the other to use his name for any statement or declaration, even without previous reference or consultation.

It was this personal factor that went a long way to establish the Swaraj Party firmly and give it strength and prestige in the country. From the earliest days there were fissiparous tendencies in it, for many careerists and opportunists had been drawn into it by the possibilities of personal advancement through the Councils. There were also some genuine moderates in it who were inclined to more co-operation with the Government. As soon as these tendencies appeared on the surface after the elections, they were denounced by the Party leadership. My father declared that he would not hesitate 'to cut off a diseased limb' from the Party, and he acted up to this declaration.

From 1923 onwards I found a great deal of solace and happiness in family life, though I gave little time to it. I have been fortunate in my family relationships, and in times of strain and difficulty they have soothed me and sheltered me. I realised, with some shame at my own unworthiness in this respect, how much I owed to my wife for her splendid behaviour since 1920. Proud and sensitive as she was, she had not only put up with my vagaries but brought me comfort and solace when I needed them most.

Our style of living had undergone some change since 1920. It was much simpler, and the number of servants had been greatly reduced. Even so, it was not lacking in any essential comfort. Partly to get rid of superfluities and partly to raise money for current expenditure, many things had been sold off—horses and carriages, and household articles which did not fit in with our new style of living. Part of our furniture had been seized and sold by the police, For lack of furniture and gardeners, our house lost its prim and clean appearance, and the garden went wild. For nearly three years little attention had been paid to house or garden. Having become accustomed to a lavish scale of expenditure, father disliked many economies. He decided therefore to go in for chamber practice in his spare time and thus earn some money. He had very little spare time, but, even so, he managed to earn a fair amount.

I felt uncomfortable and a little unhappy at having to depend financially on father. Ever since I had given up my legal practice I had practically no income of my own, except a trifle from some dividends on shares. My wife and I did not spend much. Indeed, I was quite surprised to find how little we spent. This was one of the discoveries made by me in 1921 which brought me great satisfaction. Khadi clothes and third-class railway travelling demand little money. I did not fully realise then, living as we did with father, that there are innumerable other household expenses which mount up to a considerable figure. Anyhow, the fear of not having money has never troubled me; I suppose I could earn enough in case of necessity, and we can do with relatively little.

We were not much of a burden on father, and even a hint of this kind would have pained him greatly. Yet I disliked my position, and for the next three years I thought over the problem without finding a solution. There was no great difficulty in my finding paying work, but the acceptance of any such work necessitated my giving up or, at any rate, my curtailing the public work I was doing. So far I had given all my working time to Congress work and Municipal work. I did not like to withdraw from them for the sake of making money. So I refused offers, financially very advantageous, from big industrial firms. Probably they were willing to pay heavily, not so much for my competence as for the opportunity to exploit my name. I did not like the idea of being associated with big industry in this way. To go back to the profession of law was also out of the question for me. My dislike for it had grown and kept on growing.

A suggestion was made in the 1924 Congress that the General Secretaries should be paid. I happened to be one of the secretaries then, and I welcomed the proposal. It seemed to me quite wrong to expect whole-time work from any one without paying him a maintenance allowance at least.

Otherwise some person with private means has to be chosen, and such gentlemen of leisure are not perhaps always politically desirable, nor can they be held responsible for the work. The Congress would not have paid much; our rates of payment were low enough. But there is in India an extraodinary and thoroughly unjustified prejudice against receiving salaries from public funds (though not from the State), and my father strongly objected to my doing so. My co-secretary, who was himself in great need of money, also considered it below his dignity to accept it from the Congress. And so I, who had no dignity in the matter and was perfectly prepared to accept a salary, had to do without it.

Once only I spoke to father on the subject and told him how I disliked the idea of my financial dependence. I put it to him as gently and indirectly as possible so as not to hurt him. He pointed out to me how foolish it would be of me to spend my time, or most of it, in earning a little money, instead of doing public work. It was far easier for him to earn with a few days' work all that my wife and I would require for a year. The argument was weighty, but it left me unsatisfied. However, I continued to act in consonance with it.

These family affairs and financial worries carried us from the beginning of 1923 to the end of 1925. Meanwhile the political situation had been changing and, almost my will, I was dragged into various combinations and acceptance of responsible office in the All-India Congress. The position in 1923 was a peculiar one. Mr. C. R. Das had been the President of the preceding Congress at Gaya. As such, he was the *ex-officio* Chairman of the All-India Congress Committee for the year 1923. But in this Committee there was a majority against him and the Swarajist policy, though the majority was a small one, and the two groups were pretty evenly balanced. Matters came to a head in the early summer of 1923 at a meeting of the A.I.C.C. in Bombay. Mr. Das resigned from the chairmanship, and a small centre group emerged and formed the new Working Committee. This centre group had no backing whatever in the A.I.C.C., and could only exist with the goodwill of one of the two main parties. Allied to either, it could just defeat the other. Dr. Ansari was the new President, and I was one of the secretaries.

We soon got into trouble on both sides. Gujrat, which was a no-change stronghold, refused to carry out some of the directions of the central office. Late in the summer of the same year another meeting of the A.I.C.C. was held, this time in Nagpur, where the National Flag Satyagraha was being carried on. Our Working Committee, representing the unfortunate Centre Group, came to an end here after a brief and inglorious career. It had to go because it represented nobody in particular, and it tried to boss it over those who held the real power in the Congress organisation. The resignation was brought about by the failure of an attempt to censure Gujrat for its indiscipline. I remember how gladly I sent in my resignation and how relieved I felt. Even a short experience of party manoeuvres had been too much for me, and I was quite shocked at the way some prominent Congressmen could intrigue.

At this meeting Mr. C. R. Das accused me of being 'cold-blooded'. I suppose he was right; it depends on the standard used for comparison. Compared to many of my friends and colleagues I am cold-blooded. And yet I have always been afraid of being submerged in or swept away by too much sentiment or emotion or temper. For years I have tried my hardest to become 'cold-blooded', and I fear that the success that has attended me in this respect has been superficial only.

In December 1923 the annual session of the Congress was held at Coconada in the South. Maulana Mohamad Ali was the President and, as was his wont, he delivered an enormously long presidential address. But it was an interesting one. He traced the growth of political and communal feeling among the Moslems and showed how the famous Moslem deputation to the Viceroy in 1908, under the leadership of the Aga Khan, which led to the first official declaration in favour of separate electorates, was a command performance and had been engineered by the Government itself.

Mohamad Ali induced me, much against my will, to accept the All-India Congress secretaryship for his year of presidentship. I had no desire to accept executive responsibility, when I was not clear about future policy. But I could not resist Mohamad Ali, and both of us felt that some other secretary might not be able to work as harmoniously with the new President as I could. He had strong likes and dislikes, and I was fortunate enough to be included in his 'likes'. A bond of affection and mutual appreciation tied us to each other. He was deeply and, as I considered, most irrationally religious, and I was not, but I was attracted by his earnestness, his overflowing energy and keen intelligence. He had a nimble wit, but sometimes his devastating sarcasm hurt, and he lost many a friend thereby. It was quite impossible for him to keep a clever remark to himself, whatever the consequences might be.

We got on well together during his year of office, though we had many little points of difference. I introduced in our A.I.C.C. office a practice of addressing all our members by their names only, without any prefixes or suffixes, honorific titles and the like. There are so many of these in India—Mahatma, Maulana, Pandit, Shaikh, Syed, Munshi, Moulvi, and latterly Sriyut and Shri, and, of course, Mr. and Esquire—and they are so abundantly and often unnecessarily used that I wanted to set a good example. But I was not to have my way. Mohamed Ali sent me a frantic telegram directing me 'as president' to revert to our old practice and, in particular, always to address Gandhiji as Mahatma.

Another frequent subject for argument between us was the Almighty. Mohamed Ali had an extraordinary way of bringing in some reference to God even in Congress resolutions, either by way of expressing gratitude or some kind of prayer. I used to protest, and then he would shout at me for my irreligion. And yet, curiously enough, he would tell me later that he was quite sure that I was fundamentally religious, in spite of my superficial behaviour or my declarations to the contrary. I have often wondered how much truth there was in his statement. Perhaps it depends on what is meant by religion and religious.

I avoided discussing this subject of religion with him, because I knew we would only irritate each other, and I might hurt him. It is always a difficult subject to discuss with convinced believers of any creed. With most Moslems it is probably an even harder matter for discussion, since no latitude of thought is officially permitted to them. Ideologically, theirs is a straight and narrow path, and the believer must not swerve to the right or the left. Hindus are somewhat different, though not always so. In practice they may be very orthodox; they may, and do, indulge in the most out-of-date, reactionary and even pernicious customs, and yet they will usually be prepared to discuss the most radical ideas about religion. I imagine the modern Arya Samajists have not, as a rule, this wide intellectual approach. Like the Moslems, they follow their own straight and narrow path. There is a certain philosophical tradition among the intelligent Hindus, which, though it does not affect practice, does make a difference to the ideological approach to a religious question. Partly, I suppose, this is due to the wide and often conflicting variety of opinions and customs that are included in the Hindu fold. It has, indeed, often been remarked that Hinduism is hardly a religion in the usual sense of the word. And yet, what amazing tenacity it has got, what tremendous power of survival! One may even be a professing atheist—as the old Hindu philosopher, Charvaka, was—and yet no one dare say that he has ceased to be a Hindu. Hinduism clings on to its children, almost despite them. A Brahman I was born, and a Brahman I seem to remain whatever I might say or do in regard to religion or social custom. To the Indian world I am 'Pandit' so and so, in spite of my desire not to have this or any other honorific title attached to my name. I remember meeting a Turkish scholar once in Switzerland, to whom I had sent previously a letter of introduction in which I had been referred to as 'Pandit Jawaharlal Nehru'. He was surprised and a little disappointed to see me for, as he told me, the 'Pandit' had led him to expect a reverend and scholarly gentleman of advanced years.

So Mohamad Ali and I did not discuss religion. But he did not possess the virtue of silence, and some years later (I think this was in 1925 or early in 1926) he could not repress himself on this subject any more. He burst out one day, as I was visiting him in his house in Delhi, and said that he insisted on discussing religion with me. I tried to dissuade him, pointing out that our view-points were very different, and we were not likely to make much impression on each other. But he was not going to be diverted. "We must have it out," he said. "I suppose you think that I am a fanatic. Well, I am going to show you that I am not." He told me that he had studied the subject of religion deeply and extensively. He pointed out shelves full of books on various religions, especially Islam and Christianity, and including some modern books like H.G. Wells's *God, the Invisible King*. During the long years of his war-time internment, he had gone through the Quran repeatedly, and consulted all the commentaries on it. As a result of this study he found out, so he told me, that about 97 per cent of what was contained in the Quran was entirely reasonable, and could be justified even apart from the Quran. The remaining 3 per cent was not prima facie acceptable to his reason. But was it more likely that the Quran, which was obviously right in regard to 97 per cent, was also right in regard to the remaining 3 per cent, than that his feeble reasoning faculty was right and the Quran wrong? He came to the conclusion that the chances were heavily in favour of the Quran, and so he accepted it as 100 per cent correct.

The logic of this argument was not obvious, but I had no wish to argue. What followed really surprised me. Mohamad Ali said that he was quite certain that if any one read the Quran with an open and receptive mind, he would be convinced of its truth. He knew (he added) that Bapu (Gandhiji) had read it carefully, and he must, therefore, have been convinced of the truth of Islam. But his pride of heart had kept him from declaring this.

After his year of presidentship, Mohamad Ali gradually drifted away from the Congress, or, perhaps, as he would have put it, the Congress drifted away from him. The process was a slow one, and he continued to attend Congress and A.I.C.C. meetings, and take vigorous part in them for several years more. But the rift widened, estrangement grew. Perhaps no particular individual or individuals were to blame for this; it was an inevitable result of certain objective conditions in the country. But it was an unfortunate result, which hurt many of us. For, whatever the differences on the communal question might have been, there were very few differences on the political issue. He was devoted to the idea of Indian independence. And because of this common political outlook, it was always possible to come to some mutually satisfactory arrangement with him on the communal issue. There was nothing in common, politically, between him and the reactionaries who pose as the champions of communal interests.

It was a misfortune for India that he left the country for Europe in the summer of 1928. A great effort was then made to solve the communal problem, and it came very near success. If Mohamad Ali had been here then, it is just conceivable that matters would have shaped differently. But by the time he came back the break had already taken place and, inevitably, he found himself on the other side.

Two years later, in 1930, when large numbers of our people were in prison and the Civil Disobedience movement was in full swing, Mohamad Ali ignored the Congress decision, and attended the Round Table Conference. I was hurt by his going. I believe that in his own heart he was unhappy about it, and there is enough evidence of this in his activities in London. He felt that his real place was in the fight in India, not in the futile conference chamber in London. And if he had returned to his country he would, I feel sure, have joined that struggle. Physically, he was a doomed man, and for years past the grip of disease was tightening upon him. In London his overwhelming anxiety to achieve, to do something worth while, when rest and treatment was what he needed, hastened his end. The news of his death came to me in Naini Prison as a blow.

I met him for the last time on the occasion of the Lahore Congress in December 1929. He was not pleased with some parts of my presidential address, and he criticised it vigorously. He saw that the Congress was going ahead, and becoming politically more aggressive. He was aggressive enough himself, and, being so, he disliked taking a back-seat and allowing others to be in the front. He gave me solemn warning: "I warn you, Jawahar, that your present colleagues will desert you. They will leave you in the lurch in a crisis. Your own Congressmen will send you to the gallows." A dismal prophecy!

The Coconada Congress, held in December 1923, had a special interest for me, because the foundations of an all-India volunteer organisation, the Hindustani Seva Dal, were laid there. There had been no lack of volunteer organisations even before, both for organisational work and for gaol-going. But there was little discipline, little cohesion. Dr. N. S. Hardiker conceived the idea of having a well-disciplined all-India corps trained to do national work under the general guidance of the Congress. He pressed me to co-operate with him in this, and I gladly did so, for the idea appealed to me. The beginnings were made at Coconada. We were surprised to find later how much opposition there was to the Seva Dal among leading Congressmen. Some said that this was a dangerous departure, as it meant introducing a military element in the Congress, and the military arm might over-power the civil authority! Others seemed to think that the only discipline necessary was for the volunteer to obey orders issued from above, and for the rest it was hardly desirable for volunteers even to walk in step. At the back of the mind of some was the notion that the idea of having trained and drilled volunteers was somehow inconsistent with the Congress principle of non-violence. Hardiker, however, devoted himself to this task, and by the patient labour of years he demonstrated how much more efficient and even non-violent our trained volunteers could be.

Soon after my return from Coconada, in January 1924, I had a new kind of experience in Allahabad. I write from memory, and I am likely to get mixed up about dates. But I think that was the year of the *Kumbh*, or the *Ardh-Kumbh*, the great bathing *mela* held on the banks of the Ganges at Allahabad. Vast numbers of pilgrims usually turn up, and most of them bathe at the confluence of the Ganges and the Jumna—the *Triveni*, it is called, as the mythical Saraswati is also supposed to join the other two. The Ganges river-bed is about a mile wide, but in winter the river shrinks and leaves a wide expanse of sand exposed, which is very useful for the camps of the pilgrims. Within this river-bed, the Ganges frequently changes its course. In 1924 the current of the Ganges was such that it was undoubtedly dangerous for crowds to bathe at the *Triveni*. With certain precautions, and the control of the numbers bathing at a time, the danger could be greatly lessened.

I was not at all interested in this question, as I did not propose to acquire merit by bathing in the river on the auspicious days. But I noticed in the Press that a controversy was going on between Pandit Madan Mohan Malaviya and the Provincial Government, the latter (or the local authorities) having issued orders prohibiting all bathing as the junction of the rivers. This was objected to by Malaviyaji, as, from the religious point of view, the whole point was to bathe at that confluence. The Government was perfectly justified in taking precautions to prevent accidents and possible serious loss of life, but, as usual, it set about its work in the most wooden and irritating way possible.

On the big day of the Kumbh, I went down to the river early in the morning to see the *mela*, with no intention of bathing. On arrival at the river bank, I learnt that Malaviyaji had sent some kind of polite ultimatum to the District Magistrate, asking him for permission to bathe at the *Triveni.* Malaviyaji was agitated, and the atmosphere was tense. The Magistrate refused permission. Thereupon Malaviyaji decided to offer Satyagraha, and, accompanied by about two hundred others, he marched towards the junction of the rivers. I was interested in these developments and, on the spur of the moment, joined the Satyagraha band. A tremendous barrier had been erected right across the open space, to keep away people from the conflueuce. When we reached this high palisade, we were stopped by the police, and a ladder we had was taken away from us. Being non-violent Satyagrahis, we sat down peacefully on the sands near the palisade. And there we sat for the whole morning and part of the afternoon. Hour after hour went by, the sun became stronger, the sand hotter, and all of us hungrier. Foot and mounted police stood by on both sides of us. I think the regular cavalry was also there. Most of us grew impatient, and said that something should be done. I believe the authorities also grew impatient, and decided to force the pace. Some order was given to the cavalry, who mounted their horses. It struck me (I do not know if I was right) that they were going to charge us and drive us away in this fashion. I did not fancy the idea of being chased by mounted troopers, and, anyhow, I was fed up with sitting there. So I suggested to those sitting near me that we might as well cross over the palisade, and I mounted it. Immediately scores of others did likewise, and some even pulled out a few stakes, thus making a passage-way. Somebody gave me a national flag, and I stuck it on top of the palisade, where I continued to sit. I grew rather excited, and thoroughly enjoyed myself, watching the people clambering up or going through and the mounted troopers trying to push them away. I must say that the cavalry did their work as harmlessly as possible. They waved about their wooden staffs, and pushed people with them, but refrained from causing much injury. Faint memories of revolutionary barricades came to me.

At last I got down on the other side and, feeling very hot

after my exertions, decided to have a dip in the Ganges. On coming back, I was amazed to find that Malaviyaji and many others were still sitting on the other side of the palisade as before. But the mounted troopers and the foot police now stood shoulder to shoulder between the Satyagrahis and the palisade. So I went (having got out by a roundabout way) and sat down again near Malaviyaji. For some time we sat on, and noticed that Malaviyaji was greatly agitated : he seemed to be trying to control some strong emotion. Suddenly, without a hint to any one, he dived in the most extraordinary way through the policemen and the horses. For any one, that would have been a surprising dive, but for an old and physically weak person like Malaviyaji, it was astounding. Anyhow, we all followed him; we all dived. After some effort to keep us back the cavalry and the police did not interfere. A little later they were withdrawn.

We half expected some proceedings to be taken against us by the Government, but nothing of the kind happened. Government probably did not wish to take any steps against Malaviyaji, and so the smaller fry got off too.

Early in 1924 there came suddenly the news of the serious illness of Gandhiji in prison, followed by his removal to a hospital and an operation. India was numbed with anxiety; we held our breaths almost and waited, full of fear. The crisis passed, and a stream of people began to reach Poona from all parts of the country to see him. He was still in hospital, a prisoner under guard, but he was permitted to see a limited number of friends. Father and I visited him in the hospital.

He was not taken back from the hospital to the prison As he was convalescing, Government remitted the rest of his sentence and discharged him. He had then served about two years out the six years to which he had been sentenced. He went to Juhu, by the sea-side near Bombay, to recuperate.

Our family also trekked to Juhu, and established itself in a tiny little cottage by the sea. We spent some weeks there, and I had, after a long gap, a holiday after my heart, for I could indulge in swimming and running and riding on the beach. The main purpose of our stay, however, was not holiday-making, but discussions with Gandhiji. Father wanted to explain to him the Swarajist position, and to gain his passive co-operation at least, if not his active sympathy. I was also anxious to have some light thrown on the problems that were troubling me. I wanted to know what his future programme of action was going to be.

The Juhu talks, so far as the Swarajists were concerned, did not succeed in winning Gandhiji, or even in influencing him to any extent. Behind all the friendlly talk, and the courteous gestures, the fact remained that there was no compromise. They agreed to differ, and statements to this effect were issued to the Press.

I also returned from Juhu a little disappointed, for Gandiji did not resolve a single one of my doubts. As is usual with him, he refused to look into the future, or lay down any long-distance programme. We were to carry on patiently 'serving' the people, working for the constructive and social reform programme of the Congress, and await the time for aggressive activity. The real difficulty, of course, was that even when that time came, would not some incident like Chauri Chaura upset all our calculations and again hold us up? To that he gave no answer then. Nor was he at all definite in regard to our objective. Many of us wanted to be clear in our own minds what we were driving at, although the Congress did not then need to make a formal declaration on the subject. Were we going to hold out for independence and some measure of social change, or were our leaders going to compromise for something very much less ? Only a few months before, I had stressed independence. This Conference was held in the autumn of 1923, a little after my return from Nabha. I was just recovering from the illness with which Nabha Gaol had presented me and I was unable to attend the Conference, but my address, written under fever in bed, went to it.

While some of us wanted to make the issue of independence clear in the Congress, our friends the Liberals had drifted so far from us—or perhaps the drifting had been done by us—that they publicly gloried in the pomp and power of the Empire, although that Empire might treat our countrymen as a doormat, and its dominions keep our countrymen as helots or refuse them all admittance. Mr. Sastri had become an Imperial Envoy, and Sir Tej Bahadur Sapru had proudly declared at the Imperial Conference in London in 1923: "I can say with pride that it is my country that makes the Empire imperial."

A vast ocean seemed to separate us from these Liberal leaders; we lived in different worlds, we spoke in different languages, and our dreams—if they ever had dreams—had nothing in common. Was it not necessary then to be clear and precise about our goal?

But such thoughts were then confined to a few. Precision is not loved by most people, especially in a nationalist movement which by its very nature is vague and somewhat mystical. In the early months of 1924, public attention was largely concentrated on the Swarajists in the Legislative Assembly and the Provincial Councils. What were these groups going to do after their brave talk about "opposition from within" and wrecking the Councils? Some fine gestures took place. The budget for the year was rejected by the Assembly; a resolution demanding a round-table discussion to settle the terms of Indian freedom was passed. The Bengal Council, under Deshbandhu's leadership, also bravely voted down supplies. But both in the Assembly and in the province, the Viceroy or the Governor certified the budgets and they became law. There were some speeches, some excitement in the legislatures, a momentary feeling of triumph among the Swarajists, headlines in the Press, and nothing more. What else could they do? They could repeat their tactics, but the novelty wore off, the excitement vanished, and the public mind grew accustomed to budgets and laws being certified by the Viceroy or Governor. The next step, of course, was beyond the competence of the Swarajists inside the Councils. It lay outside the Council chamber.

Some time in the middle of that year (1924) a meeting of the All-India Congress Committee was held at Ahmedabad. At this meeting, unexpectedly, a sharp conflict appeared between Gandhiji and the Swarajists, and there were some dramatic situations. The initiative was taken by Gandhiji. He proposed a fundamental alteration in the Congress constitution, changing the franchise and the rules for membership. So far, every one who subscribed to the first article of the Congress constitution, which laid down the objective of Swaraj and peaceful methods, and paid four annas could become a member. He now wanted to limit membership to those who gave a certain amount of self-spun yarn instead of the four annas. This was a serious limitation of the franchise, and the A.I.C.C. was certainly not competent to do this. But Gandhiji has seldom cared for the letter of a constitution when this has come in his way. I was shocked at what I considered a violence to our constitution, and I offered to the Working Committee my resignation from the secretaryship. But some new developments took place and I did not press it. In the A.I.C.C. the proposal was fiercely resisted by my father and Mr. Das, and ultimately, to show their entire disapproval of it, they marched out with a goodly number of their followers just before the voting. Even then some people, opposed to the resolution, still remained present in the Committee. The resolution was passed by a majority, but ultimately it was withdrawn. For Gandhiji had been tremendously affected by the walk-out of the Swarajists and the unbending attitude on this subject of Deshbandhu and my father. He was emotionally worked up, and a chance remark of a member upset him and he broke down. It was obvious that he had been cut to the quick. He addressed the Committee in a most feeling manner and reduced a number of members to tears. It was a moving and extraordinary sight.[1]

1. The above account was written in prison memory. I find now that my memory was defective and I had overlooked an important aspect of the A.I.C.C. discussions, thus giving a wrong impression of

I could never make out why he was so keen on that exclusive form of spinning franchise then, for he must have known that it would be bitterly opposed. Probably he wanted the Congress to consist only of people who were believers in his constructive programme of Khadi, etc., and was prepared to drive out the others or make them conform. But although he had the majority with him, he weakened in his resolve and began to compromise with the others. During the next three or four months, to my amazement, he changed several times on this question. He seemed to be completely at sea, unable to find his bearing. That was the one idea that I did not associate with him, and hence my surprise. The question itself was not, so it seemed to me, a very vital one. The idea of labour being made the qualification for franchise was a very desirable one, but in the restricted form in which it came up,

what happened. What moved Gandhiji was a resolution relating to a young Bengali terrorist (Gopinath Saha) which was moved in the meeting and was altimately lost. The resolution, so far as I remember, condemned his deed but expressed sympathy for his motives. More than the resolution itself, the speeches accompanying it distressed Gandhiji, and it was this feeling that many people in the Congress were not serious about its profession of non-violence that upset him. Writing of this meeting in *Young India* soon after, he said : "I had a bare majority always for the four resolutions. But it must be regarded by me as a minority. The house was fairly evenly divided. The Gopinath Saha resolution clinched the issue. The speeches, the result and the scenes I witnessed after were a perfect eye-opner. . . Dignity vanished after the Gopinath Saha resolution. It was before this house that I had to put my last resolution. As the proceedings went on, I must have become more and more serious. I felt like running away from the oppressive scene. I dreaded having to move a resolution in my charge... I do not know that I have made it clear that no speaker had any malice in him. What preyed upon my mind was the fact of unconscious irresponsibility and disregard of the Congress creed or policy of non-violence . . .That there were seventy Congress representatives to support the resolution was a staggering revelation." This incident, with Gandhiji's commentary on it, is very significant, as it shows the extreme importance attached by Gandhiji to non-violence, and the reactions on him of any attempt, even though this might be unconscious and indirect, to challenge it. Much that he has subsequently done is probably due fundamentally to some such reactions. Non-violence has been, and is, the sheet-anchor of his policy and activities.

it lost some of its meaning.

I came to the conclusion that Gandhiji's difficulties had been caused because he was moving in an unfamiliar medium. He was superb in his special field of Satyagraphic direct action, and his instinct unerringly led him to take the right steps. He was also very good in working himself and making others work quietly for social reform among the masses. He could understand absolute war or absolute peace. Anything in between he did not appreciate. The Swarajist programme, of struggle and opposition inside Councils, left him cold. If a person wants to go to the legislature, let him do so with the object of co-operating with the authorities for better legislation, etc., and not for the sake of opposition. If he does not want to do so, let him stay out, The Swarajists adopted neither of these positions, and hence his difficulty in dealing with them.

Ultimately he adjusted himself to them. The spinning franchise became an alternative form, the old four-anna franchise remaining. He almost blessed the Swarajist work in the legislatures, but for himself he kept severely aloof. It was said that he had retired from politics, and the British Government and its officers believed that his popularity was waning and that he was a spent force. Das and Nehru, it was said, had driven Gandhi into the background; they seemed to dominate the political scene. Such remarks, with suitable variations, have been repeated many times in the course of the last fifteen years, and they have demonstrated every time how singularly ignorant our rulers are about the feelings of the Indian people. Ever since Gandhiji appeared on the Indian political scene, there has been no going back in popularity for him, so far as the masses are concerned. There has been a progressive increase in his popularity, and this process still continues. They may not carry out his wishes, for human nature is often weak, but their hearts are full of goodwill for him. When objective conditions help they rise in huge mass movements, otherwise they lie how. A leader does not create a mass movement out of nothing, as if by a stroke of the magician's wand. He can take advantage of the conditions themselves when they arise; he can prepare for them, but not create them.

But it is true to say that there is a waning and a waxing of Gandhiji's popularity among the intelligentsia. In moments of forward-going enthusiasm they follow him; when the inevitable reaction comes they grow critical. But even so the great majority of them bow down to him. Partly this has been due to the absence of any other effective programme. The Liberals and various groups resembling them, like the Responsivists, do not count; those who believe in terroristic violence are completely out of court in the modern world and are considered ineffective and out of date. The socialist programme is still little known, and it frightens the upper-class members of the Congress.

After a brief political estrangement in the middle of 1924, the old relations between my father and Gandhiji were resumed and they grew even more cordial. However much they differed from one another, each had the warmest regard and respect for the other. What was it that they so respected? Father has given us a glimpse into his mind in a brief Foreword he contributed to a booklet called *Thought Currents*, containing selections from Gandhiji's writings :

"I have heard," he writes, "of saints and supermen, but have never had the pleasure of meeting them, and must confess to a feeling of scepticism about their real existence. I believe in men and things manly. The 'Thought Currents' preserved in this volume have emanated from a man and are things manly. They are illustrative of two great attributes of human nature—Faith and Strength . . .

" 'What is all this going to lead to?' asks the man with neither faith nor strength in him. The answer 'to victory or death' does not appeal to him . . . Meanwhile the humble and lowly figure standing erect . . . on the firm footholds of faith unshakable and strength unconquerable, continues to send out to his countrymen his message of sacrifice and suffering for the motherland. That message finds echo in millions of hearts . . . ."

And he finishes up by quoting Swinburne's lines :

> Have we not men with us royal,
> Men the masters of things ? . . . .

Evidently he wanted to stress the fact that he did not admire Gandhiji as a saint or a Mahatma, but as a man. Strong and unbending himself, he admired strength of spirit in him. For it was clear that this little man of poor physique had something of steel in him, something rock-like which did not yield to physical powers, however great they might be. And in spite of his unimpressive features, his loin-cloth and bare body, there was a royalty and a kingliness in him which compelled a willing obeisance from others. Consciously and deliberately meek and humble, yet he was full of power and authority, and he knew it, and at times he was imperious enough, issuing commands which had to be obeyed. His calm, deep eyes would hold one and gently probe into the depths; his voice, clear and limpid, would purr its way into the heart and evoke an emotional response. Whether his audience consisted of one person or a thousand, the charm and magnetism of the man passed on to it, and each one had a feeling of communion with the speaker. This feeling had little to do with the mind, though the appeal to the mind was not wholly ignored. But mind and reason definitely had second place. This process of 'spell-binding' was not brought about by oratory or the hypnotism of silken phrases. The language was always simple and to the point and seldom was an unnecessary word used. It was the utter sincerity of the man and his personality that gripped; he gave the impression of tremendous inner reserves of power. Perhaps also it was a tradition that had grown up about him which helped in creating a suitable atmosphere. A stranger, ignorant of this tradition and not in harmony with the surroundings, would probably not have been touched by that spell, or, at any rate, not to the same extent. And yet one of the most remarkable things about Gandhiji was, and is, his capacity to win over, or at least to disarm, his opponents.

Gandhiji had little sense of beauty or artistry in man-made objects, though he admired natural beauty. The Taj Mahal was for him an embodiment of forced labour and little more. His sense of smell was feeble. And yet in his own way he had discovered the art of living and had made of his life an artistic whole. Every gesture had meaning and grace, without a false touch. There were no rough edges or sharp corners about him, no trace of vulgarity or commonness, in which, unhappily, our middle classes excel. Having found an inner peace, he radiated it to others and marched through life's tortuous ways with firm and undaunted step.

How different was my father from him! But in him too there was strength of personality and a measure of kingliness, and the lines of Swinburne he had quoted would apply to him also. In any gathering in which he was present he would inevitably be the centre and the hub. Whatever the place where he sat at table it would become, as an eminent English judge said later, the head of the table. He was neither meek nor mild, and, again unlike Gandhiji, he seldom spared those who differed from him. Consciously imperious, he evoked great loyalty as well as bitter opposition. It was difficult to feel neutral about him; one had to like him or dislike him. With a broad forehead, tight lips and a determined chin, he had a marked resemblance to the busts of the Roman Emperors in the museums in Italy. Many friends in Italy who saw his photograph with us remarked on this resemblance. In later years especially, when his head was covered with silver hair—unlike me, he kept his hair to the end—there was a magnificence about him and a grand manner, which is sadly to seek in this world of to day. I suppose I am partial to him, but I miss his noble presence in a world full of pettiness and weakness. I look round in vain for that grand manner and splendid strength that was his.

I remember showing Gandhiji a photograph of father's some time in 1924, when he was having a tug-of war with the Swaraj Party. In this photograph father had no moustache, and, till then, Gandhiji had always seen him with a fine moustache.

He started almost on seeing this photograph and gazed long at it, for the absence of the moustache brought out the hardness of the mouth and the chin, and he said, with a somewhat dry smile, that now he realised what he had to contend against. The face was softened, however, by the eyes and by the lines that frequent laughter had made. But sometimes the eyes glittered.

Father had taken to the work in the Assembly like a duck to water. It suited his legal and constitutional training, and, unlike Satyagraha and its offshoots, he knew the rules of this game. He kept his party strictly disciplined and even induced other groups and individuals to give support. But soon he had to face difficulties with his own people. During the early days of the Swaraj Party, it had to contend against the No changers in the Congress, and many undesirables were taken in to increase its strength within the Congress. Then came the elections, and these demanded funds which had to come from the rich. So these rich folk had to be kept in good humour, and some were even asked to become Swarajist candidates. "Politics," says an American socialist (quoted by Sir Stafford Cripps), "is the gentle art of getting votes from the poor and campaign funds from the rich by promising to protect each from the other."

All these elements weakened the Party from the very beginning. Work in the Assembly and the Councils necessitated daily compromises with other and more moderate groups, and no crusading spirit or principles could long survive this. Gradually a decline in the discipline and temper of the Party set in, and the weaker elements and the opportunists began to give trouble. The Swaraj Party had invaded the legislatures with the declared object of "opposition from within". But two could play at this game, and the Government decided to have a hand in it by creating opposition and disruption within the ranks of the Swarajists. High office and patronage in innumerable ways was placed in the way of the weaker brethren. They had just to pick them up. Their ability and their qualities of statesmanship and sweet reasonableness were praised. A pleasant and agreeable atmosphere was created round them—so different from the dust and tumult of the field and market-place.

The general tone of the Swarajists went down. Individuals here and there began to slip away to the other side. My father shouted and thundered and talked about cutting 'the diseased limb'. But this threat has no great effect when the limb is eager to walk away by itself. Some Swarajists became ministers, some became Executive Councillors in the provinces later. A number formed a separate group calling themselves 'Responsivists' or 'Responsive Co-operators', a name originally used by Lokamanya Tilak in entirely different circumstances. As used now it seemed to mean : take a job when you have the chance and make the best of it. The Swaraj Party carried on in spite of these defections, but father and Mr. Das became a little disgusted with the turn of events and somewhat weary of what seemed to be their profitless work in the legislatures. To add to this weariness of spirit was the growing Hindu-Muslim tension in North India, leading occasionally to riots.

Some Congressmen who had been to prison with us in 1921 and 1922 were now ministers and holders of high offices in the Government. In 1921 we had had the satisfaction of being declared unlawful and being sentenced to prison by a Government of which some Liberals (also old-time Congressmen) were members. In future we were going to have the additional solace of being imprisoned and outlawed by some of our own old colleagues in some provinces at least. These new ministers and Executive councillors were far more efficient for this job than the Liberals had been. They knew us and our weaknesses and how to exploit them; they were well acquainted with our methods; and they had some experience of crowds and the feelings of the masses. Like the Nazis, they had flirted with revolutionary methods before changing sides, and could this knowledge to suppress more efficiently their old colleagues of the Congress than either the official hierarchy or the Liberal ministers in their ignorance could have done.

In December 1924 the Congress session was held at Belgaum, and Gandhiji was President. For him to become the Congress President was something in the nature of an anticlimax, for he had long been the permanent super-president. I did not like his presidential address. It struck me as being very uninspiring. At the end of the session I was again elected, at Gandhiji's instance, the working secretary of the A.I.C.C. for the next year. In spite of my own wishes in the matter, I was gradually becoming a semi permanent secretary of the Congress.

In the summer of 1925 my father was unwell and his asthma troubled him greatly. He went with the family to Dalhousie in the Himalayas, and I joined him for a short while later. We made a little trip from Dalhousie to Chamba in the interior of the Himalayas. It was a June day when we arrived, and we were a little tired after our journey by mountain paths. A telegram came. It told us that Chitta Ranjan Das had died. For a long time father sat still without a word, bowed down with grief. It was a cruel blow to him, and I had seldom seen him so affected. The one person who had grown to be a closer and dearer comrade to him than any one else had suddenly gone and left him to shoulder the burden alone. That burden had been growing, and both he and Deshbandhu had grown aweary of it and of the weakness of their people. Deshbandhu's last speech at the Faridpur Conference was the speech of a person who is a little tried.

We left Chamba the next morning and tramped back over the mountains to Dalhousie, and from there to the distant railhead by car, and then to Allahabad and Calcutta.

My illness in the autumn of 1923, after my return from Nabha prison, when I had a bout with typhus germ, was a novel experience for me. I was unused to illness or lying in bed with fever or physical weekness. I was a little proud of my health, and I objected to the general valetudinarian attitude that was fairly common in India. My youth and good constitution pulled me through, but, after the crisis was over, I lay long in bed in an enfeebled condition, slowly working my way to health. And during this period I felt a strange detachment from my surroundings and my day-to-day work, and I viewed all this from a distance, apart. I felt as if I had extricated myself from the trees and could see the wood as a whole; my mind seemed clearer and more peaceful than it had previously been. I suppose this experience, or something like it, is common enough to those who have passed through severe illness. But for me it was in the nature of a spiritual experience—I use the word not in a narrow religious sense—and it influenced me considerably. I felt lifted out of the emotional atmosphere of our politics and could view the objectives and the springs that had moved me to action more clearly. With this clarification came further questioning for which I had no satisfactory answer. But more and more I moved away from the religious outlook on life and politics. I cannot write much about that experience of mine; it was a feeling I cannot easily express. It was eleven years ago, and only a faded impression of it remains in the mind now. But I remember well that it had a lasting effect on me and on my way of thinking, and for the next two years or more I went about my work with something of that air of detachment.

Partly, no doubt, this was due to developments which were wholly outside my control and with which I did not fit in. I have referred already to some of the political changes. Far more important was the progressive deterioration of Hindu-Muslim relations, in North India especially. In the bigger cities a number of riots took place, brutal and callous in the extreme. The atmosphere of distrust and anger bred new causes of dispute which most of us had never heard of before. Previously a fruitful source of discord had been the question of cow sacrifice, especially on the Bakr-id day. There was also tension when Hindu and Muslim festivals clashed, as, for instance, when the Moharram fell on the days when the Ram Lila was celebrated. The Moharram revived the memory of a past tragedy and brought sorrow and tears; the Ram Lila was a festival of joy and the celebration of the victory of good over evil. The two did not fit in. Fortunately they came together only once in about thirty years, for the Ram Lila is celebrated according to the solar calendar at a fixed time of the year, while the Moharram moves round the seasons, following a lunar year.

But now a fresh cause of friction arose, something that was ever present, ever recurring. This was the question of music before mosques. Objection was taken by the Muslims to music or any noise which interfered with their prayers in their mosques. In every city there are many mosques, and five times every day they have prayers, and there is no lack of noises and processions (including marriage and funeral processions.) So the chances of friction were always present. In particular, objection was taken to processions and noises at the time of the sunset prayer in the mosques. As it happens, this is just the time when evening worship takes place in the Hindu temples, and gongs are sounded and the temple bells ring. *Arti*, this is called, and *arti-namaz* disputes now assumed major proportions.

It seems amazing that a question which could be settled with mutual consideration for each other's feelings and a little adjustment should give rise to great bitterness and rioting. But religious passions have little to do with reason or consideration or adjustments, and they are easy to fan when a third party in control can play off one group against another.

One is apt to exaggerate the significance of these riots in a few northern cities. Most of the towns and cities and the whole of rural India carried on peacefully, little affected by these happenings, but the newspapers naturally gave great prominence to every petty communal disturbance. It is perfectly true, however, that communal tension and bitterness increased in the city masses. This was pushed on by the communal leaders at the top, and it was reflected in the stiffening up of the political communal demands. Because of the communal tension, Muslim political reactionaries, who had taken a back seat during all these years of non-co-operation, emerged into prominence, helped in the process by the British Government. From day to day new and more far-reaching communal demands appeared on their behalf, striking at the very root of national unity and Indian freedom. On the Hindu side also political reactionaries were among the principal communal leaders, and, in the name of guarding Hindu interests, they played definitely into the hands of the Government. They did not succeed, and indeed they could not, however much they tried by their methods, in gaining any of the points on which they laid stress; they succeeded only in raising the communal temper of the country.

The Congress was in a quandary. Sensitive to and representative of national feeling as it was, these communal passions were bound to affect it. Many a Congressman was a communalist under his national cloak. But the Congress leadership stood firm and, on the whole, refused to side with either communal party, or rather with any communal group, for now the Sikhs and other smaller minorities were also loudly voicing their particular demands. Inevitably this led to denunciation from both the extremes.

Long ago, right at the commencement of non-co-operation or even earlier, Gandhiji had laid down his formula for solving the communal problem. According to him, it could only be solved by goodwill and the generosity of the majority group, and so he was prepared to agree to everything that the Muslims might demand. He wanted to win them over, not to bargain with them. With foresight, and a true sense of values he grasped at the reality that was worth while; but others who thought they knew the market price of everything, and were ignorant of the true value of anything, stuck to the methods of the market-place. They saw the cost of purchase with painful clearness, but they had no appreciation of the worth of the article they might have bought.

It is easy to criticise and blame others, and the temptation is almost irresistible to find some excuse for the failure of one's plans. Was not the failure due to the deliberate thwarting of others, rather than to an error in one's own way of thinking or acting? We cast the blame on the Government and the communalists, the latter blame the Congress. Of course, there was thwarting of us, deliberate and persistent thwarting, by the Government and their allies. Of course, British governments in the past and the present have based their policy on creating divisions in our ranks. Divide and rule has always been the way of empires, and the measure of their success in this policy has been also the measure of their superiority over those whom they thus exploit. We cannot complain of this or, at any rate, we ought not to be surprised at it. To ignore it and not to provide against it is in itself a mistake in one's thought.

How are we to provide against it? Not surely by bargaining and haggling and generally adopting the tactics of the market-place, for whatever offer we make, however hight our bid might be, there is always a third party which can bid higher and, what is more, give substance to its words. If there is no common national or social outlook, there will not be common action against the common adversary. If we think in terms of the existing political and economic structure and merely wish to tamper with it here and there, to reform it, to 'Indianise' it, then all real inducement for joint action is lacking. The object then becomes one of sharing in the spoils, and the third and controlling party inevitably plays the dominant role and hands out its gifts to the prize boys of its choice. Only by thinking in terms of a different political framework—and even more so a different social framework—can we build up a stable foundation for joint action. The whole idea underlying the demand for independence was this: to make people realise that we were struggling for an entirely different political structure and not just an Indianised edition (with British control behind the scenes) of the present order, which Dominion Status signifies. Political indendence meant, of course, political freedom only, and did not include any social change or economic freedom for the masses. But it did signify the removal of the financial and economic chains which bind us to the City of London, and this would have made it easier for us to change the social structure. So I thought then. I would add now that I do not think it is likely that real political freedom will come to us by itself. When it comes it will bring a large measure of social freedom also.

But almost all our leaders continued to think within the narrow steel frame of the existing political, and of course the social, structure. They faced every problem—communal or constitutional—with this background and, inevitably, they played into the hands of the British Government, which controlled completely that structure. They could not do otherwise, for their whole outlook was essentially reformist and not revolutionary, in spite of occasional experiments with direct action. But the time had gone by when any political or economic or communal problem in India could be satisfactorily solved by reformist methods. Revolutionary outlook and planning and revolutionary solutions were demanded by the situation. But there was no one among the leaders to offer these.

The want of clear ideals and objectives in our struggle for freedom undoubtedly helped the spread of communalism. The masses saw no clear connection between their day-to day sufferings and the fight for swaraj. They fought well enough at times by instinct, but that was a feeble weapon which could be easily blunted or even turned aside for other purposes. There was no reason behind it, and in periods of reaction it was not difficult for the communalists to play upon this feeling and exploit it in the name of religion. It is nevertheless extraordinary how the *bourgeois* classes, both among the Hindus and the Muslims, succeeded, in the sacred name of religion, in getting a measure of mass sympathy and support for programmes and demands which had absolutely nothing to do with the masses, or even the lower middle class. Every one of the communal demands put forward by any communal group is, in the final analysis, a demand for jobs, and these jobs could only go to a handful of the upper middle class.

There is also, of course, the demand for special and additional seats in the legislatures, as symbolising political power, but this too is looked upon chiefly as the power to exercise patronage. These narrow political demands, benefiting at the most a small number of the upper middle classes, and often creating barriers in the way of national unity and progress, were cleverly made to appear the demands of the masses of that particular religious group. Religious passion was hitched on to them in order to hide their barrenness.

In this way political reactionaries came back to the political field in the guise of communal leaders, and the real explanation of the various steps they took was not so much their communal bias as their desire to obstruct political advance. We could only expect opposition from them politically, but still it was a peculiarly distressing feature of an unsavoury situation to find to what lengths they would go in this respect. Muslim communal leaders said the most amazing things and seemed to care not at all for Indian nationalism or Indian freedom; Hindu communal leaders, though always speaking apparently in the name of nationalism, had little to do with it in practice and, incapable of any real action, sought to humble themselves before the Government, and did that too in vain. Both agreed in condemning socialistic and such-like "subversive" movements; there was a touching unanimity in regard to any proposal affecting vested interests. Muslim communal leaders said and did many things harmful to political and economic freedom, but as a group and individually they conducted themselves before the Government and the public with some dignity. That could hardly be said of the Hindu communal leaders.

There were many Muslims in the Congress. Their numbers were large, and included many able men, and the best-known and most popular Muslim leaders in India were in it. Many of those Congress Muslims organised themselves into a group called the 'Nationalist Muslim Party', and they combated the communal Muslim leaders. They did so with some success to begin with, and a large party of the Muslim intelligentsia seemed to be with them. But they were all upper middle-class folk, and there were no dynamic personalities amongst them. They took to their professions and their businesses, and lost touch with the masses. Indeed, they never went to their masses. Their method was one of drawing-room meetings and mutual arrangements and pacts, and at this game their rivals, the communal leaders, were greater adepts. Slowly the latter drove the Nationalist Muslims from one position to another, made them give up, one by one, the principles for which they stood. Always the Nationalist Muslims tried to ward off further retreat and to consolidate their position by adopting the policy of the 'lesser evil', but always this led to another retreat and another choice of the 'lesser evil', There came a time when they had nothing left to call their own, no fundamental principle on which they stood except one, and that had been the very sheet-anchor of their group : joint electorates. But again the policy of the lesser evil presented the fatal choice to them, and they emerged from the ordeal minus that sheet-anchor, So to-day they stand divested of every shred of principle or practice on the basis of which they formed their group, and which they had proudly nailed to their masthead—of everything, all, except their name !

The collapse and elimination of the Nationalist Muslims as a group—as individuals they are, of course, still important leaders of the Congress—forms a pitiful story. It took many years, and the last chapter has only been written this year (1934). In 1923 and subsequent years they were a strong group, and they took up an aggressive attitude against the Muslim communalists. Indeed, on several occasions, Gandhiji was prepared to agree to some of the latter's demands, much as he disliked them, but his own colleagues, the Muslim Nationalist leaders, prevented this and were bitter in their opposition.

During the middle 'twenties many attempts were made to settle the communal problem by mutual talks and discussions—'Unity Conferences' they were called. The most notable of these was the conference convened by M. Mohamad Ali, the Congress president for the year, in 1924, and held in Delhi under the shadow of Gandhiji's twenty-one-day fast. There were many earnest and well meaning people at these conferences, and they tried hard to come to an agreement. Some pious and good resolutions were passed, but the basic problem remained unsolved. It could not be solved by those conferences, for a solution could not be reached by a majority of votes but by virtual unanimity, and there were always extremists of various groups present whose idea of a solution was a complete submission of all others to their views. Indeed, one was led to doubt whether some of the prominent communalists desired a solution at all. Many of them were political reactionaries, and there was no common ground between them and those who desired radical political change.

But the real difficulties went deeper and were not just the result of individual back-sliding. The Sikhs were now loudly advancing their communal demands, and an extraordinarily complicated triangle was created in the Punjab. The Punjab, indeed, became the crux of the matter, and the fear of each group of the others produced a background of passion and prejudice. In some provinces agrarian trouble—Hindu zamindars and Muslim tenants in Bengal—appeared under communal guise. In the Punjab and Sind, the banker and richer classes generally were Hindus, the debtors were Muslim agriculturists, and all the feeling of the impoverished debtors against the creditor, out for his pound of flesh, went to swell the communal tide. As a rule, the Muslims were the poorer community, and the Muslim communal leaders managed to exploit the antagonism of the have-nots against the haves for communal purposes, though, strangely enough, these purposes had nothing whatever to do with the betterment of those have-nots. Because of this, these Muslim communal leaders did represent some mass elements, and gained strength thereby. The Hindu commual leaders, in an economic sense, represented the rich banker and professional classes; they had little backing among the Hindu masses although, on occasions, they had their sympathy.

The problem, therefore, is getting a little mixed up with economic groupings, though unhappily this fact is not realised. It may develop into more obvious conflicts between economic classes, but if that time comes, the present-day communal leaders, representing the upper classes of all groups, will hasten to patch up their differences in order to face jointly the common class foe. Even under present conditions it should not be difficult to arrive at a political solution, but only if, and it is a big if, the third party was not present.

The Delhi Unity Conference of 1924 was hardly over when a Hindu-Muslim riot broke out in Allahabad. It was not a big riot, as such riots go, in so far as casualties were concerned, but it was painful to have these troubles in one's home town. I rushed back with others from Delhi to find that the actual rioting was over; but the aftermath, in the shape of bad blood and court cases, lasted a long time. I forget why the riot had begun. That year, or perhaps later, these was also some trouble over the Ram Lila celebrations at Allahabad. Probably because of restrictions about music before mosques, these celebrations, involving huge processions as they did, were abandoned as a protest. For about eight years now the Ram Lila has not been held in Allahabad, and the greatest festival of the year for hundreds of thousands in the Allahabad district has almost become a painful memory. How well I remember my visits to it when I was a child! How excited we used to get! And the vast crowds that came to see it from all over the district and even from other towns. It was a Hindu festival, but it was an open-air affair, and Muslims also swelled the crowds, and there was joy and lightheartedness everywhere. Trade flourished. Many years afterwards when, as a grown-up, I visited it I was not excited, and the procession and the tableaux rather bored me. My standards of art and amusement had gone up. But even then, I saw how the great crowds appreciated and enjoyed the show. It was carnival time for them. And now, for eight or nine years, the children of Allahabad, not to mention the grown-ups, have had no chance of seeing this show and having a bright day of joyful excitement in the dull routine of their lives. And all because of trivial disputes and conflicts! Surely religion and the spirit of religion have much to answer for. What kill-joys they have been!

3

Hindu-Muslim Unity

At this point of time, Rafi Ahmad began to show interest in the sessions of the Indian National Congress which he attended as a young delegate. He attended the session of the Congress at Cocanada in 1923 where Maulana Mohamed Ali was the President of the Congress. His name appeared in the Subjects Committee along with Motilal Nehru, Jawaharlal Nehru, Khaliquzzaman and several others. As a young man he felt much encouraged in the company of political stalwarts. But he had no contribution in the initial sessions which he happened to attend.

Soon his disciplined work and devotion paid him rich dividends. When the session of the Congress was held at Kanpur under the presidentship of Sarojini Naidu, Rafi Ahmad was one of the Secretaries of the Reception Committee. The other two Secretaries were Ganesh Shankar Vidyarthi and Krishna Dutt Paliwal. Besides Jawaharlal Nehru, a youngman of thirty-six and Shuaib Qureshi were the General Secretaries of the Congress. Undoubtedly, Rafi Ahmad's began to be recognised as a popular mass leader in the United Provinces.

'Rafi Ahmad's politics in those days was in conformity with that of his leader Motilal who, along with Deshbandhu C.R. Das and Vithalbhai Patel, was in favour of entering the legislatures "to wreck the Government from within". "Congressmen instead of boycotting the elections would stand as candidates", he had declared, "at the polls and after capturing the elected seats would carry on a policy of uniform, continuous and consistent opposition to the Government". Thus they found themselves opposed to the 'No Change' policy of Mahatma's adherents who formed the majority in the Congress. It was at Gaya where the Congress met in December, 1922 under the presidentship of Deshbandhu that Motilal declared the formation of the Swarajya Party which was confirmed by Mr. Das who also resigned his office of President. Rafi Ahmad worked hard during all those strenuous years which preceded and followed the formation of the Swarajya Party. He, with Motilal, undertook a tour of Upper India to educate the people, especially the Congressmen, on the aims and objectives of the newly formed party within the Congress. Intense propaganda was carried on by the leaders of the Swarajya Party who divided the country into zones amongst themselves, Deshbandhu in south India, central India and Bengal; Motilal in upper India and Vithalbhai in Bombay. It was mainly due to the efforts of Motilal and his energetic secretary that the Swarajist Conference was called soon after, at the residence of Motilal where the constitution and plan of the campaign of the Swarajya Party were drawn up. It is a tribute to the hard work done by these leaders of the Swarajya Party that by the middle of the year 1923, the Working Committee of the Congress composed entirely of No-Changers could no longer command a majority in the All India Congress Committee, and had therefore to resign. All this required a great deal of manoeuvres, intense propaganda, and considerable organising ability. Rafi, the Secretary, necessarily played with his leader a most notable role in achieving these marvellous results. It was at this time that he learnt the art of dislodging and disarming his opponents—the strategy which he employed so often during his later career with remarkable success. Gandhites or, more appropriately, the 'No-Changers' were dislodged and the so-called 'Centre Party' which did not accept the Swarajya Party plan but was not die-hard Gandhite either, came into power. These were the circumstances when the Congress session was called at Delhi (September, 1923) under the presidentship of Maulana Abul Kalam Azad, one of the most intelligent and distinguished Muslim leaders. It was mainly through the efforts, influence and wisdom of Maulana Azad that a compromise was arrived at and the "Congressmen were permitted to take part in the forthcoming elections and carry on a uniform, continuous and consistent opposition against the Government within the legislatures. But the Congress as an organisation would have no responsibility in the matter." Though there were then only two months left for elections, the Swarajists put up a strong fight and produced excellent results in C.P. and Bengal. Even to the Centre they returned a strong contingent of which Motilal was elected as the leader. Rafi did not stand as a candidate in these elections as he had passed on the nomination offered to him by Pandit Motilal to a friend. But he had much to do in securing the resounding success with which the efforts of the Swarajya Party met. He perhaps played a more prominent role in elections to the local bodies in Uttar Pradesh in which the Swarajists won a large number of seats and even formed the majority in many cases. It was now that he had the opportunity to show his organising ability which made a deep impression on all those who came into contact with him. Soon he had to shoulder still greater responsibilities. The sudden death of Deshbandhu on June 16, 1925 left Motilal as the sole leader not only of the Swarajya Party but also of the majority of the Congress. According to Gandhi-Das Pact, Mahatma was to devote himself to the Khadi campaign while the Swarajists were to be in charge of the political campaign. Rafi, with his leader, had naturally to bear the burden which increased monifold when dissentions among the Swarajists led to the secession of the Maharashtrians who formed the Responsive Party. At the Cawnpore Congress the Swarajist ideology of entering the Councils was approved of by the Congress. Mainly through the efforts of Pandit Motilal and Rafi, a 'National Demand' which represented the greatest common measure of agreement among the non-official members of the Assembly on the immediate grant of Dominion Status was put forward. But as the Government turned it down, Motilal along with other members of the Swarajya Party withdrew from the Assembly in March

1926. In the latter half of 1926 the Legislatures were dissolved and fresh elections were held in November. These were contested by the Nationalists in the name of the Congress but the results were not very satisfactory as the Muslim Bloc and the Responsivist Bloc emerged in most of the provincial assemblies as well as the Central Assembly. But in these elections Rafi Ahmad was returned to the Central Legislature Assembly from Lucknow and Fyzabad Division Muhammadan rural constituency. On Wednesday, the 19th January 1927, he took the oath of office. It was his good fortune that among his contemporaries in the Assembly were personalities like Madan Mohan Malaviya, Lajpat Rai, Motilal Nehru, M.A. Jinnah, Fazl-i-Hussain, Dr. B.S. Moonje, M.S. Aney, T.A.K. Shervani and Abdul Matin Choudhury, all of whom played important roles in India's struggle for freedom. Rafi soon acquainted himself wilh the procedure of the Assembly. In the very second session, he could put questions and elicit information on various matters of public importance. His questions in the Assembly had a peculiarity of their own. Almost all of them concerned the welfare of the man in the street. It appears that the employment and transfer of the staff of the former Oudh and Rohilkhand Railway from Lucknow to Calcutta had greatly agitated his mind in those days, for he put a number of questions to draw the attention of the Government to the matter. The cancellation of the passport of Salklatwala, M.P., who was to visit India in December, 1926 also formed a subject of his questions. He criticized the Government for its indifferent and callous attitude towards the Indians who had been repatriated from South Africa and expressed concern over their welfare. Again he took up the case of Town Inspectors of Post Officers of Bombay and U.P. circles, many of whom were retrenched under orders of the Government of India. He put in a number of supplementaries to help the cause of the poor employees, little knowing that he was destined to be the first Communications Minister of Free India. Of course he was free from all religious narrow-mindedness. He did not approve, for instance, the move of the 16 Muslim members of the Central Assembly who desired that the Sarda Act should not apply to them on the ground that "the marriage institution of the Muslims is within the category of their personal law and legislation on any aspect of the institution is an invasion thereof", they said in a memorandum. "Sarda's Bill as at present before the Assembly aims at making an offence of what is permissible according to Shariat that is the Islamic law. This is an unwarranted encroachment on the personal rights of a Muslim. It is therefore clear that the Bill should not apply to Muslims". Rafi had two skirmishes with their leader, Maulvi Mohammed Shafee Daoodi, on that score".

He soon made his mark in the party and was selected as the Chief Whip, an enviable position considering the personalities that composed the Swarajya group in the Central Assembly. In the House were a number of groups such as the Nationalist Party, the Swarajya Party, the Muslim Bloc, Responsive Bloc, European Bloc, etc., all with different ideologies. It was indeed very hard for Rafi, who happened to be the Chief Whip of the main opposition party whose numerical strength in the House was not great, to muster any effective number of votes. It is indeed a tribute to Rafi's tact and intelligence that on many an occasion he was able to manoeuvre a majority of votes to get adjournments of the Assembly, inspite of stiff opposition from the Government benches.'

In the All-Parties Conference convenel at Calcutta under the presidentship of M.A. Ansari on 22 Dec. 1928—1 January 1929, Rafi Ahmad was elected as the Secretary of this forum. He contributed Introduction to the brochure broughtout at the time of this convention. He elucidated several issues like the constitutional status for India, fundamental rights, the communal problem and the functioning of the princely States. He greatly praised the Nehru Report and called it a political solution of the prevailing communal problem in our sub-continent. But inspite of his efforts and the efforts of other leaders, the desired results could not be achieved. At this point of time, Muslim League under the chairmanship of M.A. Jinnah began to oppose the Nehru Report and came out with his demand of Fourteen Points by which one-third of the elected seats in both Houses of Legislature for Muslims, reservation of seats for Muslims in Bengal and Punjab on the basis of population of the community, vesting of residuary powers in the provinces and other demands which were not acceptable to the Congress in toto. The Sikhs also demanded a few concessions and the Hindu Mahasabha refused to make any concessions. The Nehru Report thus met with much criticism on account of new issues which Jinnah had raised.

Pattabhi Sitaramayya stated thus : "The All Parties Convention was really lying in Calcutta on its sickbed, one might say, its death-bed. The longer it lived, the more numerous became the demands of the poor relations that gathered around it. Like the calf at Sabarmati, it could not live but would not die. It was therefore necessary to smoothen its way to heaven," and Mahatma Gandhi performed this sacred duty by moving that the Convention may be adjourned *sine die.* This was not all. Opposition to the Nehru Report also came from friendly quarters. The Calcutta session of the Indian National Congress presided over by Motilal Nehru found itself divided into two camps, the elder group which was contented if the demand for Dominion Status was acceded to and was therefore in favour of accepting the Nehru Report while the younger element led by Jawaharlal and Subhash Chandra stood for nothing less than complete independence. The main resolution of the Congress was moved by Mahatma Gandhi which stated that "subject to the exigencies of the political situation, the Congress will adopt the Nehru Constitution in its entirely, if it is accepted by the British Parliament on or before December 31, 1929; but in the event of its non-acceptance by that date or its earlier rejection, the Congress will organise non-violent non-co-operation by advising the country to refuse taxation and in such other manner as may be decided upon".

When Gandhi landed in India in 1915 he was not well-aware of the numerous socio-religious and political problems facing millions of masses in our country. Though hardly forty-six at that point of time, he had gained rich and fruitful political experience during his stay in South Africa for about two decades. The problems in India were, however, quite different and as advised by his *guru*, Gopal Krishna Gokhale, he had to be a passive spectator for one year. The Indian National Congress was three decades old and it so far could not launch a mass movement against the *Raj*.

Gandhi was well-conversant to mobilize people and organize them under a well disciplined leadership. At this time, Congress was deprived of two prominent leaders. Pherozeshah Mehta and Gokhale, and this gave Gandhi an opportunity to come forward on the political scene of India in a few years. The great task he planned and envisaged soon after the end of the global war was the attainment of swaraj for India.

The occurrence of tragic events like the dismemberment of Turkey and the Jallianwala Bagh tragedy at Amritsar afforded Gandhi an opportunity to mobilize the people against the *Raj* by launching mass movement along with Ali Brothers—Mohamed and Shaukat Ali—he took up the cause of Khilafat, and along with the famous Congress leaders he took up the cause of Punjab and the swaraj.

Gandhi had the realization that his great task for the achievement of swaraj would remain unfulfilled unless he sought the sympathy and support of each and every community of India. He became a pioneer to seek Hindu Muslim unity by raising the slogan of secularism in all his political programmes under the banner of the Indian National Congress. Thus he planned to mobilize a huge population of all communities for the national cause for which he launched an incessant non-violent satyagraha for more than three decades. And on this road of rebellion he always wished to have a united action with complete strength and unity.

When the Khilafat issue greatly agitated the minds of the Muslims during 1915—18, he was consulted by the prominent Muslim leaders whom he advised to show patience and to avoid any kind of violent posture against the government.[1] His visit to the Aligarh Muslim University and other places where he pleaded the cause of the Khilafat in large audience proved his sincerity for the Turkish problem.[2]

Thus the means Gandhi adopted to achieve Hindu-Muslim unity were pure and simple. He had to face numerous, complexities to attain this goal. He always condemned clashes, riots and ill-will among communities. Whereas he gave the messege of peace and friendship, he was much critical of murder, loot and arson. He opined, Murder can never he avenged by either murder or taking compensation. The only way to avenge murder is to offer oneself as a willing sacrifice, with no desire for retaliation. Revenge or compensation may furnish some satisfaction to the individual, but I am quite definite that it can never restore peace to or uplift society.[3]

In a letter to M.A. Ansari, on 16 February, 1930, Gandhi showed much concern about the communal problem and agreed that Hindu-Muslim problem was the 'problem of problems'.[4] He however advised him to seek solution of the problem with the cooperation of one and all. He stated, 'I fancy that I see my way clear now'.[5]

It is now 3.30 a.m. I have been struggling to find time to give you a few lines. Your letter I appreciate. It was first seen by Motilalji and Jawaharlal and then read to the Working Committee. There were various comments. No one, however, thought that there was anything in it to warrant a departure from the Lahore programme. I agree that the Hindu-Muslim problem is the problem of problems. But I feel that it has to be approached in a different manner from the one we have hitherto adopted—not (as) at present by adjustment of the political power but by one or the other acting on the square under all circumstances. Give and take is possible only when there is some trust between the respective communities and their representatives. If the Congress can command such trust the matter can proceed further, not before. The Congress can do so only by becoming fearless and strictly just. But meanwhile the third party—the evil British power—has got to be sterilized. There will be no charter of independence before the

Hindus and the Muslims have met but there can be virtual independence before the charter is received. Hence must civil disobedience be forged from day to day by those who believe that there is no escape from non-violence and that violence will never bring freedom to India.

I do not know if I have made myself clear. Anyway my own personal line is cast. I fancy that I see my way clear now. There will be no turning back. I can live if God will and if He finds work for me. I have no interest in living if there is no work for me in the direction for which He appears to me to have called me. If all this be hallucination I must perish in the flames or my own lighting. I want you then to cheer up. It does not matter at all if we do not see eye to eye. It is well with us if our hearts are pure, as I know they are.[6]

(PS)

I had a heart to heart chat with Shuaib. He has promised to meet you. I would love to see as he does. You may share this with him or any friend you like.[7]

M.K.G.

The occurrence of communal riots resulting into loss of lives greatly pained Gandhi's conscience. He was much critical of such riots in Kanpur, Banaras and Mirzapur in 1931.[8] He felt ashamed whenever either of the two communities committed atrocities, but those committed by the Hindus naturally put him to greater shame.[9] He called it an utterly uncivilized practice, and opined that not even a blow should be returned for a blow. In this regard, he begged the Ulema to assist him.[10]

There are many gentlemen belonging to the Jamiat-ul-Ulema with whom I am acquainted. Many of them are persons who have made great sacrifices during satyagraha and have helped us in many ways. I am grateful to them for this. Everyone feels that at present the atmosphere in India has become noxious. Hindus and Muslims lost their sanity in Kanpur, Banaras and Mirzapur. I have heard that the Hindus started the riots in Kanpur. I admit that it was a grave error. Ever since the time of the non-co-operation movement, I have been shouting from the house-tops that if we wish to accomplish our task peacefully, we should try to reason with all people and make an impression upon their minds. If we carry out our task through the use of force, we shall be held guilty in the court of God. Even while picketing foreign cloth and liquor shops, the people overstepped the limits. It is possible that this may have had immediate good results, but we have seen, in Kanpur, how it is fraught with danger. When reports of the atrocities committed by Hindus reached me, my head bent low in shame, I was ashamed of myself. I should feel ashamed whenever either of the two communities commits atrocities, but those committed by the Hindus naturally put me to greater shame. It is a matter of regret that till today neither of the two communities—Hindus or Muslims—has regained its sanity. Nowadays we have established the practice of returning a blow for a word of abuse and a bullet for a blow. This is an uncivilized practice. I say that not even a blow should be returned for a blow. In this matter, I humbly beg the Ulema to assist me. Please use whatever influence you have with the Muslims.[11]

In political matters also, we quarrel with one another. Here, took I wish to take as much help from you as possible. If we do not succeed in this, it will be practically futile to attend the Round Table Conference. I do not desire that this, Government should become an arbitrator between the two of us and give an award. I shall humbly tell the Jamiat-ul-Ulema that it can be of great help in this matter. As a Congressman and as a Hindu, I say that I wish to give the Muslims what they want. I do not wish to act like a Bania. I wish you to put down whatever you want on a blank sheet of paper and I shall agree to it. Jawaharlal too had said the very same thing in prison. The Pathans of the Frontier Province carry rifles and swords, but in this war they did not make use of either, like brave men they received the bullets upon their chests, they bore in silence whatever suffering fell to their lot. Jawaharlal said: "I would put a pen into the hands of such people and ask them to write down what they wanted and I would affix my signature to it." It has become the duty of the Congress to settle matters now with minority communities in this way alone. Those who belong to the Congress cannot make any distinctions between Hindus and Muslims. From here we shall be proceeding to Delhi. We have received a telegram from Maulana Shaukat Ali asking us to send a delegation on behalf of the Congress to a conference of Muslims which is being held there. Sardar Patel has already sent in the names of the members of this delegation. That conference is being held on the 4th and the 5th, where every effort will be made (for a settlement). A mountain of difficulties faces us, but if you too try, the problem will be solved within two or three days. I too shall do likewise. I am aware that the Muslims are greatly enraged by the incidents which took place in Kanpur and other places but, at this juncture, it is our duty to resolve this issue somehow.[12]

The Congress has, by passing a long resolution, set its own standards, from which it can be seen that the swaraj which will be established will be for benefit of the poor. The Congress belongs to the poor, it belongs to the peasants.

It is not right to say that the Congress is a Hindu organization. What is the Congress to do if Muslims would not care to go into it? The Congress is based on adult franchise, and any adult Hindu or Mussalman can join the Congress. No community is excluded. Ask the Muslim friends who are members of the Congress, and they well tell you that they have not come to grief by having joined the Congress. I ask you therefore not to suspect that the Congress is a Hindu organization. I ask every one of you to join the Congress and to take charge of it. But one cannot take charge of it by force. It can be done only by willing service. Ever since the Congress was started, those who have served it have had charge of it. And yet the Congress does not belong only to them, does not stand only for them, it belongs to and stands for all. It is the swaraj Government in embryo. Its prestige is ever so much superior to that of the British Government, and the Congress President is greater than the Viceroy. Only moneyed people and men in high places know the Viceroy. One needs a motor-car to reach the Viceregal House. But the poorest man knows the Congress President (at present Sardar Vallabhbhai) and can walk up to him. The Sardar has dedicated himself to the service of the country, and he who serves the poor is great in the eyes of God. If you want to be in power under swaraj, I invite you to assume the reins of the Congress now by joining it in large numbers. It is the most powerful organization in the country, join it. We will welcome you.

At this juncture, I am reminded of the simplicity and determination of Hazrat Umer. He could not permit for himself or for his wealthy associates any luxuries or adornments. He made those who wore muslim or velvet discard those garments and made them wear khadi. He made those who were fond of finely ground flour give it up. Will not the Muslims today make such sacrifice for the sake of the poor?

The Spinners' Association, which is an organization under Congress, has to date spent Rs. 30 lakhs for this purpose. Who received this money? I would like to inform you that the larger portion of this amount has gone to poor Muslim women, as they form the majority among the spinners. The larger quantity of fine khadi is woven from yarn spun by sacred Muslim hands. Many of the weavers of khadi are Muslims. Is khadi made in this manner prohibited to you under a religious injunction, whereas cloth made in Manchester is something permissible? But forget the Muslims, for that matter. It is merely an accident that the major portion of that amount goes to the Muslims, but are not Hindu weavers your brothers? Cannot articles made by them be fit enough for your use? You refer to God as Rahim, you recite *kalamas*. I am an insignificant individual, but I too have read the Koran Sharif. But there is not a single *kalama* in it which gives you the right to wear foreign cloth. Although thus the Koran permits you to do nothing else, only a handful of Muslims are wearing khadi. At the most, some wear mill-made cloth, but the majority wear only foreign cloth. If the Jamiat-ul-Ulema has any love for the poor, it is its duty to take up khadi work. I know of an old woman of sixty who earns her living by spinning yarn. How much must she be earning in this way? And yet she breaks into tears if no one buys her yarn. Whether a cowrie his any value for you or not, that poor woman values it. From the money she gets from yarn every week, she does not buy tobacco or cigarettes, but lentils, vegetables, ghee and milk for her child. I have merely cited an instance to you. Do you feel no compassion for thousands of such poor people? If you do feel no compassion towards them, I tell you that you cannot attain heaven even by performing the *namaz* five times. A Hindu, with great humility, wishes to tell this to you learned Ulema. Moreover, I would humbly tell you that you may as well not recite *namaz*, but fear God and fear no man. If I am mistaken in saying this, forgive me, but understand the feeling in my heart.[13]

Now I wish to address a few words to the Muslim zamindars of Sind. I am of opinion that Sind should be made a separate province. However, nowadays I receive hundreds of telegrams and letters from the Hindus of Sind. Today too a deputation of Hindus met me. I replied to them in accordance with my understanding of the situation, but I also asked them to go and meet Muslims first as they came and met me. Now I ask you why are they afraid of meeting you? Why do you not go to them to see their privations? Why is it that the Hindus of Sind distrust you so much? They are afraid of you. Why are they afraid of you? Is it not your duty to rid them of their fear? If they are afraid of you, is it not a matter of shame to you? With a great deal of humility, I appeal to you, the Ulema, to persuade the Muslims of Sind to win the confidence of the Hindus there. I wish that the Hindus and the Muslims would jointly send me telegrams that both are agreeable to having Sind made into a separate province. Sind does not belong to the Muslims only but to both the communities. It is in your hands to make it into the best province. There are fakir-devotees like Jamshed Mehta in Sind. The

Sind Muslims are a wealthy people. There are intelligent, rich Amils residing in Sind. Sindhis have gone forth to all the corners of the world. By combining all your abilities, you can turn Sind into the most advanced province. If the Hindus stop sending me telegrams, the country will save money, I can spin more yarn and devote my time to more important work. If you can do this, your achievement will produce a good impression on other provinces. This is my humble request. It is my prayer to God that my words may touch your hearts and that He cleanse the hearts of all of us.[14]

In an article on 'Save the Cow' in *Young India,* Gandhi believed that it must be an article of faith for every Hindu that the cow could only be saved by the Mussulman friendship.[15] He asked Hindus to be patient as it must take time for it to react upon the Muslim masses.[16] He advised Hindus that they should develop their *Goshala* so as to make it a model dairy farm as well as a home for aged and infirm cattle.[17]

Professor Vaswani has unfurled the banner of the cow's freedom. The danger has come sooner than I had expected. I had hoped that it would come when India could regard it with equanimity. In my humble opinion, Professor Vaswani might have started the movement under better auspices. Any movement started by Hindus for protecting the cow, without wholehearted Mussulman co-operation, is doomed to failure.

The Hindu's participation in the Khilafat is the greatest and the best movement for cow-protection. I have therefore called Khilafat our *Kamadhuk*.

The Mussulmans are striving their utmost to respect Hindu susceptibilities in this matter of life and death to the Hindu. The Muslim League under Hakim Ajmal Khan's presidentship carried a cow-protection resolution at Amritsar two years ago. Maulana Abdul Bari has written upon it. The Ali Brothers, for the sake of their Hindu countrymen, have given up the use of beef in their house. Mian Chhotani saved hundreds of cows in Bombay alone during the last *Bakr-i-Id*. We could not accuse our Mussulman countrymen of apathy in the matter.

The surest way of defeating our object is to rush Mussulmans. I do not know that Mussulman's honour has ever been found wanting. With them, as with everyone, prejudices die hard. We have got enlightened Mussulman opinion with us. It must take time for it to react upon the Mussulman masses. The Hindus must therefore be patient.

There is nothing strange about all the Shikarpur Hindus' having voted unanimously in favour of the prohibition of cow-slaughter. Is there a Hindu who will not vote it? The use of that unanimous opinion for bearing down Mussulman opposition is the way to stiffen it. The Hindu members must have known, must have ascertained, Mussulman feeling. And they should have refrained from going to a division, so long as the Mussulman opinion was against them.

Let us recognize that there is an interest actively working to keep us--Hindus and Mussulmans—divided. That very interest is quite capable of developing regard for Hindu susceptibilities in this respect. I should beware of it, and distrust it. I strongly advise the Shikarpur friends to wait for their Mussulman brethren.

Let them by all means abstain from all meat, so that their Mussulman brethren may have other meat cheaper than beef. Let them consider it a shame to have a single cow or her progeny in distress, or undergoing ill-treatment at the hands of Hindus themselves. Let them develop their *Goshala* so as to make it a model dairy farm as well as a home for aged and infirm cattle. Let them breed the finest cattle in their *Goshala*. They will do real service to *Gomata*. Let the Shikarpuris be one and become true non-co-operators, and hasten the redress of the Khilafat wrong. I promise they will save the cow when they have done their utmost to save the Khilafat.

It must be an article of faith for every Hindu that the cow can only be saved by Mussulman friendship. Let us recognize frankly that complete protection of the cow depends purely upon Mussulman goodwill. It is as impossible to bend the Mussulmans to our will as it would be for them to bend us to theirs. We are evolving the doctrine of equal and free partnership. We are fighting Dyerism—the doctrine of frightfulness.

Cow-protection is the dearest possession of the Hindu heart. It is the one concrete belief common to all Hindus. No one who does not believe in cow-protection can possibly be a Hindu. It is a noble belief. I endorse every word of what Professor Vaswani has said in praise of the cow. Cow-worship means to me worship of innocence. For me the cow is personification of innocence. Cow-protection means the protection of the weak and the helpless. As Professor Vaswani truly remarks, cow-protection means brotherhood between man and beast. It is a noble sentiment that must grow by patient toil and *tapasya*. It can be imposed upon anyone. To carry cow-protection at the point of the sword is a contradiction in terms. *Rishis* of old are said to have performed penance for the sake of the cow. Let us follow in the footsteps of the *rishis* of old said to have performed penance for the sake of the cow. Let us follow in the footsteps of the *rishis*, and ourselves do penance, so that we may be pure enough to protect the cow and all that the doctrine means and implies.[18]

Gandhi was very unhappy over the occurrence of communal riots in U.P. in early 1938. He warned that the Congressmen might not treat his warning lightly.[19] Calling himself a 'Congress expert' on non-violence, he cited examples of Ahmedabad. Viramgam violences, Bombay violence during the visit of the Prince and Chauri Chaura tragedy.[20] He opined that they must discover a solution for the Hindu-Muslim tension. Congressmen must not be afraid to find themselves in a minority. Every Provincial Congress Committee should raise a proper corps of volunteers sincerely pledged to non-violence in thought, word and deed. He argued emphatically that the Congress was the only political organization in the world which had, at his instance, adopted unadulterated non-violence for the attainment of swaraj. He feared that 'In the last heat we may be found to be cowards instead of brave men and women.[21]

My remarks arising out of the recent riots in U.P. have attracted much attention. Friends have sent me cuttings from the press. This is some of the criticism printed or spoken :

(1) My writing betrayed hysteria.

(1) I wrote without sufficient data.

(3) I had recanted my views on non-co-operation and civil resistance.

(4) I had been driven to the policy of the Liberals.

(5) Congressmen had never adopted non-violence as between themselves.

(6) I was expecting the impossible from human nature.

(7) If my position was accepted swaraj would never be obtained, for all India could never become non-violent.

There is much more I could call from the criticism. I have only taken the relevant parts.

1. If my article betrayed hysteria, the symptoms still persist, for in spite of the criticism which I have studied with the care it demanded, I see nothing to change the position I have taken up. The critics should remember that my proposition was specific and narrow. Swaraj could not be obtained through non-violent means unless our non-violence was of the brave and such as to be able to deal effectively with violence. I have not maintained that it could not be obtained by other means. But if it could be so obtained we were not ready to deliver the goods, for we were not ready for matching out force against the British.

2. All the data required were that there were riots, no

matter on how small a scale, that Congressmen were not able to deal with them non-violently, and that the aid of the police and the military had to be summoned. There was no dispute about these three broad facts. They were enough to enable me to draw the conclusions I did. In this there was no reflection on the Ministers. I have admitted that they could not have acted otherwise. The fact, however, remains that the Congress non-violence was not able to cope with the emergency.

3. There is nothing in my article to warrant the inference that I had lost my faith in non-co-operation and civil resistance. All I need say is thgt it is brighter than ever. The two are quite enough to bring swaraj, provided that non-violence practised is of the bravest.

4. I wish I could be drawn towards the policy of the Liberals. I have many personal friends among them. But they have no sanction. I claim that I have an infallible sanction. My article was written to show that during the riots it was not the sanction that had failed, the failure was of the organization which had accepted the sanction, namely, active, constructive non-violence.

5. I can only refer the critics to the many resolutions of the Congress which do not confine the use of non-violence only towards Englishmen. Indeed I remember having many discussions at the Working Committee meetings at which the necessity of non-violence among ourselves was emphasized.

6. Well, human nature has hitherto responded nobly to the call of non-violence. But I am concerned with the Congress nature. Congressmen have to sign a pledge which commits them to non-violence. My question was and is—have they non-violence in them? If they have, is it of the brave? My thesis is that if it is of the brave, it should be enough for dealing with riots and for delivering the goods.

7. This is answered in the foregoing.

But I have the fear that our non-violence is not of the kind required. Congressmen may not treat my warning lightly. After all I am supposed to be the Congress expert, however inefficient, on non-violence. I have confidence in my readings and my remedies. I cite Ahmedabad and Viramgam violences, Bombay violence during the Prince's visit, and Chauri Chaura on the eve of Bardoli. The results have amply justified the remedies applied at my instance, though on these occasions critics were not wanting who had expressed their strong disapproval of the suspensions. I have no doubt about my present diagnosis (or) about the remedies. The remedies are not beyond our ability if we have a living conviction about non-violence and its nature. Here are some of the remedies :

1. We must discover a solution for the Hindu-Muslim tension. I use that expression deliberately instead of 'communal'—for if we find this, the other will follow as a matter of course.

2. There must be a purging of the Congress registers so as to make them proof against bogus voters. From all accounts I receive, our registers contain too many bogus names to be called at all accurate.

3. Congressmen must not be afraid to find themselves in a minority.

Without delay every Provincial Congress Committee should raise a proper corps of volunteers pledged to non-violence in thought, word and deed. And there should be a manual of instructions as to training, etc., prepared for universal use.

There is nothing heroic or impracticable in these suggestions. But they are impracticable if those who lead have no living faith in non-violence. If they have not, the sooner non-violence is removed from the Congress vocabulary the better it is for the Congress and the nation. The alternative is certainly not unadulterated violence. The Congress is the only political organization in the world which has, at my instance, adopted unadulterated non-violence for the attainment of swaraj. It is its only sanction. I dare say that if its quality is not what it should be, it will do great harm to the nation.

In the last heat we may be found to be cowards instead of brave men and women. And there is no disgrace greater than cowardice for fighters for freedom. Surely there is nothing to be ashamed of in retracing our steps. If we feel that we shall not be able to displace the British power without a violent struggle, the Congress must say so to the nation and prepare accordingly. We must do what is being done all the world over—'forbear when we can, hit when we must'. If that is to be our creed or policy, we have lost precious seventeen years. But it is never too late to learn and mend. Seventeen years in the life of a nation is nothing. It will go hard with Congressmen if having received the warning they do not make the choice.[22]

He called Moplah revolt as a test for Hindus and Muslims. He stated that Hindus must have the courage and the faith to feel that they could protect their religion in spite of such fanatical eruptions. He argued that a verbal disapproval of the Mussulmans or Moplah madness was no test of Mussulman friendship.[23] He also warned that the Muslims must naturally feel the shame and humiliation of the Moplah conduct about forcible conversions and looting, and they must work away silently and effectively that such things might become impossible even on the part of the most fanatical among them.[24]

A correspondent from Scotland takes me to task for not dealing sufficiently with the Moplah rising in these columns. The result, he says, has been that those in Great Britain who are in the habit of studying Indian affairs have been induced to believe that an Islamic kingdom is established in India. The reproof is not wholly underserved, but I have not shirked duty in the matter. I have been simply helpless. I wanted to go to Calicut and reach the bottom of the trouble. They certainly do not wish to give non-cooperators the credit for peacefully ending the trouble. They are desirous of showing once more, that it is only the British soldier who can maintain peace in India. And I could not then give battle to the Government by disregarding the instructions not to enter the disturbed area.

I should like to think better of the men on the spot. It is contrary to my nature to believe in the depravity of human beings. But there is so much evidence about me of the depravity of the bureaucratic mind that it will stop at nothing to gain its end. It is the literal truth I tell, when I say that before I went to Champaran, I did not believe the stories I was told of atrocities committed against the peasantry of Champaran. When I went there, I found the state much worse than was described to me. I had refused to believe that innocent people could have been murdered in cold blood without warning as they were in Jallianwala Bagh. I had refused to believe that human beings could be made to crawl upon their bellies. But on reaching the Punjab, I found to my horror that much more than what I was told had happened. And all this was done in the name of peace and order-so-called, but in reality for the purpose of sustaining a false prestige, a false system and an unnatural commerce. It is true that a strong Lieutenant-Governor was able to attain justice in Champaran in the face of overwhelming opposition. But that was really an exception due to exceptional causes. And so I feel the Moplah revolt has come as a blessing to a system that is crumbling to pieces by the weight of its own enormity.

The Moplah revolt is a test for Hindus and Mussulmans. Can Hindu friendship survive the strain put upon it? Can Mussulmans in the deepest recesses of their hearts approve of the conduct of the Moplahs? Time alone can show the reality. A verbal and forced philosophic acceptance of the inevitable is no test of Hindu friendship. The Hindus must have the courage and the faith to feel that they can protect their religion in spite of such fanatical eruptions. A verbal disapproval by the Mussulmans of Moplah madness is no test to Mussulman friendship. The Mussulmans must naturally feel the shame and humiliation of the Moplah conduct about forcible conversions and looting, and they must work away so silently and effectively that such things might become impossible even on the part of the most fanatical among them. My belief is that the Hindus as a body have received the Moplah madness with equanimity and that the cultured Mussulmans are sincerely sorry for the Moplah's perversion of the teachings of the Prophet.

The Moplah revolt teaches another lesson, *viz.*, that each individual must be taught the art of self-defence. It is more a mental state that has to (be) inculcated than that our bodies should be trained for retaliation. Our mental training has been one of feeling helpless. Bravery is not a quality of the body, it is of the soul. I have seen cowards encased in tough muscles, and rare courage in the frailest body. I have seen big bulky and muscular Zulus cowering before an English lad and turning tail if they saw a loaded revolver pointed at them. I have seen Emily Hob-house with a paralytic body exhibiting courage of the highest order. She was the one noble women who kept up the drooping spirits of brave Boer generals and equally brave Boer women. The weakest of us physically must be taught the art of facing dangers and giving a good account of ourselves. What was more detestable, the ignorant fanaticism of the Moplah brother, or the cowardliness of the Hindu brother who helplessly muttered the Islamic formula or allowed his tuft of hairs to be cut or his vest to be changed? Let me not be misunderstood. I want both the Hindus and Mussulmans to cultivate the cool courage to die without killing. But if one has not that courage, I want him to cultivate the art of killing, and being killed, rather than in a cowardly manner flee from danger. For the latter in spite of his flight does commit mental *himsa*. He flees because he has not the courage to be killed in the act of killing.

There is yet another lesson the Moplah outbreak teaches us. We dare not leave any section of our countrymen in utter darkness and expect not to be overtaken by it ourselves. Our English "masters" were uninterested in the Moplahs becoming orderly citizens and learning the virtue of toleration and the truth of Islam. But we too have neglected our ignorant countrymen all these long centuries. We have not felt the call of love to see that no one was left ignorant of the necessity of humanness or remained in want of food or clothing for no fault of his own. If we do not wake up betimes, we shall find a similar tragedy enacted by all the submerged classes. The present awakening is affecting all classes. The "untouchables" and all the so-called semisavage tribes will presently bear witness to our wrongs against them if we do not do penance and render tardy justice to them.[25]

References

1. *See* for details S.R. Bakshi, *Gandhi and Khilafat*, Delhi, 1985, Chapter I.
2. *Ibid.*
3. *Harijan*, 18 August 1946.
4. *Ansari Papers* : *Gandhi to Ansari*, 16 February 1930.
5. *Ibid.*
6. *Ibid.*
7. *Ibid.*
8. *Navajivan*, 19 April 1931.
9. *Ibid.*
10. *Ibid.*
11. *Ibid.*
12. *Ibid.*
13. *Ibid.*
14. *Ibid.*
15. *Young India*, 8 June 1921.
16. *Ibid.*
17. *Ibid.*
18. *Ibid.*
19. *Harijan*, 9 April 1938.
20. *Ibid.*
21. *Ibid.*
22. *Ibid.*
23. *Young India*, 20 October 1921.
24. *Ibid.*
25. *Ibid.*

4

The Khilafat

"Islam compels obedience to the Khalif as much as it does to the word of Allah and to the Prophet. A Muslim has to obey the Khalif unless the latter goes against the order of God and the Prophet. Disobedience to the Khalif is the source of displeasure of God and his Prophet. There is a tradition quoted by Ibni Omar which runs thus : "He who rebelled against the authority of the Khalif would not be forgiven on the day of Resurrection".[1]

In the second decade of the twentieth century, when the Ottoman Empire had greatly weakend and began to be nick-named as the 'sickman of Europe',[2] some European powers made it their convenient target and made plans for its extinction. So far so, in 1911, Tripoli, a part of the Turkish Empire, became a victim of European aggression : Italy could have an easy edge over it and occupied it.[3] This occupation led to the inhuman treatment of Italy towards Arabs. The massacre of captives—innocent men, women and children—was indiscriminate. Meanwhile the Balkan States also revolted. The Turks resisted but ultimately met with a crushing defeat, and the result was that the Ottoman Empire came to an end.[4]

Gandhi moved a comprehensive resolution in a meeting of the citizens of Bombay reaffirming the following resolution of the Congress Working Committee which was passed on 5th October 1921. 'The working Committee congratulates the Ali Brothers and their comrades upon their prosecution and having considered the Resolution of the Khilafat Conference held at Karachi, regarding Military Service under the Government, the Working Committee is of opinion that the Resolution virtually reaffirms the principle laid down by the Congress at its special session in Calcutta, and its ordinary session in Nagpur last year, that it is contrary to national dignity and national interest for any Indian to engage or remain in the service of a Government in any capacity whatsover; a Government that has used the soldiers for the purpose of crushing the national spirit of the Egyptians, the Turks, the Arabs and other nations. The Working Committee has been only deterred from calling out the soldiers and the civilians in the name of the Congress because the Congress is not yet ready to support these Government servants who may have to leave Government Service and who may not be able themselves to find means of livelihood. The Working Committee, however, is of opinion that in pursuance of the spirit of the Congress Resolution on non-cooperation, it is a clear duty of every Government employee, whether soldier of civilian, who can support himself without Congress assistance to leave such service.

'The Working Committee draws the attention of all Indian soldiers and police to the fact that carding and handspinning and hand-weaving afford them, by undergoing training for a brief period, an honourable means for independent livelihood. The Working Committee is further of opinion that the reasons given for the prosecution with reference to the said Karachi Resolution constitute an undue interference with religious liberty'.[5]

Lala Lajpat Rai opined in *The Political Future of India in* 1919 thus: 'With 70 million Moslems India is the most important centre of Mohammedan sentiment. With Christians as their present rulers, the Hindus and Mohammedans of India are coming to realise that their best interests require a closing up of their ranks . . . The Hindus will stand by their Mohammedan countrymen in all their efforts to revive the glory of Islam, and to regain political independence for it.

There is no fear of a Pan-Islamic movement if the new spirit of internationalism prevails. If, however, it does not, the Pan-Islamic movement might find a sympathetic hand in India, . . .'[6]

The series of Khilafat conferences held at various places, from time to time, under the presidentship of prominent leaders, proved effective in inculcating the anti-*Raj* spirit amongst Muslims and their supporters. They favoured the idea of boycotting British goods and recommended the use of *swadeshi* goods. They offered their services and wealth to any of the workers who were willing to bear death or jail if need be in the case of Islam. They spoke at length on the point of migration to Afghanistan and urged the people to take advantage of the Amir's offer and leave India.

Maulvi Ahmed Said accused Muslims of not being united and of not respecting leaders as Hindus respected Gandhi. He accused the British of having arrested *Sheikh-ul-Islam* of Turkey by treachery and pointed out that the British did everyhing by the methods of treachery. He called upon the title-holders to return their titles to government and follow the example set by Hakim Ajmal Khan.

Maulvi Muhammad Daud Ghaznavi upbraided the government for its tyranny and drew comparisons between the Turkish massacres of Armenians and the Punjab disturbances. He asked the Muslims if they were waiting for the mosque of Sophia at Constantinople to be turned into Church and *Khalifat-ul-Muslemen* to be murdered. He called upon them to follow God, encouraged them by saying that they had nothing to fear from the British government.

Syed Ataullah of Amritsar prefixed his speech by reading out verses from the Quran. He urged Muslims to attain their aim by *jehad* or *hijrat*. He referred to Englishmen as elephants and sheep of Christ, and themselves as ants. When an ant got into the trunk of an elephant and bit him, he was dead. So also would they bite and Englishmen would not live.[7]

Maulana Abdul Bari stated on 15 October 1920 at Lucknow thus: 'If at Englishman has given his life here, lacs of Hindus and Muhammadans have been killed there. If lacs of Muhammadans have been Massacred there is Smyrna, and if after this anyone killed Christians they have wreaked vengeance on Constantinople. If that man has killed for the sake of religion, he will become a martyr. If he is killed, paradise is waiting for him and the virgins are standing with cups for him . . . It is duty of the Muhammadans to do everything by which liberty may be secured.'[8]

As a protest against the terms of the Treaty of Peace with Turkey, Hakim Ajmal Khan returned the *Kaisar-i-Hind* Medal as well as the silver medal granted to him on the occasion of the Coronation of His Majesty. He apprised Gandhi of the relationship between Hindus and Muslims on 17 March 1922. He stated, 'I have no doubt that the secret of the progress of our country lies in the unity of the Hindus, the Mussalmans and other races of India . . . I prize the unity of races inhabiting our country that, if the country gave up all other activities and achieved that alone, I would consider the Khilafat and the swaraj questions automatically solved to our satisfaction . . . We can only achieve it by the sincerity and purity of our hearts.

'I do not consider the question of the Khilafat, in other words, the question of the evolution of Islamic policy, a passing phase . . . God alone knows how and when it will finally be solved . . . It is an admitted fact that looking to the present condition of India, next to Hindu-Muslim unity in importance is the question of non-violence . . . Unity of the races inhabiting India and non-violence are the two essential conditions for the success of the present movement'.[9]

The members of the Khilafat Deputation presented a Memorial to the Viceroy on the subject of the Turkish Peace Terms. '. . . The preservation of the Khilafat as a temporal no less than a spiritual institution is not so much a part of their faith as the very essence thereof, and no analogies from other creeds that tolerate the lacerating and devitalising distinction between things spiritual and things temporal between the Church and the State, can serve any purpose save that of clouding and befogging the clearest of issues. Temporal power is of the very essence of the institution of the Khilafat, and Mussalmans can never agree to any change in its character or to the dismemberment of its Empire.'

The no less important question of the Jazirat-ul-Arab, over no portion of which can any kind of non-Muslim control be tolerated, is equally clearly not one of Muslim sentiment, but of Islamic faith.

Similarly Islam also declares and defines the sanctity of the Holy Places of Islam, and places this and similar matters beyond the uniformed interpretation of people of alien faiths. Mussalmans insist and with perfect reason, that the Khalifat alone shall be the warden of the Holy Places.[10]

As representative of the Central Khilafat Committee, Maulana Shaukat Ali gave vent to his feelings at Lucknow on 15 October 1920, '. . . The sympathy of Sir Harcourt Butler has been exploded. You will know that all, whether Butler or O'Dwyer are birds of the same feather . . . It is my religious belief and that of the Muhammadans that to die and to kill in the path of God, to die and kill in the path of righteouseness, to die and kill in the path of truth, are acts which will both please God . . . so long as the question of Khilafat and the liberty of India is not settled, they will act according to the dictates of their leader Mahatma Gandhi, they will sacrifice their lives, they will go to jail, they will be hanged . . . If God forbid, he (Gandhi) is not successful, I would make a challenge that there is not a single wordly power which can stand against 33 crores of persons, who, relying on God, will use their physical power . . . Both Hindus and Muhammadans, for the sake of their prophet, for the sake of their religion, for the sake of their salvation should be determined sincerely that so long as their demands are not satisfied they, men and women, young and old, poor and rich, should, shoulder to shoulder, leave no stone unturned until they secure complete victory.'[11]

On 26-27 February 1921, Shaukat Ali in his speech at Lucknow stated, '. . . . Our voice is the voice of God. We number thirty crores. Sacrifice your own lives, strong soldiers . . . We have now to be manly. What can they do? I declare today that the Indian army is the army of Mahatma Gandhi. The Indian police is police of Mahatma Gandhi . . . We will be given *swaraj*. They will come with folded hands, bend down on their knees and rub their noses on the ground and say, "For God's sake take *sawraj*, Khilafat and the Punjab but allow us to stay in India". I say, they must repent and apologise . . . The thirty crores of Indians have to become brave . . . Call at every house and take one rupee per head not excluding even a poor man. Realize five or ten rupees from those who are rich . . . The Government will oppress us. Let us have one month more, so that we may realize money . . . Therefore, I request you to be generous and help us, as far as you can, in this work. God will bless you.'[12]

Mohamed Ali preached Pan-Islamism from the Khilafat Committee as well as the Congress platforms. He wanted to accomplish this in India. He opined in his presidential address, 'To die for a cause is not difficult. The harder thing is to live for a cause, and if need be, suffer for it . . . and the cause we must live and suffer for must be the realization in India of the Kindom of God'.

Undoubtedly, Mohamed Ali was fully conscious of the religious differences between the two major communities of the country. He, however, maintained his linkage with the Indian National Congress as well as with Mahatma Gandhi's ideology. But there were a few factors which impelled him to give up this linkage and take a separate line of action. The cause of Khilafat, supported and sponsored for a few years, could not come to fruition on account of some international developments. The communal riots perpetrated in various regions of India had marred the atmosphere and the efforts of the Congress leaders, at various levels, to contain these riots and to maintain peace and goodwill could not bear the desired results. These factors combined with a few others lead to doubts in the minds of the leaders. Also serious differences began to develop with the Congress leadership. Mohamed Ali began to give vent to his feelings in a way which ultimately made him severe his relationship with Gandhi and the Indian National Congress.[13] He said, 'I do not wish to create a home-made incubus of a caste of shopkeepers of our own. To my mind most of the agitation is being financed, and partly for selfish reasons, by the Banias of Bombay and Gujarat'.[14]

The future of the Khilafat became uncertain after the decision made at the Paris Conference, and this was taken as a serious challenge by the Muslims with a wave of resentment, anger and dissatisfaction in their hearts. The issue was raised in numerous meetings, public speeches and deputations. A few demands were however made, and these were Turkish independence and autonomy; restoration of Thrace, Smyrna, Adrianpole and other regions of Asia Minor.

The subservience shown by Mohmed VI, the Sultan of Turkey, to the Allies made his position weak and untenable in the estimation of the Nationalists and on 1st November, 1922, the Sultanate was abolished. The Sultan—Caliph fled from Constantinople and the Turkish National Assembly elected his cousin as Caliph, with purely spiritual and on temporal power over the faithful. On 29 October 1923, a republic was proclaimed in Turkey. Mustafa Kemal, the saviour of Turkey's independence who emphasised his country's Asiatic outlook and her desire to build a national life in Anatolia by changing the capital from Constantinople to Ankara, became the first President. His main aim was to free Turkey from foreign influence and domination and this he achieved by the Treaty of Lausanne.[15]

The arrest of Ali Brothers greatly pained Gandhi. He

called them brave Brothers and staunch lovers of their country.[16] Their role in the Khilafat cause was also eulogised. They were the pioneers of Hindu Muslim unity. He reminded the nation that the foundation of the movement was on non-violence, whereas violence was the final refuge of the Government.[17] He lamented that Hindus and Muslims had lost much in moral stamina. They had become poor representatives of their respective faiths.[18] 'We shall therefore find favour in the sight of God only by choosing methods which are different in kind from those of our opponents.'[19]

Dear Countrymen,

Whilst the arrest of Maulana Shaukat Ali and Mohamed Ali has touched every Indian heart, I know what it has meant to you. The brave Brothers and staunch lovers of their country, but they are Mussulmans first and everything alse afterwards. It must be so with every religiously-minded man. The Brothers have for years past represented all that is best and noblest in Islam. No two Mussulmans have done more then they to raise the status of Islam in India. They have promoted the cause of the Khilafat as no two other Mussulmans of India have. For they have been true, and they dared to tell what they felt even in their internment in Chhindwara. Their long internment did not demoralize or weaken them. They came out just as brave as they went in.

And since their release from internment, they have shown themselves true nationalists, and you have taken pride in their being so.

The Brothers have by their simplicity, humility and inexhaustible energy fired the imagination of the masses as no other Mussulman has.

Ali these qualities have endeared them to you. You regard them as your ideal men. You are therefore sorry for their separation from you. Many besides you miss their genial pressence. For me, they had become inseparable. I seem to be without my arms. For anything connected with Mussulmans. Shaukat Ali was my guide and friend. He never once misled me. His judgment was sound and unerring is most cases. With the Brothers among as I felt safe about Hindu-Muslim unity, the value of which they understood as few of us have.

But whilst we all miss them, we must not give way to grief or dejection. We must learn, each one of us, to stand alone. God only is our infallible and eternal guide.

To be dejected is not only not to have known the Brothers, but it is, if I may venture to say so, not to know what religion is.

For do we not learn in all religions, that the spirit of the dear ones abides with us even when they physically leave us? Not only is the spirit of the Brothers with us, but they are serving better by their sufferings, than if they were in our midst giving us some of their own courage, hope and energy. The secret of non-violence and non co-operation lies in our realizing, that it is through suffering that we are to attain our goal. What is the renunciation of titles, councils, law-courts and schools but a measure (very slight indeed) of suffering? That preliminary renunciation is a prelude to the larger suffering, the hardships of a jail life and even the final consummation of the gallows if need be. The more we suffer and the more of us suffer, the nearer we are to our cherished goal.

The earlier and the more clearly we recognize, that it is not big meetings and demonstrations that would give us victory, but quiet suffering, the earlier and more certain will be our victory.

I have made your cause my own, because I believe it to be just. Khilafat, I have understood from your best men, is an ideal. You are not fighting to sustain any wrong or even . . . . . You are backing the Turks, because they represent the gentlemen of Europe, and because the European and especially the English prejudice against them is due, not to the Turks being worse than others as men, but to their being Mussulmans and not assimilating the modern spirit of exploitation of weaker, people and their lands. In fighting for the Turks, you are fighting to raise the dignity and the purity of your own faith.

You have naturally therefore chosen pure methods to attain your end. It cannot be denied, that both Mussulmans and Hindus have lost much in moral stamina. Both of us have become poor representatives of our respective faiths. Instead of each one of us becoming a true child of God, we expect others to live our religion and even to die for us. But we have now chosen a method that compels us to turn, each one of us, our face towards God. Non-co-operation presumes, that our opponent with whom we non-co-operate resorts to methods which are as questionable as the purpose he seeks to fulfil by such methods. We shall therefore find favour in the sight of God only by choosing methods which are different in kind from those of our opponents. This is a big claim we have made for ourselves, and we can attain success within the short time appoined by us, only if our methods are in reality different from those of the Government.

Hence the foundation of our movement rests on complete non-violence, whereas violence is the final refuge of the Government. And as no energy can be created without resistance, our non-resistance to Government violence must bring the latter to a stand-still. But our non-violence to be true must be in word, thought and deed. It makes no difference that with you non-violence is an expedient. Whilst it lasts you cannot consistently, with your pledge harbour designs of violence. On the contrary we much have implicit faith in our programme of non-violence, which presupposes perfect accord between thought, word and deed. I would like every Mussulman to realize, whilst the occasion for anger is the greatest, that by non-violence alone can we gain complete victory even during this year.

Nor is non-violence a visionary programme. Just imagine

what the united resolve of seven crores of Mussulmans (not to count the Hindus) must mean. Should we not have succeeded already, if all the titled men had given up their titles, all the lawyers had suspended their practice and all the students had left their schools and all had boycotted councils? But we must recognize, that with many of us the flesh has proved too weak. Seven crores are called Mussulman and twenty-two crores are called Hindus, but only a few are true Mussulmans or true Hindus. Therefore, if we have not gained our objective, the cause lies within us. And if ours is, as we claim it is, a religious struggle, we dare not become impatient save with ourselves, not even with one another.

The Brothers, I am satisfied, are as innocent as I claim I am, of incitement to violence. Theirs, therefore, is a spotless offering. They have done all in their power for Islam and their country. Now, if the Khilafat and the Punjab wrongs are not redressed and swaraj is not established during this year, the fault will be yours and mine.

We must remain non-voilent, but we must not be passive. We must repeat the formula of the Brothers regarding the duty of soldiers and invite imprisonment. We need not think that the struggle cannot go on without even the best of us. If it cannot, we are neither fit for swaraj nor for redressing the Khilafat or the Punjab wrong. We must declare from a thousand platforms, that it is sinful for any Mussulman or Hindu to serve the existing Government whether as soldier or in any other capacity whatsoever.

Above all we must concentrate on complete boycott of foreign cloth, whether British, Japanese, American, French or any other, and begin, if we have not already done so, to introduce spinning-wheels and handlooms in our homes and manufacture all the cloth we need. This will be at once a test of our belief in non-violence for our country's freedom and for saving the Khilafat. It will be a test also of Hindu-Muslim unity, and it will be a universal test of our faith in our own programme: I repeat my conviction that we can achieve our full purpose within one month of a complete boycott of foreign cloth. For we are then in a position having confidence in our ability to control forces of violence, to offer civil disobedience, if it is at all found necessary.

I can therefore find no balm for the deep wounds inflicted upon you by the Government other than non violence translated into action by boycott of foreign cloth and manufacture of cloth in our own homes."

Gandhi clarified that our advocacy of the Khilafat would be wrong if Islam were based on force. He argued that there was nothing in the Koran to a warrant the use of force for conversion. 'Islam would cease to world religion if it were to rely upon force for its propagation'. He also made it clear that acceptance of non-violence for organizing India's freedom involved acceptance of non-violence for Hindu-Muslim solidarity. He stated that the Moplahs had certainly broken the rule. They were prevented from having access to the new manifestation.

I paraphrase below what a friend writes regarding the influence of the Moplah outbreak on Hindu-Muslim unity :

> I am a staunch believer in Hindu-Muslim unity. But this Moplah outbreak has raised doubts in me. Success in the Khilafat means strength to Islam. Strength to Islam means attempts at conversion. Have we not often been given the choice between Islam and the sword? Can people such as the Moplahs learn the beauty of non-violence? And even if they appreciate non-violence for the sake of their faith, will they not use violence for the sake spreading their faith? My belief in the necessity of Hindu-Muslim unity is there. But do you not think that the questions I have raised are relevent ?

The questions are indeed relevant, if only because they have occurred to one so sane as the writer is. But in my opinion there is a misunderstanding about the whole question. Our advocacy of the Khilafat would be wrong if Islam were based on force. There is nothing in the Koran to warrant the use of force for conversion. The holy book says in the clearest language possible, "There is no compulsion in religion". The Prophet's whole-life is a repudiation of compulsion in religion. No Mussulman, to my knowledge, has ever approved of compulsion. Islam would cease to be a world religion if it were to rely upon force for its propagation.

Secondly, historically speaking, the charge of conversion to Islam by force cannot be proved against its followers as a body. And whenever attempts have been made to convert by force, responsible Mussulmans have repudiated such conversion.

Thirdly, the conception of Hindu-Muslim unity does not pre-suppose a total absence for all time of wrong by any of the parties. On the contrary it assumes, that our loyalty to the unity will survive shocks such as the forcible conversions by Moplahs, that in every such case we shall not blame the whole body of the followers but seek relief against individuals by way of arbitration and not by way of sale.

Fourthly, acceptance of non-violence for organizing India's freedom involves acceptance of non-violence for Hindu-Muslim solidarity. The Moplahs have certainly broken the rule. But they were prevented from having access to the new manifestation. Whilst they had heard something about the Khilafat vaguely, they knew nothing of non-violence.

Fifthly, we need not suspect any evil befalling India under swaraj; for it is tolerably certain, that had the Congress and the Khilafat workers been permitted to penetrate the Moplah territories, they would have been able to nip the evil in the bud. As it was, it is a matter capable of proof that the Khilafat workers, wherever they could go, were able to exercise great restraining influence. To me the Moplah madness is proof of the Hindu-Muslim solidarity, because we kept calm. As members of a family, we shall sometimes fight, but we shall always have leaders who will compose our differences and keep us under check.

Sixthly, in the face of possibilities of such madness in future, what is the alternative to Hindu-Muslim unity ? A perpetuation of slavery ? If we regard one another as natural enemies, is there any escape from eternal foreign domination for either of us ? Is not the present domination worse than the possibility of forcible conversions or worse ? Is Hinduism worth anything, if it cannot survive force ? Cannot the Mussulmans too ask the same question as the friend has asked ? Is there no possibility of a repetition of pillage and murder on the part of Hindus as happened in Shahabad three years ago ? Is not the remedy therefore clearly. Hindu-Muslim unity at all hazards ? The Hindus as also the Mussulmans, whenever one of them goes mad, have two courses left open. Either to die vallantly without relation, that will at once arrest the progress of mischief; or to retaliate and live or die. For individuals both the courses will abide as long as the world lasts. All questionings arise, because we have become helpless. We have forgotten the divine art of dying for our faiths without retaliation, and we have equally forgotten the art of using force in self-defence at the peril of our lives. And Hindu-Muslim unity is nothing, if it is not a partnership between brave men and women. We must trust each other always, but in the last resort, we must trust ourselves and our God.

In his opinion, attainment of swaraj was the quickest method of righting the Khilafat wrong.[21] He warned that more ignorant, thoughtless and angry outburst of violence might give vent to pent-up rage but could bring no relief to Turkey.[22] 'And the measures taken to put down violence may well lessen the speed with which we are marching to our goal'.[23]

At Lucknow I found natural impatience on the part of the Mussulmans regarding the Khilafat. Maulvi Salamatulla voiced in moderate language the public feeling regarding the position of the Angora Government when he said that the British attitude was becoming anbearable. There is no doubt about the growing distrust of the British declarations about friendliness towards the Turks. Nobody believes either that the British declarations are genuine or that the British Government is powerless to afford relief. In their impatient anger the Mussulmans ask for more energetic and more prompt action by the Congress and Khilafat organizations. To the Mussulmans swaraj means, as it must mean, India's ability to deal effectively with the Khilafat question. The Mussulmans therefore decline to wait if the attainment of swaraj means indefinite delay or a programme that may require the Mussulmans of India to become impotent witnesses of the extinction of Turkey in European waters.

It is impossible not to sympathize with this attitude. I would gladly recommend immediate action if I could think of any effective course. I would gladly ask for postponement of swaraj activity if thereby we could advance the interest of the Khilafat. I would gladly take up measures outside non-co-operation, if I could think of any in order to assuage the pain caused to the millions of Mussulmans.

But, in my humble opinion, attainment of swaraj is the quickest method of righting the Khilafat wrong. Hence it is that for me the solution of the Khilafat question is attainment of swaraj and *vice versa.* The only way to help the afflicted Turks is for India to generate sufficient powers to be able to assert herself. If she cannot develop that power in time, there is no way out for India and she must resign herself to the inevitable. What can a paralytic do to stretch forth a helping hand to a neighbour but to try to cure himself of his paralysis ? Mere ignorant, thoughtless and angry outburst of violence may give vent to pent-up rage but can bring on relief to Turkey. Nor can it increase the power of India to assert herself. And the measures taken to put down violence may well lessen the speed with which we are marching to our goal.

But there is no cause whatsoever for despair. The whole of the Congress programme has been framed and measures are being adopted to meet the Khilafat crisis. There is no doubt that two months for finishing the swadeshi work is a most intensive measure calculated to bring the best out of the nation. And if India completes the boycott by September and comes to her own in October, surely it must satisfy the most sanguine temperament and the most impatient and ardent Khilafatist as I claim myself to be.

The fact is that all the workers are not convinced of the possibility of completing the swadeshi programme during the time fixed or of its power to effect all that is claimed for it. Such doubters have to stand out, unless they can suggest a better and quicker method and get it accepted by the country. In spite of their doubt, they should faithfully plunge themselves into swadeshi work and give the experiment a fair trial. And does not this doubting of India's ability to go through the swadeshi programme show, if the doubt is justified, that India has really no interest in the Khilafat or it has no desire to sacrifice anything for it? Is it a big sacrifice for every Hindu and Mussulman to discard all foreign cloth and to use only khadi? And if India is not to have that ability, will it not also be proof that India is unfit for any higher sacrifice and therefore unfit for helping Turkey? Let us all work for complete boycott of foreign cloth and the manufacture of the required quantity of khadi and we shall be in sight of the heaven.

A suggestion was seriously put forth at Lucknow that we should boycott Ralli Bros., a Greed firm, and avenge ourselves against the Greeks and should invite the labourers to stop work on the export cargo. The suggestions, it seems to me, are as absurd as they are impossible to carry out. Assume for one moment that we can in a moment extinguish the business of Ralli Bros., how can that affect the Greeks? Ralli Bros. do not send all or a great pact of their flour to Greece. Theirs is a world trade. And it is more difficult to deal with their trade than with swadeshi. Any such attempt apart from its inherent wrong can only expose us to well-deserved ridicule. Interference with the labourers working on export cargo is equally fantastic. If we had such absolute control over the masses, we should have won our battle long ago. To stop the export of cargo requires not only a permanent of an indefinitely long stoppage of work by the existing labourers, but it presupposes our ability to stop any replacement of withdrawn labour. I fear we are not organized enough for the work. Any such attempt can only end in failure, if not worse.

The only feasible suggestion is the immediate taking up of civil disobedience. I am convinced that the country is not ready for its adoption on an extensive scale. It can be safely and successfully adopted, if the country evinces sufficient organizing ability, resourcefulness and discipline necessary for bringing the eminently practical swadeshi enterprise to a successful end. Let us hope and pray that the country will.[24]

References

1. For a detailed study *see* Syed Mahammad *The Khilafat and England*, Patna, 1921, pp. 26 ff.
2. Charles Downer Hazen, *Europe Since 1815*, rep. Calcutta, 1955, pp. 56.
3. *Ibid.*
4. *Ibid.*
5. *The Bombay Chronicle*, 10 October 1921.
6. Lajpat Rai, *The Political Future of India*, New York, 1919, p. 207.
7. Home Deptt. Pol. Deposit, May 1920, File 9.
8. Home Deptt. Pol. Deposit, January 1921, File 4.
9. Home Deptt. Pol. Deposit, April 1921, File 72.
10. Home Deptt. Pol. Deposit, January 1921, File 60. *See* full text in this File.
11. Home Deptt. Pol. Deposit, January 1921, File 5.
12. Home Deptt. Pol. Deposit, May 1921, File 8.
13. See S.R. Bakshi, *Gandhi and Khilafat*, Delhi, 1985, pp. 56-7.
14. Home Deptt. Pol. A, December 1920, File 210-216, and K.W.
15. See R.S. Bakshi, *op.cit.*
16. *Young India*, 29 September 1921.
17. *Ibid.*

18. *Ibid*
19. *Ibid.*
20. *Ibid.*
21. *Young India*, 18 August 1921,
22. *Ibid.*
23. *Ibid.*
24. *Ibid.*

5

Congress Ideology

As usual the prominent Labour leaders showed much sympathy and concern for the cause of the Indian National Congress for which it always stood.[1] 'Indians of all shades of opinion always resented the preamble to the Government of India Act, 1919 in which it is stated that "the time and manner of each advance towards responsible government can be determined by Parliament". Quite understandably, Indians felt that this was a slight on them and maintained that they were best fitted to judge of the pace by which they should advance to the full measure of complete self-government as an integral part of the British Commonwealth of Nations with all the freedom and privileges of that status. The die-hards in this country stood by the letter of the preamble, whilst Indians as firmly insisted on a Round Table Conference between representatives of their varying religious, political parties and interests and the British Government at which the whole matter could be discussed and thrashed out.

'There is now a unique opportunity. We have a Labour Government installed at Westminster, with a courageous and imaginative Secretary of State who regards himself as the representative of Indian interests. An invitation has been offered to all political parties and interests in India to meet the Government here, and in a frank and full discussion at a Round Table Conference not merely to place their views before the Government but to advise them as to what are, in their opinion, the best steps to take to solve that most intricate of problems, the future Government of India.

'From this Conference no point of view will be excluded. I would beg my friends in India to accept this genuine offer, honestly and frankly made, and send delegation to London composed of their best men who are prepared to meet the Secretary of State in the same spirit as he has shown.

'What is the alternative? A barren agitation with spasmodic riots—and in the unfortunate possibility of a change of Government here—a policy of repression and "black and Tan" government that will make of India another Ireland. That will merely play into the hands of the diehards and put back for generations the day of freedom and equality for India for which some of us have given much of the best of our lives.

'More and more bitterness and misunderstanding would inevitably follow. I ask my Indian friends not to be put off by the fulminations in the British Press (of the *Daily Mail* and *Morning Post* type) of the U'Dwyer's Gaurehills and Birkenheads. They represent a very small, though very vocal, proportion of the British public.

'The Labour Party is solidly in favour of Indian freedom and self-government, and ranged behind them are many of the best of the Tories and Liberals. Lord Reading and Mr. Lloyd George by no means represent the most progressive part of the Liberal Party. Similarly, Lord Birkenhead's views are diametrically opposed to those of Mr. Baldwin.

'This is the opportunity we have been working for years. Do not let us down. On the contrary, I bed to you to accept this invitation and so strengthen the hands of the Friends of India, and complete the "Wreck of the Birkenhead".[2]

A. Fenner Brockway, M.P. wrote, 'I hope the Indian National Congress will realise that there is in reality a new spirit in the attitude of the British Government, and that it will decide to task part in the Round Table Conference and insist there upon Dominion Status. The need on the British side is that the new spirit should be expressed in the administration of justice. Congress can rely upon a group of friends here pressing for an ending of the persecution of political opinion and for an amnesty.'[3]

William Lawther, M.P. opined, 'It is always difficult for those who are far off, to understand what is the opinion of those on the spot on any particular question, and although Indian questions have for generations been the subject of debates and discussions in the Mother of Parliaments, there yet remains much misunderstanding as to what are the desires of the Indian People.

'Therefore, the Indian National Congress has an unique opportunity of helping to bring before the great mass of the people in this country, their considered judgment and opinions by accepting the invitation to the proposed Round Table Conference. Might I put it in this form; before coming to the House of Commons, I was a Miners' representative, and the Miners in this country never neglected an opportunity of putting forward their views before any assembly. No section of workers in the world have laboured more to redress the injustices they suffer from and today we are within the borderlines of the beginning of the end of these injustices. And feel that the steps that are initiated by the Labour Government on Indian matters will likewise lead to the redressing of their grievances. No cause ever suffers from the taking of opportunities at all times and on all occasions to state their ideals and principles. My message to you, my comrades of the Indian National Congress, is to follow the pathway, by way of a Round Table Conference, there to place your views on those subjects for which you have laboured so long and earnestly.'[4]

'William Bennett, M.P. remarked thus : 'The present time seems to me to offer more hope and encouragement to the Indian people than any previous period.

'I can assure you of the heartiest sympathy and appreciation of the demand for Dominion Status from all the members of the Labour Parliamentary Party with whom I am acquainted. The Round Table Conference is an absolutely genuine invitation.'[5]

John Scurr, M.P. opined, 'The time has come for every man and woman who sincerely desired the welfare of the people of India to do everything they can to promote a real understanding between the two nations.

'I have always stood for the realisation of Dominion Status for India at the earliest opportunity, and it has been a matter of personal regret that the counsels of extremists on both sides has produced such a cloud of misunderstanding.

'The Labour movement in this country desires to render justice to the people of India. It is whole-heartedly in favour of self-government.

'How this ideal can best be carried out can be settled by the proposed conference between the representatives of the peoples of India and of Britain.

'I trust sincerely that as a result of complete cooperation between these representatives, the world may be able to hail India as a self-governing nation, before the British Labour Government leaves office.[6]

James Barr, M.P. stated, 'I am most anxious to see India attaining full Dominion Status. Adapting a well-known poem of Robert Burns, I would say :

> 'Never but by Indian Hands
> Shall Indian wrongs be righted.'[7]

Will Thorne, M.P. opined, 'During my forty years in the Socialist and Trade Union Movement, I have always been in favour of the right of self-determination for the Indian peoples: more especially after digesting the late Mr. Hyndman's book on India.

'I think the British Nation have everything to gain and nothing to lose by making the Indian peoples responsible for their own Government.'[8]

Ernst Thurtle, M.P. wrote thus : 'I hope the National Congress meeting at Lahore will effectively demonstrate Indias' determination to achieve national freedom, and will at the same time show to the world that she knows how to maintain national unity for the purpose of reaching this objective.

'Indian leaders must necessarily be the best judges of the policy and tactics to be pursued in furtherance of the national cause but as an outsider, I would like to express the hope that it may be possible for the Congress to decide to be represented at the forthcoming Round Table Conference, in order that all whom it may concern may know without misunderstanding the programme for which the Congress stands.'[9]

Peter Freeman, M.P. stated, 'Cordial greetings and every good wish for a successful Congress. At the present moment, India and Great Britain have been drawn closer together in mutual respect, understanding and comradeship than perhaps ever before to consider their respective interests and common ideals. . .

'The workers of England regard the workers of India as comrades in a common struggle for freedom from Capitalism and Imperialism. I urge the Indian leaders to cooperate with the British Labour Government as I feel sure in that way lies the best hope of securing not only Dominion Status but equality of status. The time must come for both people when caste on the one side and colour prejudice on the other must give way to ideal of freedom and equality for all.'[10]

E.S. Palmer, M.P. opined, 'As a Labour member of the British House of Commons I am glad to be supporting a Government having proper appreciation of the Indian National Congress point of view. The highest hopes and aspirations of the Indian people are nearer realisation today than ever. Self-determination is the general principle under which a Labour

Government must operate and there can be no doubt India's demand for Dominion Status will be conceded at an early date'.[11]

Ben Tillett,[12] M.P. remaked, 'I hope you will forgive my inability to write a long note, but a very sincere and anxious wish is given to you and your movement that freedom may come to the people of India, and that democracy may carry with it its own spiritual sense and responsibility and alliance with the workers of the world. . .

F.G. Watkins, M.P. remarked, 'During the recent years, the people of Great Britain have become more understanding with regard to the question of self-government to India, and this has become much more marked during the last twelve months. It is now true to say that in this country there is an enormous volume of public opinion in support of granting Dominion Status at the very earliest suitable opportunity. Everyone in the Labour Movement is praying that great and beneficial results may come from the forthcoming Conference. The rights of all people to govern themselves in harmony with their own genius and traditions is a fundamental principle of the Labour Party, and by the application of that principle alone can the problem of India be solved.

'A large contribution to the disentanglement of world complication can be made by the Indian people, and Labour would welcome their cooperation and fellowship in the task of creating a relationship between the Mother Country and India based on mutual toleration and respect. I am confident that Great Britain will respond to the best possible spirit to all the aspirations of India which conform to the highest teaching of Indian philosophy and tradition.'[13]

Dr. Norton Phillips, M.P. stated, 'Members of the Labour Party look forward to the entrance of India into the British Commonwealth of Nations as a self-governing Dominion. Therefore they have welcomed very warmly the proposal for a Round Table Conference after the presentation of the Simon Report and urge their Indian brothers to participate to the fullest extent. A representative conference will, we believe, help materially towards the establishment of Dominion Home Rule. May I, as an Australian add the eager hope that it will not be long before India and Australia, Commonwealths of the East and of the South, are standing side by side in a world wide federation with the British peoples of the West?'[14]

J. Horrabin, M.P. stated in equally favourable tone. 'I am very glad to send greetings to the Indian National Congress. I hope very much that representatives of Indian National opinion will accept the invitation to a Round Table Conference and that this will lead to a better understanding between English and Indian people and provide a basis for the realisation of India's just demands.'[15]

Besides, among the messages read or mentioned by Dr. Ansari as having been received from outside India, were those of the Kabul Congress Committee, the American Branch of the Indian Congress, the Fiji Congress, the Socialist Party of Persia, the South African Indian Federation, the Indian National Association, Cape Province, the South African Indian Congress and the Indian Oppressed Peoples' Association, Nanking China. The message from Mahendra Pratap from Kabul, specially requests the Congress to sympathise with Afghanistan and accepts the principle of world federation and push on organisation and activity to achieve independence.

Among the messages from several parts of India was one of C. Vijiaraghavachariar, formerly president of the Indian National Congress, hoping that wisdom and long-sighted statesmanship would characterise the discussions and decisions for on both depended how well a free India shall be started in the year 1930.' Mahendra Pratap in his letter from Kabul said, 'We must quite openly sympathise with Soviet Russia, accept the principle of Pan Asian Unity and solemnly agree to work for the complete freedom of all nations and federations of the world.'[16]

The following two condolence resolutions were moved from the chair and passed by the Congress, the whole House standing in reverence.

'This congress expresses its appreciation of the supreme self-sacrifice of Jatindra Nath Das and Phoongi U. Wizaya and offers its condolence to their families, and is further of opinion that the foreign Government in India is responsible for their self-immolations'.[17]

This Congress expresses its sorrow at the death of Pandit Gokarannath Misra, ex-General-Secretary of All-India Congress Committee and Prof. S.M. Paranjpaye and Messrs Bhaktavatsalu Naidu, Rohinikanta Hatibarua, R.K. Lahiri and Byomkesh Chakravarti'.[18]

After the Messages had been read, Mahatma Gandhi moved the first resolution which ran as follows :

'The Congress deplores the bomb outrage perpetrated on the Viceroy's train and reiterates its own conviction that such action is not only contrary to the creed of the Congress, but results in harm being done in the national cause. It congratulates the Viceroy and Lady Irwin and their party including the poor servants on their fortunate and narrow escape.'

Gandhi spoke as follows in English after his speech in Hindustani. 'I have been asked to give you the substance of what I said in English. In my opinion, it is or it will be a good beginning with our resolutions dealing with the duty of the Congress, if we begin by passing this unanimously. In coming here to propose it, I have realised my responsibility fully. My certain conviction is that the Congress will fail in its obvious duty if it does not record this resolution. You find the reasons stated in the resolution itself. So long as the Congress creed remains what it is, namely, we want to attain Swaraj not by any means, but by peaceful and legitimate means, it is our bounden duty to take note of anything that happens in India in breach of that creed. You might be told, as I dare say, you will be told, that when people who do not belong to the Congress organisation, and are not connected with it in any shape or form, do particular acts which may be contrary to our creed, we are in no way and in no sense responsible. Those who think like that have, I say in all humility, little sense of the tremendous responsibility that rests on their shoulders, and they have little sense also of the great status that belongs to the Congress. We claim to represent the thirty crores of Hindustan or we not. If we claim to represent them as I, a humble Congress worker do, and as I hope you also do, then it is our duty to consider ourselves responsible for anything that a single person in Hindustan may do, if he is born in Hindustan. It does not matter to me in the least whether that person is a responsible human being or whether he belongs to the C.I.D. I hope you consider C.I.D. Indians also to be our kith and kin. Everyone we expect to convert to our creed, and use his services in the attainment of our goal. Not only that but the resolution stated and I hope you believe it, that such acts do great narm in the national cause.

'I do not wish to take up your time by drawing your attention to the various landmarks in the history of the Congress which would enable me to prove to your own satisfaction that each bomb outrage has cost India. You may say, if you wish, that the reforms that were obtained could not have been obtained without bomb outrages or without violence. Let me tell you, that everyone of these reforms have cost far more than you would care to face. You have paid in millions in exchange for your toys.

'The Congress resolution also congratulates the Viceroy and Lady Irwin and their party including the poor servants. In my humble opinion, it is a natural corollary to what has been said in the previous part of the resolution. We lose nothing by showing common coutesy. Not only so, we would be guilty of not having understood the implications of our creed if we forget that those Englishmen, whether in authority or not in authority, who choose to remain in India are our charge, that we who profess this creed of non-violence should consider ourselves trustees for the safety of their lives. We have a tremendous military burden which is crushing the starving millions who are living in the seven hundred thousand villages in India. The burden is not due to the necessity of our Frontier. That is due, let me assure you to the fact, that thirty crores of people are held bond slaves by a few thousand Englishmen coming all the way from England. If we would get rid of this military burden at any stage, it would be the necessity of the case that we hold the life of those whom we may even consider our enemies as a sacred trust. That is the clearest possible implication, in my humble opinion, of the creed of non-violence in the political salvation of India If you hold with me, it is not only a matter of courtesy on your part to tender our congratulations to the Viceroy and Lady Irwin and their party, including their servants, and tender congratulations if you will to ourselves also. I hope that you, after having listened to everything that might be said against this resolution, pass it unanimously and heartily.[20]

Dr. Ansari seconded the resolution.[21] His first remark that freedom was never won by such outrages, roused a protest from certain sections in the *pandal*, while little red flags were waved from one enclosure along with shouts of protest. This encloure was occupied by students for two hundred of whom the Reception Committee had issued tickets. Dr. Ansari retorted, 'Even those who waving the red flag should remember that Communist people do not believe in individual violence, but believe in mass violence. So, even the Communist creed does not permit such an outrage. Let me emphasise that India's whole history and culture is against this cowardly outrages. I hope you will not say one thing and do another. The world will trust you. On the other hand, consider the resolution cooly, and adopt this righteous course.'[22]

Swami Govindananda opposing the resolution said that the creed of non-violence should not be forced on those who were not Congressmen and believed in different means to achieve the freedom of the country. The Congress should not therefore condemn those who did not believe in the Congress creed. It was very difficult today to say which party was serving the country better. The time for pronouncing any judgment would be when India was free. He further deplored that while the resolution condemned the outrage it did not say a word against the Government for having arrested several innocent youngmen at Lahore who had nothing to do with the outrage.'[23]

Dr. Alam opposing the resolution, appealed to the delegates not to vote out of regard for any personality. A new era was dawning and so they should see that their vote followed the dictates of conscience. It had been said that the non-violent method was the best. Indeed, if that was not to be so, he himself would not have followed it for ten years. The question, however, was not whether the method of violence or non-violence was to be preferred. The latter was indeed preferable, but that had nothing to do with the present resolution. The resolution was unimportant, improper and harmful, and hence needed rejection. Where was the need of repealing the declaration of belief in non-violence? Was it due to their having lost faith in their belief in non-violence? By such resolutions, the hands of the administration were strengthened, so that several innocent persons were harassed. Again, did the administration at all express any grief at the death of Lalaji which had been medically declared to have been precipitated by the beating by the police officials. Indeed, the Government had not even agreed to hold any enquiry into the affair in spite of his efforts in the Council.[24]

H.D. Raja declared that the resolution was contrary to the anti-Imperialist outlook of the Congress. What mattered it to them whether the bomb hit the Viceroy or any other.[25]

Baba Gurdit Singh of *Komagata Maru* fame felt that by this resolution they were deceiving Englishmen and provoking youngmen to greater acts of violence. Even old men, he thought did not dislike such outrages, but also did not like to see youngmen to go to the gallows. He asked, if a man had a right to do *Hijarat* to another country, had he not the right to sacrifice himself in order not to live under conditions of slavery? Moreover; so long as the Lawrence and Outram statues showed the sword by which they won India, youngmen would be provoked to draw the sword.[26]

Abdur Rahman, supporting the resolution, said that he honoured everyone who worked for the cause of the country, yet, as the perpetrator of the outrage in question had gone against the Congress creed, it was the duty of the Congress to maintain its dignity by passing this resolution. He, therefore, supported the resolution.[27] Concluding, the speaker said that if any one of those who made such cries and considered himself capable of leading the country in place of Gandhiji would come forward to lead them, then, the speaker would oppose the resolution.

Purushotamdas Tandon did not agree that the bomb thrower was a coward, for he played upon his life. The question was whether such brave acts were in the country's interest. He felt that the resolution was truthful, and also politically expedient.[28]

Mahatma Gandhi's reply to the debate did not agree about the interpretation put on young men's mind. He came into touch with them by thousands either personally or by correspondence, but even if young men were of a different view, he must fight for the creed he believed in. "Indian National Congress cannot say one thing and act another, 'he observed. Voting then proceeded and the task of judging which side had won by a show of hands was impossible owing to the almost balanced strength of both sides. Tellers were then appointed to undertake the counting which showed that the resolution was carried in Gandhi's favour.[29]

The next resolution was on complete independence. Introducing this resolution as adopted by the Subjects Committee, Gandhi characterised it as the root of the future Congress work. The resolution declared complete independence as the meaning of Swaraj for the purposes of the Congress creed and resolved on the complete boycott of the legislatures as a preliminary step towards organising a campaign for independence.

In a short Hindi speech, Gandhi explained the various parts of the resolution emphasising the independence and boycott clauses. He reserved arguments till the reply to the debate. The following is the text of the resolution.

'The Congress endorses the action of the Working Committee in connection with the manifesto signed by party-leaders, including Congressmen, on the Viceregal pronouncement of the 31st October relating to Dominion Status and appreciates the efforts of the Viceroy towards the settlement of the national movement for Swaraj. The Congress, however, having considered all that has since happened, and the result of the meeting between Mahatma Gandhi, Pandit Motilal Nehru and other leaders and the Viceroy, is of opinion that nothing is to be gained in the existing circumstances by the Congress being represented at the proposed Round Table Conference. This Congress, therefore, in pursuance of the resolution passed at its session at Calcutta last year declares that the word "Swaraj" in Article I of the Congress Constitution shall mean Complete Independence, and further declares the entire scheme of the Nehru Committee report to have lapsed and hopes that all Congressmen will henceforth devote their exclusive attention to the attainment of Complete Independence for India. As a preliminary step towards organising a campaign for Independence and in order to make the Congress policy as consistent as possible with the change of creed, this Congress resolves upon complete boycott of the Central and Provincial Legislatures and committees constituted by the Government and calls upon the Congressmen and others taking part in the national movement to abstain from participating, directly or indirectly, in future elections, and directs the present Congress members of the Legislatures and Committees to resign their seats. This Congress appeals to the nation zealously the constructive programme of the Congress and authorises the All-India Congress Committee, wherever it deems fit, to launch upon a programme of Civil Disobedience, including non-payment of taxes, whether in selected areas or otherwise and under such safeguards as it may consider necessary.'[80]

Motilal Nehru emphasised the importance of the resolution as one by which the present session of the Congress would be known. So far as his experience and observation told him he felt that if they changed even a word of the resolution as passed by the Subjects Committee, they would be failing in their duty to the Congress. If they wished to maintain the dignity of the Congress and stand by their undertaking, they would adopt the resolution in the given form. He divided the resolution into three parts, one dealing with the past happenings, the other with their duty at present, and the third with their programme in future.[31]

Reiterating the terms of the Calcutta resolution, Motilal Nehru described the circumstances under which, he said, the talk of the Congress participation in the Round Table Conference had broken down owing to the Congress representatives' terms for the same not being accepted by the Viceroy. The resolution merely asked them to endore the Working Committee's action which had been entirely within the scope of the Calcutta resolution. The appreciation of the Viceroy's efforts was a mere act of human courtesy. Undoubtedly by granting Dominion Status to India, Britain stood to gain more than India, as the only other alternative for Britain was to wash her hands clean in India. As the talk of Dominion Status and Round Table Conference had ended, the present resolution declared Independence as the goal as the only alternative left.

Dealing with the boycott of Councils, he confessed that their attention had been diverted from their real goal by joining the Councils. Indeed the Government had entrapped most public workers in one Committee or other. And they had failed to achieve the object which they hoped to. Moreover, if they were declaring Independence as the creed, then going into the Councils would be entirely inconsistent with that creed. Those who insisted on the triple boycott, he conselled to benefit by past experience and move forward step by step. Perhaps it might be said that 'because he had himself reiterated the practice of the law, he desired to exempt the boycott of law-courts.' But he had no mind to take any further briefs. The third part of the resolution empowered the All-India Congress

Committee to launch on further steps of the campaign which could all be taken in 1930 if the country whole-heartedly helped it forward. He exhorted the Congress to accept the resolution, without which there was no other course left for work for freedom.[32]

Madan Mohan Malaviya moved an amendment for postponing the change in the creed till after an All-Parties' Conference in March or April next. He reiterated the arguments used in the Subjects Committee, and narrated the developments that led to the announcement of the Round Table Conference, and held that the Government had shown a clear intention of fulfilling the national demand. He drew attention to the sympathy exhibited by the British Parliament on Brockway's motion. Then, again, both the Butler report and the Simon Commission had been put on the shelf. He advised them not to be hasty in taking a revolutionary step. He asked, could the Viceroy give any promise regarding Dominion Status at this stage ? It was premature to say that they would not participate in the Round Table Conference.[33]

N.C. Kelkar in moving his amendment to delete the words, in the resolution, relating to the boycott of legislatures, said, 'It is unfortunate that the flood-gates of the miserable controversy as to entry into Councils have been reopened. No one need introduce any heat of feeling in this matters. I am a cool and collected man, but I am a man all the same with the firmest convictions. I think definitely that it is politically unwise to boycott the Councils. The resolution merely seeks to renew the exploded stunt, and I predict it is not going to get much support in the country. The situation in 1920 was quite different. Standing on this platform, Gandhiji spoke words in depreciation of Council work, and said that so far as work for independence was concerned, not one inch of ground was covered. In reply to that, I will say, measure the other peoples' work by the same foot-rule and you will find they also have not covered one inch of ground. In this demand for boycott of the legislatures, there is nothing more than party vendetta, political unwisdom and mental perversity. Congressmen in the Councils have not given any cause for complaint. There may be quarrels here and there and lack of discipline, but such quarrels and lack of discipline are to be found in the other departments of the Congress as well Congressmen in the Council have carried on obstruction and assisted in the constructive programme. That Congressmen outside the Councils devote their whole time and energy to the constructive programme is a fallacy. All along they had been showing a sneaking kind of partiality for Council work, and for receiving assistance from Council friends. They did interfere in elections and seized any public advantage that could be got from the Councils. Was this not against the discipline of the Congress ? This sort of boycott, I say, is useless. After all, in this world, there are workers and shirkers. Workers will always work and shirkers will always shirk whether they go into Councils or stand outside. But the legislatures are the supreme powerhouse of the Government, and if you want to organise against the Government, and lead an attack on it, you must capture the legislatures. Take the simple example of a dacoity. When the dacoits want to enter a house and commit a loot, some of them enter into it and the others keep outside on watch, both serving a common purpose. Similarly, Congress work in the Councils and outside is co-related and linked for achieving freedom for the country. Follow the example of Ireland, and settle a programme which will suit the capacities of the people. I plead for an all-round understanding. Let me do what I can. You do what you can, and let us all work for the common cause of the Motherland'.[34]

Subhas Chandra Bose next moved the counter resolution which he had placed before the Subjects Committee for a parallel government. He said, 'Before I proceed to lay my case I take this opportunity of conveying my cordial and hearty thanks to Mahatma Gandhi for coming forward to move a resolution which declares Swaraj to mean complete Independence. But I move this amendment because I believe that the programme laid down in his resolution is not such as to carry us towards the goal of complete Independence. My amendment is consistent with the goal and in keeping with the spirit of the times. I have no doubt it will find favour with the younger generation in this country, if not now, at least in the next Congress.

'Mine is a programme of all-round boycott and I do not think it will be of any use to take up one item in the programme of boycott and leave out others. It will not be consistent with our creed of Independence to go and practise in the law courts. It will not be consistent either to enter local bodies, some of which like the Calcutta Corporation, require the path of allegiance to be taken. There is another reason why you should give them all up. The task before us is so arduous and the responsibility on our shoulders is so great that we shall have to concentrate our whole time and energy on the programme of work. I should like to submit, at this stage if you are not prepared to go in for complete boycott, it will be no use for you to boycott the Councils only.

'Atter all, let us be consistent. Let us be for complete boycott or none at all. I am an extremist and my principle is—all or none. If I am to advocate a policy of the capture of public bodies, I would like to capture every public body. If we are to boycott at all, why not boycott completely and concentrate our attention and energy on some other programme? Therefore, I would earnestly plead for the acceptance of my amendment, because I know public opinion in India to-day requires it.

'Now a word or two on Mahatmaji's resolution. In the preamble, you are asked to endorse the action of the Working Committee in subscribing to the Delhi manifesto. It is for you to consider whether on the 31st December 1929, you are prepared to endorse it. I am not prepared to advise any one to do it. Again, are you prepared to accept reference to the Round Table Conference? I would not call it a round table. It is certainly not round. I would call it square. A Round Table Conference is a conference between two belligerent parties, between plenipotentiaries representing opposite sides. I ask you whether the people in India are invited to send any of their representatives with full powers to negotiate with the representatives of the British Government, or, are we assured that the conclusions arrived at this conference are to be ratified by both parties? Are we sure that the conclusions of the conference are not to go up for the reconsideration before the British Parliament? You know when the treaty was drawn between Britain and South Africa, the conclusions were arrived at the conference of both parties. I know for a fact that in the case of South African constitution drawn up at the conference, in spite of its grammatical errors, it had to be ratified by the British Government, and the British Parliament could not even correct those grammatical errors. That is what a round table conference means. What is the character of the conference that has been offered to India? The Simon Commission and its paraphernelia are to be there and the conclusions of the conference are to go before the Parliament. It is not merely the people of India that should send representatives to the conference, but the European Chambers of Commerce and the Ruling Chiefs. Is there a fight between the British Government on the one hand and the European Chambers and Ruling Chiefs on the other? Is there any fight proceeding between Government and loyalists? I know of no such fight. When there are these bodies to send in their representatives to this conference, I say it is not a round table conference. But unfortunately, people in this country insist on calling it so and Britishers are equally insistent in not calling it a round table conference.

One argument more and I have done. The resolution refers to the constructive programme as a method whereby we have to achieve the political emancipation of India. I would like the House to consider whether the constructive programme, which the Congress has been pursuing for the last few years, is something which is sufficient to enable us to reach the goal of complete independence. No doubt, there is a reference to civil disobedience in the resolution. But I submit that civil disobedience will never come until we can organise the workers and peasants and depressed classes on their specific grievances. If my programme is adopted, it shall be sufficiently effective to march on the road to Independence. I appeal to the supporters of the resolution to note the altered circumstances and feeling of the people, particularly the younger generation, and accept my motion'.

Dr. Alam objected to the appreciative reference to the Viceroy because on the day, they were handing down to posterity the Charter of Liberty the same resolution should not bear the trace of slavery. H.D. Raja moved an amendment that besides civil disobedience, the Congress should organise labour in order to bring about a general strike. Hardly had Mr. Raja begun his speech, when he was greeted by shouts of 'No, go back'. At this the president intervened and silenced the audience. Mr. Raja, however, emphasised the point that a dynamic programme with the help of labour and the peasantry was necessary to rid the country of slavery. Madhavan Nair moved for the elimination of the boycott of the legislatures. Govindachar moved for the boycott of law courts besides the legislatures, as it was dishonest and inconsistent to boycott only the legislatures.[35]

Satyamurti moved an amendment to omit the words indicative of non-cooperation with the proposed Round Table Conference and the boycott of legislatures. He said, 'I wholeheartedly subscribe to the ideal of independence. I believe no self-respecting nation can have any goal other than complete independence. But the history of the countries like Ireland, Egypt and South Africa, who fought for independence, showed that they accepted Dominion Status as a compromise. The fourth sentence of the resolution is, however, most mischievous and I ask you to reject it. For it asks you to repeat history and the tragic mistake committed of a futile boycott of legislatures. I with Desabandhu Das and Lalaji were here to fight this resolution for Council boycott.

'The reasons given for the boycott are wholly unconvincing, It is stated that this is a preliminary step towards organising a campaign of independence. I emphatically say, 'no' to it. You can fight elections and win them, God willing, on the issue of complete independence. Is it nothing that you get sixty lakhs of voters to vote in favour of those who are for complete independence? I say that the fight for independence may be carried on both inside and outside the legislatures. I say again that the experience of countries like England, Egypt and South Africa must convince us that we lose considerably and gain nothing by the boycott of legislatures. We are told that the oath of allegiance cannot be taken by those who are pledged to independence. May I ask how these estimable gentlemen agreed not to the boycott of law courts administering the law which the legislatures make? How can you take part in local bodies which are statutory creatures of legislatures in most of which you have to take oath of allegiance? Then it seems to me if you are not going to have a complete programme of immediate civil disobedience for achieving independence, the boycott of legislatures is a great mistake.

'Another reason given is that the Congress policy should be as consistent as possible with the change of creed, I agree, but beginning with the boycott of legislatures in the beginning at the wrong end. What about insurance companies and cooperative societies which are creatures of Government statutes and ought to depend on Government assistance? Gandhiji himself admitted that it is impossible to have complete non-cooperation today. Therefore, I say that Congressmen capturing the legislatures is perfectly consistent with the Congress declaration of independence.

'You are told that the legislatures absorb too much of time of the Congressmen. After all you want only about six to seven hundred men for about fifty days in the year in those bodies. Is the country so bankrupt in her resources as not to be able to give the necessary number of men to work inside the councils and outside? Can anybody deny that President Patel has done something to take the nation along the path of Swaraj? Mahatmaji himself has spoken in praise of the work of the Swarajists, in the columns of *Young India* in the central and provincial legislatures. Experiences of countries which have won freedom recently convince me, and must convince you also, that you have to capture the strategic positions of power and give battle to those arrayed against you from every platform. I suggest that we ought to sympathise our national activity. We must act on the maxim that those who are not with us are against us, and those who are not against us, are with us. There is no immediate programme alternative to the boycott of legislatures. Those who have been asked to come out of the legislatures, what are they to do? It is impossible to accept the boycott with contingent civil disobedience, and with no other programme before you. I suggest it is a most suicidal step.'

T. Prakasam speaking on his amendment to postpone the change of creed, boycott of legislatures and the starting of civil disobedience, said. 'It is a matter of great thankfulness for the country that two great leaders had at last given the right lead to the country by refusing to send in any representative from the Congress to the so-called Round Table 'Conference. Sir John Simon, when he was here with his Commission hinted that all those who did not give any evidence before him would be called for some conference there. That is the conference which is now developed by Mr. Wedgwood Benn. It is not the Round Table Conference at which our constitution would be settled but it is one to which the different warring elements would be invited. They would be made to quarrel and then they would say, "You are quarrelling here and therefore not for self-government. The Englishmen are so clever and they put their case in such a way as to make the world believe that they have made a gesture to India, and it is for India to respond. With that object Mr. Benn laboured hard and made a fallacious speech that India is already enjoying Dominion Status. That is how the trap was laid. The Congress leaders discovered it and declared that it would be an ignominy and humiliation to send any representative across the waters to London on behalf of the Congress.

Having next pleaded for the postponement of the decision on the questions referred to by him till after the results of the

Conference were known, Mr. Prakasam said that the boycott of the legislatures took his breath away. 'I cannot understand how Gandhiji has reconciled himself to put in the boycott of the legislatures when the boycott of courts is more important when you are having an independence resolution. Independence means complete severance of the British connection. A lawyer goes to the court and swears loyally. If we pass a resolution for the boycott of legislatures without the boycott of courts, we will make ourselves ridiculous. This means independence on the one hand and loyalty on the other. Have complete boycott by all means, whether there is response or not. Response will come in due course. I have faith in the leaders and the followers. If you do not have all boycotts, do not have any boycott at all. Lord Irwin was touring Southern India a couple of weeks back, and all the time he was anxiously enquiring in his interviews with non-officials whether, if the Congress refused to attend the Round Table Conference, there would be any other strong party. I am an admirer of parties in the legislatures, but still in India where once it was not possible to have party Government it was left to the Congress to send candidates into the legislatures and declare to the world that they would make a party on the lines on which Pandit Motilal Nehru was able to do it.'[36]

M.S. Aney put forward an amendment proposing the postponement of the question of change of creed to a special session of the Congress, and permitting participation in the Round Table Conference, provided adequate representation on it was given to the Congress, and the political prisoners were released, and enjoining Congress representatives to place before the conference an approved scheme of Dominion Status. He argued that nothing had happened to show that the Indian leaders' terms would not be accepted. The presence in Gandhiji's resolution of the clause appreciating the Viceroy's efforts was itself a certificate of the chage of heart. If that were granted, there was evidently cause to give more time for settlement of the matter.'

Maulana Zafar Ali moved an amendment which proposed

to remove the preamble, and to set up arbitration courts to administer justice in the place of law courts, and asked the Congress definitely to take upon itself the duty of organising labour and peasants. He asked what did this cry of Dominion Status mean? England was hardly of the size of the Punjab. Therefore, it was for England to become a Dominion of India and not for India to work for becoming England's Dominion.[37]

Abhyankar supported Dr. Alam and held that the reference to the Viceroy was a symptom of hypocrisy or cowardice. Could they appreciate the acts of a Viceroy whose Government was responsible for killing Lalaji or showering *lathis* on Padit Jawaharlal at Lucknow? 'I wonder why Pandit Jawaharlal is sitting there dumb-founded today. Gandhiji had told you to pass this resolution as something which would be manly. My definition of a man is one who will give sweet words for a kind act, but kick for kick and blow for blow. I warn you against being deceived.'[38]

J.M. Sen Gupta while supporting the resolution said, 'This resolution goes as far as the Calcutta resolution expected us to go, and as far as the present political conditions warrant us to go. The main point is : Do you have in India today another commander who can lead the country to victory than Gandhi? You have not. You know that today Gandhiji has come out of his seclusion to lead us again. He has given you his programme.

After referring to the Delhi manifesto, Sen Gupta said, 'It was necessary for the Congress leaders before the Congress met to see whether this Viceroy's offer was a hoax or not. Most of us know it was a hoax. Now that the Viceroy has given a clear answer, we have a clear duty under the Calcutta resolution to declare Swaraj which means complete independence. As for the appreciation of the Viceroy's service, the feelings expressed by Dr. Alam are probably in my breast, but I am not going to quarrel with my commander whom the nation has selected for that little piece of appreciation of the

Viceroy. The Mahatma says that he found the Viceroy sincere in this matter, and that does not apply either to other past acts or to the future. As for the boycott of councils, I stood for council work in 1923, but today the circumstances have changed. We must change means as circumstances change. We, in the Bengal Council, have been entirely successful in our Congress creed of obstruction; but now boycott is necessary, when we are going to change our creed. As regard local bodies, I feel that so far as Bengal is concerned, it will be a good thing if there is a proper boycott of local bodies also.'[39]

Jamnadas Mehta supported the resolution of Mahatma Gandhi although it was good only in parts. He opined that the boycott of the legislatures was a blunder and asserted that not all the men on the dais of the Congress platform could jointly do as much work as President Patel had done in the Assembly. Indeed, barring the Congress platform, there was no better place in the country to carry on national propaganda[40]

Mahatma Gandhi replied to the debate which lasted for about seven hours. He first spoke in Hindi and later in English. He spoke with much warmth and feeling commending his resolution for the acceptance of the Congress session without change of even a comma. He said, 'This resolution has to be considered as a whole. Even if a part of the picture is destroyed, the whole of it is destroyed. To this picture, which I have presented to you, was given by the Working Committee all the skill that it is capable of in the framing of it, and after a hot discussion it has come to you. It is for you either to reject it in toto or accept it in toto, but not to interfere with it or disturb it. The four words "in the existing circumstances" have their definite place and if you want to show wisdom you ought really to understand and realise that some day or other, we shall have to meet in conference with even our enemies. Before that we want to be able to establish independence here. But in the existing circumstances, it is enough protection for you and for the nation and enough hint to the whole world. It does presuppose that your representative will not, dare not and cannot go into the conference where Dominion Status is a matter for consideration. They can only go to a conference where independence is the matter for consideration. Similarly there is the appreciation of the efforts of the Viceroy in connection with the Swaraj settlement. Either you believe the testimony of your chosen representatives or you reject it. If you really believe that your representatives have told you the truth, the whole truth, and nothing but the truth, when they say that the Viceroy seemed to mean well, he was courteous throughout and he patiently went through the whole matter as if two friends had met, does it not behove you—it is not a matter of common courtesy merely but it is your bounden duty to appreciate it? If you do not believe then you must bound us out of the committee and out of the Congress *Pandal.* You would have to say, "We don't believe that you are saying under the influence of the Viceroy who, being an Englishman and representative of the Government, is incapable of being courteous and of meaning well.' If that is your opinion you must certainly accept the amendment to delete the words. Whereas if you accept our testimony that the Viceroy did mean well or seemed to us to mean well, then it is your duty to adopt the resolution. This is a matter of courtesy.

'It is not a sign of courage that a man should be afraid of saying what he feels. It is a sign of decided courage when a man shows even to an enemy that which he believes to be good. This is what we believe to be good and we have placed it before you. So far in connection with the amendment that has been so hotly debated. As a matter of fact, people who are pledged to the creed of non-violence and truth will always go out of the way to perform an act of delicate courtesy to think well of the enemy, to see hope were there seems to be utter darkness, because a man truth-loving and non-violent, is always filled with hope, and also courage for decisive action. Therefore, pledged to a creed of this character, it is your bounden duty to accept this response in the general resolution and reject the amendment.

'Then there is the question of boycott of legislatures with reference to which I can only give you the testimony of those who went into the legislatures with high hopes and on the top of it all is Pandit Motilal Nehru. He speaks of the Assembly with bitter experience. He says it is no good for him now. He regrets having gone to it. He has discharged his duty, as even a critic admitted, in the noblest manner possible. He says, "My work, I have done there. I shall not be able to carry on the battle of Swaraj event a step further by being there." That testimony is conclusive for me. I do not go in search of any other testimony and may it be conclusive for you also. I have no such personal experience to decide, but I have that conviction now even greater than I had in 1919. Friends ask why not add boycott of law courts and schools. It is certainly a consistent and logical proposition, but mankind is not always governed by logic and by consistency either. Sometimes mankind or a nation vindicates its weakness as also its strength by being frankly inconsistent Wisdom lies in understanding our limitation, and the Working and the Subjects Committee have come to the conclusion that we may no longer go to the legislatures and we have to get strength enough to be outside the legislatures.

'There is one stock argument, viz., we will keep our places vacant. It is not the idea of the resolution that the places should remain vacant. Imagine an opium den to which fifty thousand went, amongst whom we also counted ourselves. Shall we hesitate to empty that den because somebody else will go and occupy it ? I am quite certain that we will not. If we believe the legislatures are played out, it does not matter to us who are likely to occupy them. The relevent consideration is thus; 'Can we or can we not in terms of complete independence go to those legislatures and hasten progress towards independence ?" If you feel that could be done by going to the legislatures, by all means go there. I won't speak now about oathtaking, though for a man like me it is a conclusive argument.

'As for boycott of law courts and schools, I do not see the

needed atmosphere. If there is no atmosphere, what is the use of putting a clause which is not going to be acted upon by the very people to whom it is addressed ? Hence this reservation. There is next the question of civil disobedience. It is a thing for which I live and move. Civil Disobedience I swear by because I cannot possibly conceive India vindicating her freedom by criminal disobedience. Criminal disobedience means bomb violence, the sword and the rifle. I can only conceive of freedom and independence being achieved by and on behalf of the starving millions scattered over by legitimate and special means. Hence disobedience to be peaceful and effective has got to be always civil and always non-violent. If you want that civil disobedience in the very near future inside of a few months, you will have to transform yourselves. You will not then deceive yourselves, unconsciously may it be, deceive the nation that bomb and non-violence can run parallel and side by side.

'If you believe in your creed of non-violence and civil disobedience that is wanted, then you must observe stricter discipline and patch up quarrels. There should be no passion and running in against ourselves and no ugly demonstrations that we have in the Subjects Committee meeting during the past few days. We must be calm, cool, collected and brave. We must speak to the point and never obstruct. So if you really want civil disobedience in the near future, then it becomes necessary for you to conduct the proceedings of the Congress, the Subjects Committee and also yourselves in every walk of life in a manner behaving peaceful men, truthful men, and above all, nationalists pining for freedom who in season and out of season, nay, every minute of the twenty-four hours of the day, are determined upon regaining their lost freedom in the quickest manner possible. It you get that passion for freedom, there is no room for irritation, for jealousy or quarrels, and there is room for unity, and brave, calm and collected action. Hence I ask you with all the strenght I can possibly command to carry this resolution with acclamation, because it is the central resolution. Let it not be said in the world that divided counsels prevailed on the question of independence.

Let it go forth to the world that we rose to a man to vindicate our freedom and pledged ourselves to attain that absolute freedom in the quickest manner possible. There, I ask you to reject the motion of Mr. Subhas Bose. I know he is a great worker in Bengal. He was the General Officer Commanding of our force at Calcutta. But his proposition, though it is no doubt a good one, suggests parallel government. Do you think you can establish a parallel government, when the Congress flag does not fly even in a thousand villages ? It is not bravery or wisdom and you cannot establish freedom by merely passing resolutions. We are not declaring independence as our goal. Here we go a step further and say it is not a distant goal, but it is our immediate objective towards which we are moving. Mr. Subhas Bose, however, seeks to go a slep further. I should like to follow him through and through and bring myself to believe that it is possible today to establish parallel government. That means complete declaration of independence. Have we got our organisations to which to go for adjusting our quarrels and have we national schools? No. What then are we going to do after declaring complete independence ? Heaven alone knows. That is why the Working Committee did not suggest it and recommended just the longest possible step that we can take under the existing circumstances. A step further will land us in a pitfall. That is my certain conviction. I urge you therefore with all the strength I can command to accept the resolution without a change of comma even, and to reject the amendments.

'I thank you all for the patient hearing. I don't know how long I spoke. I feel I have taken long enough of your time, but wait yet a while, whilst I live on this earth.'[41]

All the amendments were then put to vote and those of Pandit Malaviya and others were rejected summarily. Subhas Bose's amendment received some support but the opposition was so overwhelming that a count was not demanded. That relating to the bomb outrage was defeated by 897 to 816 votes, while the amendment objecting to the appreciative reference to the Viceroy in Mahatma Gandhi's resolution was rejected by

900 votes against 765. Besides, his main resolution on independence, was when put to vote, was declared carried with only a dozen voting against it. Thus the resolutions of Gandhi were passed without any alteration.

The Congress congratulated Mrs. Sarojini Naidu who went to South Africa at considerable inconvenience to herself and also the Indians in East Africa on the clear national stand they took upon the Indian problem in that sub-continent. The Congress was of opinion that no solution of the question could satisfy the nation that accepted communal electorates and was based on a discriminate franchise or that imposed disqualification on Indians holding property.[42]

The Congress condemned the refusal of passports for return to India to Shapurji Saklatvala and others who were living in England and other foreign countries.[43]

The next resolution was about the fixation of dates for holding the Congress session. 'In-as-much as the Congress is intended to be representative of the poor masses, in-as-much as the holding of the Congress at the end of December involves very considerable expense to the poor people in providing for extra clothing for themselves and is otherwise inconvenient to them, the date of holding Congress session is hereby by altered to some date in February or March to be fixed by the Working Committee in consultation with the provincial committee of the province concerned.[44]

'The Congress authorises the Working Committee to make all necessary consequential changes in the constitution.'

Pandit Jawaharlal Nehru also put from the chair the following resolution. 'This Congress is of opinion that the financial burdens directly or indirectly imposed on India by the foreign administration are such as a free India cannot bear and cannot be expected to bear. This Congress while re-affirming the resolution passed at the Gaya Congress in 1922, records its opinion for the information of all-concerned that every obligation and concession to be inherited by independent India will be strictly subject to investigation by an independent tribunal and every obligation and every concession, no matter how incurred or given, will be repudiate if it it not found by such a tribunal to be just and justifiable.'[45]

Pandit Nehru also classified the point that the repudiation included debts which England had incurred for the purpose of enslaving India and carrying on England's imperialistic designs. The resolution was carried.[46]

The following resolution urging the rulers of Indian States to confer responsible government was moved by Manilal Kothari.[47] 'In the opinion of this Congress, the time has now arrived for the Ruling Princes of India to grant responsible government to their people and to enact laws or issue proclamations safeguarding the elementary and fundamental rights of the people such as freedom of movement, freedom of speech, freedom to hold public meetings and security of person and property.'

Manilal Kothari said that at a time when they declared independence as the goal for British India, they could not omit to take note of the miserable position of the subjects of Indian States. Indian Princes considered their *Raj* as personal property. They were States in which one could not take typewriter or a cyclostyle machine. The Princes had spent one crore on the Butler Committee's work to establish direct relations with the Crown. The Congress was, therefore, right in taking up the case of the Indian States' subjects and demanding responsible government for them. H. Krishna Rao opined that the Congress had, for the first time, undertaken to deal adequately with the case of the Indian States' subjects who were under unblushing, undiluted autocracy.[48]

Satyamurti wished the Congress had gone further, He said that no permanent or satisfactory solution of the political future could be arrived at without the active cooperation of the Indian States' subjects. The resolution declared that hereafter the people of British and Indian India were linked together, for better or for worse, to secure freedom.[49] The claim of Maharajas to be spokesmen of their people was historically unsound, constitutionally incorrect and politically dangerous. A self-governing India would be much more friendly to the States than the present Political Department. The disputes regarding customs and others affected the Indian States' subjects as much as the Princes, and there must, therefore, be the subjects' voice in having a fair and equitable settlement. The resolution was passed.[50]

The Congress also passed without discussion, a resolution moved from the chair about communal settlement and giving assurances to the Sikhs.[51] 'In view of the lapse of the Nehru Report, it is unnecessary to declare the policy of the Congress regarding communal questions, the Congress believing that in an independent India communal questions can only be solved on strictly national lines. But as the Sikhs in particular, and the Muslims and the other minorities in general, had expressed dissatisfaction over the solution of communal questions proposed in the Nehru Report, this Congress assures the Sikhs, the Muslims and other minorities, that no solution thereof in any future constitution will be acceptable to the Congress that does not give full satisfaction to the parties concerned.[52]

Pandit Jawaharlal Nehru announced that he had received an application from 115 delegates wishing that the two resolutions of the Working Committee rejected by the Subjects Committee be taken up in the Congress. These proposed the grant of autonomy to the *khaddar* and other sub-committee and the reduction of the number of delegates to the Congress to one thousand. Although Mahatma Gandhi was the original author of both the resolutions, he advised them not to press them at that stage and they decided accordingly not to press their application. The president expressed his gratefulness to them all.

The Congress elected Dr. Syed Mahmud and Sri Prakasa as secretaries and reappointed Seth Jamnalal Bajaj and Shivaprasad Gupta as treasurers. It was resolved that the next session of the Indian National Congress would be held at

Karachi.[53]

In an interview to the Free Press Dr. B. Pattabhi Sitaramayya commented on the independence resolution thus :[54] 'The various amendments to Mahatma Gandhi's resolution were purely intellectual, logical and even psychological additions or substractions. Instead of treating his resolution as an organic whole, having a head, a body and limbs, the delegation began to view it piecemeal, much as the proverbial blind man view the elephant as the trunk or as the body or as the legs. It is difficult to see why people had not the wisdom to see that if Mahatma Gandhi was good enough to inaugurate non-cooperation, if he was good enough to declare for independence, it must be good enough to draw up a programme which was whole and from which no part could be taken away or to which no part could be added without making a cripple or a monster.'[55]

The chairman of the reception committee, Saifud Din Kitchlew, in his address, traced the history of the establishment of the British *Raj.* Explaining the property of India prior to the advent of the rule of the East India Company, he attributed the poverty of its people to the nature of the British rule. He said, 'We have come of the most critical stage of our national struggle, the struggle for India's freedom.'[56] According to him, no problem of India was religious or political; it was essentially economic, and it was not practicable to bring about the economic salvation of India without the sovereign control of its destinies.[57] He started with a degree of confidence, a good 'fighting programme' based on a national, political and economic basis. The masses he was sure, would immediately follow the lead. He called peasants, tillers of the soil, labourers and workers as the future masters of India's destiny.[58] Reviewing the national programme, the chairman ended his speech on an optimistic note that the Congress should declare complete independence.

The declaration of complete independence at the Lehore session was hailed by the champions of complete independence as their victory. Behind this victory, however, can be seen a real compromise between the two schools of Dominion Status and complete independence—a compromise which had been attempted at the Calcutta Congress in 1928, but failed.

The momentous resolution was enthusiastically received by the press as well as the people. *The Amrita Bazar Patrika* treated it as a departure from the speeches of the long line of his distinguished predecessors. It was not only the politically minded who spoke through him but also the masses, peasants and industrial workers who found in him their organ voice. Free from verbiage, his speech was as bold as it was full of practical suggestions, as realistic as it was idealistic.[59]

Liberty commented, 'The change was long overdue and nearly the whole presidential address is an eloquent exposition of the political truth which older leaders are so apt to overlook that India's freedom is incompatible with the existence of the British Empire as we know it today.'[60]

Once again after nine years, the Indian National Congress took a stern decision to defy the British Empire. Its proceedings showed that the leaders who sponsored the independence resolution had given their careful and anxious consideration to the implications of the momentous decisions made at Lahore. The delegates dispersed with full consciousness that soon they would be in the midst of another campaign of non-cooperation. The Congress thus concluded its session in a tense atmosphere surcharged with a grim determination to win *swaraj* at all costs, and at the earliest possible moment.

The resolution on complete independence differed from its earlier resolution considerably. Although a resolution on complete independence was first passed in 1927 at the Madras Congress, the Lahore resolution went a step further in two respects. In the first place, while, the Madras resolution made complete independence the goal of the Congress, the Lahore resolution made it its immediate objective. Secondly, the words, complete independence, which were left undefined in Madras, had now been virtually, though in not so many words, defined as isolation from England.

Another respect in which the two resolutions differed was while the authors of the Madras resolution had expressly disavowed the intention of changing the creed of the Congress, the Lahore Congress had changed the creed itself. Since the birth of nationalism in India, and more particularly since the advent of Gandhi, the Congress had undergone many farreaching changes. Its creed from its very inception till 31st December 1929 had been more or less complete freedom plus membership of the commonwealth presided over by the King of England. The Lahore Congress had, for the first time, changed all that, and change in this case was no more normal or theoretical in nature but practical and substantial in character.

A significant aspect of this session was Dr. Kitchlew's strong and unequivocal condemnation of communalism in politics. There had been rarely a speech of this kind in which the introduction of religion in politics, the talk of Hindus or Muslim political rights and demand for communal representation were denounced in more scathing terms than in the speech of Dr. Kitchlew. He said, 'We may be Hindu or Mahommedan by religious convictions, but that has nothing to do with our being Indian. That would not change the factum of our birth or our nationality'. To him the idea of Muslim or Hindu political rights was a misnomer. He believed that whatever political rights an individual had in India, these were by virtue of his being an Indian. He disdainfully rejected the venomous cry of 'religion in danger' and the dream of 'Muslim or Hindu Raj.'

Another notable feature of the Lahore session was the domination of it by what may be called the spirit of youth. Youths had been struggling for ascendancy in the Congress for years. It is true that the main political resolution was moved by Gandhi and recorded by Motilal Nehru, but they only meant that old in years, these two leaders retained in a full measure, vigour, idealism and passion for liberty that are generally associated with youths. Nor could there be any doubt that the conversion of these leaders to their creed was counted by the youths of India as their greatest achievement.

No less significant was the fact that the only strong and powerful opposition, in the beginning, offered to the resolution, came from one of the two greatest leaders of the youth movement in India. In the beginning, Nahru and Bose had jointly led the revolt against Gandhi. At that time, their respective ideologies were more or less the same, though Bose disliked. Communism while Nehru admired Russia. But this identity could not last long. Nehru's loyalty to Gandhi sealed the fate of their friendship. 'Gandhi is our biggest gun,' was the faith of Nehru. The thinking of Bose was just the opposite; '. . . .as a political leader Gandhi has failed.'[61] was his confirmed belief. Leaders with these differing views were bound to part company sooner or later, and conflict of Bose with Gandhi on the ideological plane was sooner, or later inevitable. Whatever be its manifestation, none of the two by temperament, disposition and experience could convert each other to his view.

Gandhi was too mature and experienced a leader to be readily converted to the belief that the social and economic edifice in India which had a history behind it, extending over thousands of years, could be altered in the course of a few months or even years, and who realised that the best thing to do was to concentrate the attention on limited programme and to proceed step by step. He could not conceive of India freed by any method except by Civil Disobedience. In the present atmosphere they were in a position to fight the government and gain freedom by not waving red flag.

Intellectual and political differences did not diminish Gandhi's affection for Nehru. He did not attempt to muzzle him. His reaction was characteristic and his objection was not so much to the radical views of the younger men, as to the light-hearted manner in which brave declarations were made without any serious effort to implement them. He knew that Nehru was not a 'blind follower' and had a mind of his own. Their philosophies of life diverged widely, but they were at one in their desire to free the country of foreign rule, its gross poverty and its social and economic inequalities. Gandhi indeed wanted to harness Nehru's great talents and energies and was confident of containing his impetuous and rebellious spirit. He was to become Gandhi's link with the younger generation. Nehru also realized the indispensability of Mahatma's leadership and showed receptivity and flexibility in honouring his advice. By doing so, he hoped that eventually Gandhi's weight would be thrown in favour of radicalizing India's politics and economy.

When the Congress was thinking in terms of independence and Civil Disobedience Movement for its attainment, the Muslim League had no plan of its own. Brought up and nurtured under British rule, it did not like to toe the Congress line and Mohammed Ali Jinnah who had dissociated himself with the Congress, was too stern and unbending to be treated as second to any one in leadership. He strongly denounced the independence resolution and kept the League away from the movement which he thought would not subserve Muslim interest. In an interview, Jinnah strongly denounced the independence resolution. The members of his community, except the nationalist Muslims, did not participate in this Conference, rather watched the events with concern and anxiety from outside. Jinnah said, 'I have read accounts of the proceedings of the Congress with extreme pain and disappointment. I think Gandhiji and Pandit Motilal have taken on themselves the gravest responsibility in taking decision which they did in breaking up the pourparlers with the the Viceroy and, thereafter, in getting the Congress to adopt resolutions which, in my opinion, are most misleading, unpractical, unsound and unwise. They are calculated to do enormous harm to the interest of India.

'Mahatma Gandhi, it seems to me, is mentally and constitutionally incapable of learning or unlearning. The enormous amount of harm he did in 1922—and subsequently admitted it was—a Himalayan blunder has not taught him to realise the consequences that would follow his policy in which he, no doubt, still believes but which is utterly unsuited to modern times and realities, we have to face in India.

'The proposition has only to be stated to be rejected that independence can be won by non-violent non-cooperation. Why even before the proceedings of the Congress terminated, Union Jack was destroyed not very far from the place where Mahatma Gandhi was sitting, and does Gandhiji believe that majority with which he carried this resolution will enable him to achieve independence without violence?[62]

'The whole of Gandhiji's political philosophy seems to me a bundle of contradictions impossible for any rational man to follow.

'It seems he is reported to have said in concluding his speech on the independence resolution 'what are we going to do, Heaven only knows. But the Working Comittee has taken the longest possible step that he can take and a step further might throw us in a pit.' All I can say is Heaven helps Gandhiji, but I feel quite differently towards the young men whose mentality is very different and why probably think Gandhiji is indispensable to them at the present moment.

'To the youth of India I will only say they are premature, they are precipitating the movement which I sincerely believe is likely to do the greatest possible damage to the vital interests of India.

'This is a moment when I urge on them to follow the advice of those who yield to none in honesty of purpose or patriotism.'[63]

The prominent Sikh leaders including Sardar Kharak Singh, Master Tara Singh and Sardar Mehtab Singh sought interview with Mahatma Gandhi and Motilal Nehru in order to discuss the problems of their community.[64] They suggested that the Nehru Report should be scrapped and there should be communal representation in any shape or form. They demanded that their community by given due consideration along with other communities of the country.[65]

The next proposal was that a piece of saffron colour cloth be affixed to the National flag as long as there are different colours in the flag.[66] Gandhi assured them that these resolutions would be placed before the Congress during 1931.[67] At this, the Sikh leaders assured Gandhi that if these proposals were adopted by the Congress, the Sikhs would gladly join the Congress in a large number and would 'form a limb' of the whole organisation.'[68]

Commenting on the Lahore Congress, the Viceroy who showed much concern over it, wrote to the Secretary of State, 'If they do try it (civil disobedience), we shall not hesitate to hit as hard as we can. . . .I do not think it is possible to dismiss the Lahore conclusions lightly as the mere academic statements of a remote objective. . . and that it involves very mischievous and dangerous potentialities.'[69]

This official criticism and determination to deal with the contemplated movement with a strong hand could not deter the determination of the leaders of the Indian National Congress to devote all their energies and resources in planning and executing the decision already taken.

References

1. See the sentiments expressed by prominent Labour leaders of Britain in *The Tribude*, 2 Jannary 1930.
2. *Ibid.*
3. *Ibid.*
4. *Ibid.*
5. *Ibid.*
6. *Ibid.*
7. *Ibid.*
8. *Ibid.*, Will Thorne was a prominent General-Secretary of National Union of Municipal Workers.
9. *Ibid.*

10. *Ibid.*
11. *Ibid.*
12. *Ibid.*, He was Secretary of General Workers Union.
13. *Ibid.*
14. *Ibid.*
15. *Ibid.*
16. Nripendra Nath Mitra, *The Indian Quarterly Register*, July-December 1929, Vol. II. Calcutta, n.d. pp. 297-98. For messages and some other details of the Indian National Congress see this volume.
17. *Ibid.*
18. *Ibid.*
19. See *The Tribune*, 29 December 1929, 1 January 1930.
20. *Ibid.*
21. Dr. Ansari spoke in Urdu.
22. *Ibid.*
23. *Ibid.*
24. *Ibid.*
25. *Ibid.*
26. *Ibid.*
27. Cries of 'Sit down, Go back' were raised from the audience.
28. *The Tribune*, 29 December 1929—1 January 1930.
29. *Ibid.*
30. *Ibid.*
31. *Ibid.*
32. *Ibid.*
33. *Ibid.*
34. *Ibid.*
35. *Ibid.*
36. *Ibid.*
37. *Ibid.*
38. *Ibid.*
39. *Ibid.*
40. *Ibid.*
41. *Ibid.*
42. Resolution V.
43. Resolution VI.
44. Resolution VII.
45. Resolution VIII.
46. *Ibid.*
47. Resolution IX.
48. *Ibid.*
49. *Ibid.*
50. *Ibid.*
51. Resolution X.
52. Resolution X.
53. Resolution XI.

54. *The Tribune*, 4 January 1930.
55. *Ibid.*
56. Report of the Forty-fourth Annual Session of the Indian National Congress held at Lahore, 1929, p. 20.
57. *Ibid.*
58. *Ibid.*
59. *The Amrita Bazar Patrika*, 1 January 1930.
60. Quoted in *The Tribune*, 1 January 1930.
61. Hugh Toye, *Subhas Chandra Bose*: *The Springing Tiger*: *Study of a Revolution* Bombay, 1962, p. 38.
62. *The Tribune*, 4 January 1930.
63. *Ibid.*
64. *The Tribune*, 1 January 1930.
65. *Ibid.*
66. *Ibid.*
67. *Ibid.*
68. *Ibid.*
69. *Halifax Papers*: Viceroy to Secretary of State, 9 January 1930.

6

Birth of a Party

'Bose was not greatly influenced by Gandhi with whose methods and philosophy he often vigorously disagreed. His only political *guru* was Deshbandhu Das, whose death in 1925 left him bereft of a secure anchorage. Bose had no patience with Gandhi's non-violence and was irritated by the intricate permutations and combinations of the Mahatma's political processes . . . .Temperamentally and intellectually Bose and Gandhi were poles apart. Eventually this was to influence Bose's place in the Congress heirarchy'.[1]

As early as 29 September 1929, Subhas Chandra Bose gave vent to his feelings as President of the Howrah District Political Conference thus:[2] He highlighted students' role in the forthcoming national struggle and highly recommended mass organisation for the achievement of *swaraj* for the country. 'I firmly believe that India shall be free. Sons of Mother India shall once more walk upon the ample surface of this globe with their heads high and shoulders erect, and their art and literature shall once again be approached by the comity of nations. The fight is on, Brothers and sisters, come, let us forget our petty, personal squabbles at this auspicious moment and plunge head-long into the fray.

'Only a few days, you made great preparations to show your love and repect to the memory of a great Bengali hero, the very embodiment of valour and prowess and self-sacrifice of the highest order, near this very *maidan*. The young worker, Jatindranath, unknown to fame laid down his life with calm deliberation for the sake of his country's freedom, never swerving an inch from his iron resolve. And today. I can only hope and fervently pray that his courage, his self-sacrifice, his prowess, his resolution, his patriotism and his marvellous power of action might continue to inspire us all until we have reached our common goal.

'If we are really anxious to see a new awakening, the pulsation of a new life in the whole nation today, we shall have to do away with all sorts of artificial, social inequalities forthwith and afford equal opportunities to all, calculated to help them to attain the full stature of their manhood. All kinds of man-made or economic irregularities much be given the go by and women freed from the servitude of men. In view of the intimate relation subsisting between the society and the state, I am fully convinced that we shall never get back our political power, unless we can bring about a radical change, a whole-sale revolution in our social system.

'One of the surest ways to find out our path to freedom is to look to history. Anyway, it is my firm conviction that the age of terrorism has passed for ever. Our main weapon now-a days is mass organisation. We shall have to get together our countrymen by way of safeguarding our interests and enforcing our claims. And this mass organisation movement will have to be built up round specific claims and particular grievances. Wherever will be found traces of oppression, the tyranny of vested interests, there shall we have to carry on a persistent agitation. This will perhaps bring us into an open conflict with the higher castes of society or sometime with the purse-proud capitalists or again we may find ourselves compelled to resort to civil disobedience and stop payment of taxes by way of extorting on political rights.

'The very best and foremost means of building up a non-violent mass organisation by way of making a success of the basic idea of non-cooperation is of course propaganda and more propaganda. By means of an extensive and incessant propaganda, we shall have to bring about a revolution in the mentality of countrymen.

'We shall have to concentrate our attention on two things immediately. The first is the organisation of Volunteer Corps on a military basis and the second is the whole-hearted participation in the labour movement. Looking at the present condition of the country, I feel that we shall be in a position to create a tremendous agitation throughout the length and breadth of our motherland by next year, and the policy of repression, at present being pursued by the Government won't be able to stop that movement. But we all perhaps need thousands of devoted workers during the terribly trying time. Should that contingency materialise, the students of Bengal would be called upon to come out of their schools and colleges once again. This time, not for a year but for ever. They will have to join the national movement in their thousands and hundreds of thousands. Perhaps the guardians would get angry at my words. But my reply is, if you want freedom, these is no other way.'

On 21 December 1929, in a Youth Conference held at Midnapur, Bose gave vent to his feelings thus:[8] 'The youth movement stands for the propagation of a newer and nobler ideal which will usher into a new social order, new political structure and a new economic conception . . . The youth were so long content to leave the elders in charge of the national movement for freedom, but nothing tangible having materialised as yet as a result of their labours, the resurgent youth of the country have now shaken off their lethargy and are coming forward to take the responsibility of conducting the struggle for freedom with firm determination to bring into being, if possible, a new heaven and a new earth . . . After most anxious deliberation during the last two years I have come to the definite conclusion that the programme of work which was placed before the country in 1921, requires a new orientation, as it is not sufficient to prepare our country for the grim struggle that lies ahead.

'The ideal which I have steadily been working for and which I want the youth organsiations to set before them is the absolute freedom for all from all forms of bondage, social, political and economic . . . The youth of the country will also have to deal a death-blow to the various social abuses and customs which have so long hampered the progress of our Motherland. Caste distinctions must be given the quietus once for all. Women folk of our country must be given absolute equality of status with men and the entire structure of society should be restructured in such a way that every man may have full and free scope for his talents.'

The AICC met in the afternoon of 27 December and the agenda circulated showed that the main change had occurred in respect of local bodies being included along with the councils and government committee in the boycott programme which thus marked an important change, and if acted upon, it was argued, would materially affect the personnel of the Calcutta, Madras aud Bombay corporations besides other local bodies which had been captured by Congressmen.

A large crowd of visitors collected outside the *shamiana.* Mahatma Gandhi, Motilal Nehru and Jawaharlal Nehru were given ovation as they arrived to attend the meeting.[4]

Subhas Bose wanted the House to be adjourned as the conduct of proceedings was not right and proper without the election dispute being decided and the right of membership of the House being determined [5]

Motilal Nehru said that Bose's representation of the case was misleading to say the least of it. There was history behind the case. This election dispute was referred to him for final decision. He clarified the whole case thus:[6] 'I, as referee appointed Dr. Pattabhi Sitaramayya, a member of the Working Committee, to record evidence in Bengal, and I declare and proclaim, as clearly as possible, that he was appointed with the fullest consent of Mr. Kiransankar Roy and Mr. Subhas Bose. Mr. Sen Gupta then telegraphed me, thanking me for Dr. Pattabhi's appointment. Then Mr. Subhas later sent me a telegram expressing surprise at this appointment.

'I explained to them that he was merely to take evidence. I am the judge. Thus both parties appeared before him. Later Mr. Subhas Bose's party retired from enquiry, and then I as sole judge give an interlocutory order that as the interval between them and the Congress session was short, the old members of AICC should retain the membership of AICC till the dispute was settled. The Bengal Provincial Congress Committee wired to me that they will act accordingly, thereby accepting my decision. In fact, it was the opposite party of Mr. Sen Gupta which objected. That was my order, but to be sure that I did not act unconstitutionally. I referred my interlocutory order to the Working Committee in case they had not clothed me with that authority. The Working Committee said I had the necessary authority, but I, having made a reference, they went into the question fully and upheld my decision. I admit this is higher authority, but the decisions of the subordinate authority like the Working Committee can only be dealt with by way of appeal. No such appeal has been filed. If it were made, the other party must be given notice and must be represented. And how can the matter be discussed by an adjournment motion when there are piles of telegrams to be discussed.'[7]

Subhas Bose said, 'There is already a representation on the file'. 'That is not an applied', replied Jawaharlal Nehru.[8]

When a member asked what was the form prescribed for appeal, Motilal Nehru replied, 'That letter was signed by four members who are not here. I do not know what authority Mr. Subhas Bose has to represent them. I hold, therefore, Mr. Subhas is out of order in making that motion.'[9]

Jamnadas Mehta stated, 'I want to raise an important point concerning the constitution of the committee, whether it is the right of a member of the committee to raise a point of appeal.' At this Motilal Nehru asserted that nobody had the right to question his ruling.[10]

Subhas Bose opined, 'But the representation I referred to is a clear appeal to the AICC.[11]

On being questioned by a member whether vacancies to the BPCC were filled a day earlier, Motilal Nehru replied in the affirmative and clarified that it was done in accordance with the constitution. The Working Committee authorised him to set up a sub-committee and he had done it to help him to fill these vacancies.[12]

This was contested by Bose with a statement: 'With regard to the appointment of Dr. Pattabhi Sitaramayya may I say that I have never been a consenting party to it and I say so in the name of everything I hold sacred.'[13]

Pandit Motilal Nehru replied. 'It is not true: that is all I can say.' At this Harisarvottam said, 'I move adjournment of the House.' At this Motilal Nehru told him that he was not in order.[14]

Jawaharlal Nehru said, 'I am not going to speak in favour of any friends. My suggestion is that as the matter is important, we might evolve technical objection, and if appeal is submitted in a proper form, I would like the AICC to go into it. The facts as disclosed before the Working Committee, were so extraordinary that I would not like that these facts be publicly disclosed because they do not resound to the credit of the Congress organization either in Bengal or in the Punjab. Let us consider them fully and let this House come to the decision on them.'[15]

Motilal Nehru was agreeable if the appeal was sent in the same day to have the discussion on it the next day. Harisarvottam Rao maintained that the House must adjourn because until that fact whether it was constitutionally constructed was upheld, it could not transact any business.[16]

At this, Jawaharlal Nehru said, 'There is no appeal yet. Let some one appeal if he so desires.[17]

Subhas Bose protested that while every other action of the

newly elected BPCC had been upheld as valid, only election to the AICC had not been so upheld under pressure from certain party.[18]

Harisarvottam Rao repeated his request for adjournment, but getting no hearing he walked out in protest. As he had gone out, Subhas Bose got up to join him, and he was followed by 24 other members of his group including two ladies.[19]

After this demonstration, the Committee took up the adoption of the report and the accounts.[20]

On 27 December 1929, Subhas Chandra Bose sent the following letter to the president, AICC resiging his membership of the Working Committee.[21]

'At yesterday's meeting of the Working Committee, it was decided by a large majority that new members from Bengal to the AICC should not be allowed to participate in the AICC and Subject Committee meetings. This decision is arbitrary, unconstitutional and un-precedented. It is clear from the communications received from the President that the decision of the President regarding the AICC elections was directly influenced by representations from Mr. J.M. Sen Gupta and his party who have openly opposed the present BPCC and that the President made no reference to us, and did not give BPCC a hearing before he arrived at this decision. The Working Committee, by arriving at this decision has trampled upon the rights and dignities of the BPCC and has ratified the fiat issued by Pandit Motilal Nehru from Lucknow. The Working Committee which under the Congress constitution return executive body, has not only usurped the functioning of the election dispute committee of the AICC but has over-ridden the constitution of the Indian National Congress in order to uphold the action of an important member of that body.

'I, therefore, beg to tender my resignation from the Working Committee as a protest against such illegal and un-constitutional procedure.'[22]

The AICC met on 1 January 1930 for the purpose of appointing a Working Committee for the new year.[23] Mahatma Gandhi proposed that besides Jawaharlal Nehru, Sri Prakasa, Dr. Alam, Jamnalal Bajaj and Shivprasad Gupta, who were to be members ex-officio, the following be elected members, namely, Mahatma Gandhi, Pandit Motilal Nehru, Sardar Sardul Singh, J.M. Sen Gupta, Abul Kalam Azad, Vallabhbhai Patel, C. Rajagopalachari, Dr. Satyapal, Dr. B. Pattabhi Sitaramayya, and Jairamdas Daulatram.[24]

Gandhi explained the causes of his choice. It had been made so to enable them to push as far possible, the work of civil disobedience. They had tried best to eliminate the elederly element and take as many youngmen as possible, but they had not entirely succeeded. Although the election was made by technical method yet the convention had established a cabinet system so that they could not impose any one on the President.[25] Mrs. Sarojini Naidu and Dr. Ansari were asked to be excused. Subhas Bose and Srinivasa Iyengar had sent their resignations.[26] Indeed, for the achievement of independence they needed united action.[27]

At this Abdur Rahim opined that unless a thorough cabinet system were followed, they should have real election.[28] Satyamurti proposed that the names of Srinivasa Iyengar, Subhas Bose and T. Prakasam be included. They had been valued associates of Mahatma Gandhi and also minority views should be represented.[29]

Mahatma Gandhi replying said that they wanted the Working Committee of one mind which might be able to enforce the extreme steps they were taking. A member voiced his feeling thus : 'Is it not a new departure that minority is not represented in the Working Committee.'[30] Gandhi replied, 'I should be extremely grieved if minority considered that because it is not represented on the Working Committee, its assistance is not required. If that is the belief with which we start this new year's programme, then we are done for.[31] At this Abdur Rahim opined, 'Should not the Working Committee be a miniature of AICC, I cannot think of the Working Committee without Mr. Subhas Baboo being on it.[32]

Dr. Alam suggested to Satyamurti to withdraw the name proposed as the programme was bound to fail so that let not their party share discredit for their half-hearted measure. Let them completely surrender to the new executive and obey them.[33]

Pandit Jawaharlal explained that he and Mahatma Gandhi very carefully went through all names and made the list so that there should be no incompatibility in the outlook among the cabinet.[34]

Jamnalal Bajaj suggested that the sense of the house be first taken on the whole list, and if that failed, then individual members be voted on.[35] At this, Satyamurti protested with the remark that it would involve tyranny of minority by majority.[36]

Pandit Motilal Nehru proposed *via media* that the sense of the House itself should be taken as to which of procedure be adopted, that proposed by Jamnalal Bajaj or Satyamurti's proposal for voting on individual names.[37] Satyamurti, however, contended at this suggestion and called it undemocratic. The procedure was above all majorities and minorities and could not be changed at the will of the house.[38]

At this, Jawaharlal Nehru intervened and pointed out that almost a convention had been established regarding the formation of the Working Committee. He tried Motilal Nehru's suggestion for taking the sense of the House which was by majority against Satyamurti.[39] Thereupon Satyamurti said he would as a protest against this undemocratic method walk out and advised others who thought with him to do so. Thereupon the majority of the sixty, who voted with Satyamurti, walked out and included Srinivasa Iyenger, Subhas Bose and Dr. Alam.[40]

Seeing this kind of situation, Jawaharlal Nehru opined :

'This is a most amazing position that there should be a walk-out before I give my ruling as to which procedure I am going to adopt. It is unbecoming for some members to walk out in this way. It is the right of any member to walk out, but I have not declared what I am going to do. I merely took the sense of the House. This walk-out shows some friends are bent on doing the thing at the slightest provocation.'[41]

Abdur Rahim said, 'This unbecoming procedure has been recognised by the Congress Party and has been practised by the members of the AICC in the Councils.[42]

Gaurishankar Bhargava came out to persuade the members to return, but these protestant members had in the meantime held an open air meeting under the chairmanship of Srinivasa Iyengar and decided to subscribe to a joint statement of protest against what they characterised was undemocratic procedure. They had decided to form themselves into the Congress Democratic Party with a provisional committee consisting of Srinivasa Iyengar, Baba Gurdit Singh, Satyamurti, Muthuranga Mudaliar, Swami Govindanand, Subrahmanyam Iyer, Dr. Ghosh of Peshawar, Hissam-ud-Din, S.C. Mitra, J.B. Sen, Abdul Bari, Srinivasachar with Subhas Bose and Dr. Alam as Joint Secretaries.[43]

After the walk-out by Subhas Bose and his followers, Jawaharlal Nehru reported the attitude of those who walked out because they did not even wait to listen to what he was going to say as president of the party. In fact, he thought that in view of the minority being fairly strong, there should be votes taken by ballot of ten names suggested by the Working Committee and also for names suggested by Satyamurti and his friends.[44] At this, a prominent member, Punniah remarked that there was a feeling that the whole House was being attempted into a certain course of action against its will. He, therefore, suggested that balloting be postponed till tomorrow as possibly night might cool down temper and dawn might bring about a settlement.[45] The president regretted he could not adopt the suggestion.[46]

In the end ten names, the originally proposed, were chosen as a result of the ballot and the five additional names suggested were eliminated, Gandhi received 100 votes, Motilal Nehru, 90, Abul Kalam Azad, 90, Vallabhbhai Patel 98, Sardul Singh 97, Dr. Satyapal 90, J.M. Sen Gupta, 92, Jairamdas Daulatram 89, C. Rajagopalachari 85, and B. Pattabhi Sitaramayya 90. Subhas Bose secured 18 votes, Srinivasa Iyengar 11, Prakasam 6 and Swami Govindanand 5.[47]

Subhas Chandra Bose and his associates called it an arbitrary action and issued the following statement on behalf of the Congress Democratic Party after their walk-out from the meeting of the All-India Congress Committee.[48]

At the meeting, Mahatma Gandhi proposed a list of ten names excluding five office-beares for the Working Committee. He stated that his list represented the decision of the Working Committee and it was desirable to have a Working Committee which would be of one mind.[49] Jawaharlal Nehru said that it was a convention in the AICC that the list of names proposed by the Working Committee should be accepted by the House without opposition.[50]

Several members pointed out in reply that the minority party should have representation in the Working Committee and that even last year the minority party in the Congress had representatives in the Working Committee in the persons of Pandit Jawaharlal Nehru, Srinivasa Iyengar, Sambamurti and Subhas Chandra Bose. This arrangement had worked well. It was also pointed out that on several occasions members of the AICC had moved amendments to the list of names proposed and that voting had taken place.[51]

Satyamurti proposed names of Srinivasa Iyengar, Subhas Bose and T. Prakasam as members of the Working Committee.[52] Other members expressed their surprise that these names had been omitted and said that without their inclusion, the composition could not be deemed to be satisfactory. The name of Swami Govindanand was also suggested at this stage.[53]

Seth Jamnalal Bajaj proposed that the vote of the House be first taken on the question as to whether it desired any change in the names proposed by Gandhi,[54] Serious objection was taken by several members of the House to this unconditional suggestion because the amendments which had been already moved could not be shut out in an arbitrary manner.[55] Motilal Nehru spoke in support of Jamnalal Bajaj's suggestion.[56]

Satyamurti stated that parliamentary procedure could not be lightly interfered with by the House and that it was unconstitutional for the president to take votes on Jamnalal Bajaj's motion and refuse to put amendments regarding fresh names to vote.[57]

The president thereupon took votes on Jamnalal Bajaj's motion and by 78 votes to 62 the House decided to retain the list prepared by Mahatma Gandhi.[58] 'We felt that the conduct of the president supported by the members of the Working Committee and the majority party in the House in shutting out amendments and thereby ignoring the rights of a very large section of the House, was thoroughly unconstitutional and undemocratic. We, thereupon, withdraw from the House as a protest.'[59]

Those who walked out of the AICC meeting in protest were 48 in number included Srinivasa Iyengar, Satyamurthi, K. Bhasyam, Annamalai Pillai, Venkatarangam Naidu, Perumalswami Reddiar, Kundaswamy Chetty, S. Venkataram, K.S. Gopalakrishna, Pattabi Raman, Shaktavatsalu, Muthuranga Mudaliar, Subhas Chandra Bose, Aftabdin Chaudhry, B.K. Datta, Arif-ur-Rahman, Shams-ud-Din Ahmed, Monoranjan Gupta, A.K. Ghulam Jilani, Syed Sharf-ud-Din, Syed Asadud-ullah Shirazi, L.M. Sanyal, Basant Kumar Mazumdar, Shrimati Hemprova Mazumdar, Baba Gurdit Singh, Saifud Din Ahmed, Dr. Alam, Shri Ram Sharma, C.C. Ghose and Gaurishanker Bhargava.[60]

These members were distributed among the various provinces as follows.[61]

Bengal	21
Bihar	2
Punjab	4
N.W.F. Province	1
Ajmer	1
Kerala	1
Andhra	1
Tamil Nadu	14

On the walk-out from the meeting of the AICC, J.M. Sen Gupta commented thus:[62] It breaks my heart . . . As usual the President chose ten members to complete the Cabinet of fifteen. Of course, under written rules anybody could propose fresh names and insist on turning out men from the Cabinet which the President had chosen but not under the unwritten convention.

'A convention had arisen in the Congress that it was admissible for the members to suggest other names and if the President accepted those names, there was the end of the matter. Otherwise one could easily imagine the situation in which the President would find himself when surrounded in the Cabinet by men with views opposed to the President and the Congress resolution. It is also not possible to include every person who is a supporter of the present policy of the Congress as expressed in the resolution in the Cabinet.

'There is no point in the objection that the outgoing Working President had no right to suggest the personnel of the new Working Committee. There is no question of the outgoing Committee controlling the new Committee. It is the right of the President if you admit the convention, to choose his colleagues, and he constantly has the right to consult the members of the outgoing members of the Working Committee as to the composition of his Cabinet as he can consult anybody else. And any member, whether he is or is not the member of the outgoing Working Committee, can propose names as the names which had been selected by the President. In this case Mahatma Gandhi did so.'

Interviewed by a representative of the *Free Press* with regard to the happenings in a meenting of the AICC, Subhas Chandra Bose said,[63] 'Those of us *viz*., Mr. Srinivasa Iyengar, Mr. Govindanand, Mr. Prakasam and self who, by a policy of exclusion were not given any place in the Working Committee, were not at all anxious to be there: and if we had been consulted, we could, by mutual agreement, have agreed to step side. But it amazed us, as well as they very large section of the House was the deliberate attempt on the part of the elders to shut us out. Mr. Prakasam was a member of the Working Committee in former years, and so was Mr. Iyengar. Both Mr. Iyengar and I had been in the Working Committee last year along with Mr. Satyamurti and Pandit Jawaharlal. I think we worked well though the four of us represented the Independence School, and other members of the Working Committee represented the Dominion Status School.

'When Pandit Jawaharlal and I resigned from the Working Committee after the Lucknow All-Parties Conference, we did so on the ground that our views disagreed with those of the elders. We were then asked to withdraw our resignation in spite of our differences and we did so. Only the other day at Allahabad towards the end of November both Pandit Jawaharlal Nehru and I, who had resigned from the Working Committee on the issue of the leaders' Delhi manifesto were requested to withdraw in the larger interest of the country. It was surprising to us that, soon after, the larger interest of the country demanded the exclusion of Mr. Iyengar and myself from the Working Committee, and that our President has now more in common with the erstwhile supporters of Dominion Status than with his colleagues in the independence League.

'The step taken by Mahatma Gandhi in moving a list of

ten members *en bloc* and the President's action in shutting out amendments to the names proposed were against Article 24 of the Constitution according to which the All India Congress Committee shall at its first meeting after the annual session of the Congress elect ten members who shall be the Working Committee. There was reference to convention in this connection but a convention cannot override a constitution. Moreover, there is hardly any convention of the kind mentioned. I remember clearly that at the meeting of the AICC at Nagpur a few years ago, names of myself and some other members moved by way of amendments and were defeated. I am informed that at the Gauhati Congress also there were more than ten names before the House and votes had to be taken. As far as I am aware, election of the Working Committee has always taken place by the mutual agreement or by taking votes of the members of AICC, and the question of convention can hardly arise.

'If the constitutional procedure is not adhered to and if the views of all sections in the Congress are not given due Consideration, I fail to see how the Congress can live up to its aceputation as the only national organisation in this country which is fair to all individuals and all communities.'[64]

On 2 January 1930, the Congress Democratic Party held conference of the party members at the intent of its chairman, Srinivasa Iyengar at Lajpat Rai Nagar.[65] Among others, Subhas Chandra Bose, Satyamurti, Bhasyan Iyengar, Muthuranga Mudaliar, Swami Govindanand, Dr. Muhammad Alam, Sheikh Hissan-ud-Din, Abdul Bari and Tirupathi. After prolonged discussion, the party outlined its immediate aims and objects to carry on its work in the country.[66]

It was decided that the Congress Democratic Party would be a party within the Congress and its creed would be the creeed of the Congress as adopted at Lahore, namely, the attainment of complete independence for India by all legitimate and peaceful means.[67]

However its chief aim would be (1) to prevent the Congress

from going back upon the creed of complete independence as was done at Culcutta, (2) the reform of the Congress organisations and their executives on a broader and democratic basis with special provisions for the direct representation of workers, peasants, youths and people of Indian States, and with detailed provisions devised to secure as the Congress constitution required, the effective representation of minorities within the Congress organisations; as well as the reform of the Congress franchise.[68]

The further aim of this party was to federalise the Congress and to give full provincial autonomy to provincial matters and such other subjects as might be agreed to.[69] The party would endeavour to the best of its ability without prejudice to the party's objective of complete independence for India to cooperate as far as possible with other parties in the country in such programmes and policies and such concerted activities as the party might adopt for the purpose of attaining its objective.[70] The party's further aim would be to induce the Congress to accept its democratic views and methods.

On 2 January 1930, Subhas Chandra Bose and Dr. Muhammad Alam, joint secretaries of the Congress Democratic Party issued the following statement.[71] 'A meeting of the Provincial Executive Committee of the Congress Democratic Party was held at Lajpat Nagar on Thursday on 2nd January at 2 P.M. The principles and policy of the Congress Democratic Party were drafted as follows:

(a) The Congress Democratic Party will be a party within the Congress and its creed will be the creed of the Congress as adopted at Lahore, namely, attainment of complete independence for India by all peaceful and legitimate means.

(b) Its chief ends are (i) to prevent the Congress from going back upon the creed of complete independence as was done at the Calcutta Congress when the independence resolution passed at Madras Congress was set aside (ii) To reform Congress organisations and their executives on broader and more democratic basis with special provisions for direct representation of workers, peasants, youths and people of Indian States and with detailed provisions devised to secure as the Congress constitution requires effective representation of minorities within the Congress at all stages of Congress organisations (iii) To reform Congress franchise and (iv) To federalise the Congress and give full provincial autonomy to provinces is provincial matters and such other subjects as may be agreed to.

(c) Without prejudice to the objective of complete independence for India, the party will endeavour to the best of its utility to cooperate as far as possible with other parties in the country in such programme, policies and activities as the party may adopt for the purpose of attaining its objective.

(d) The party will also endeavour to induce Indian National Congress organisations and their executives to accept the party's democratic views.

The above draft principles as well as a detailed programme of the party will come for fuller consideration at the next meeting of the party to be held in Calcutta toward the end of January or beginning of February.'

After two days of the session, Subhas Bose addressed a mass meeting in the municipal gardens outside the Mori Gate, Lahore.[72] In the absence of Dr. Muhammad Alam who was originally invited to preside over this meeting, Comrade Brahmanand Bharati took the chair.[73]

At the outset, Subhas Bose mentioned the resolution of the Indian National Congress declaring its creed as complete independence. 'They all knew that his resolution at Calcutta though supported by a large section of the House, was turned down. But those of them supported that resolution knew that if they had failed at Calcutta, would succeed at Lahore. They now stood vindicated. It was for his countrymen to say who was right and who was wrong in Calcutta. But he would say they were not wrong at Calcutta, they nor were at Lahore. If their motion had been turned down in Lahore, they were bound to succeed at Karachi. They had a moral victory at Calcutta and similarly they won a moral victory at Lahore. Though the programme that they urged had not found favour with their elders, theirs had been a moral victory. He was sure they would be vindicated at Karachi Congress. Their quarrels with the elders were over. Now they would execute in action the Congress programme although it was neither sufficiently progressive nor effective. He wanted to tell them that they would loyally stand by the Congress resolution and support it whole-heartedly. The Punjab was the last to come under the British rule, but Punjab had been the first to declare independence as the goal for India. They did not know what would happen during the next twelve months. It is just possible certain sections of their country-men might join the conference and misnamed the Round Table Conference. He wanted to repeat that nothing would be gained by Round Table Conference. They would not be satisfied by anything short of independence. They will have to go on with their propaganda for independence in addition to the execution of the programme. As they gave full effect to the Calcutta Congress resolution during the last year, similarly they would loyally carry out this year's programme. Civil Dirobedience had already been started in Bengal.

'If they wanted to make the Congress a thoroughly fighting body they must gather all the revolutionary spirits together. Who were they? There were the youths, the workers, the peasants and the oppressed. They believed that it was duty of Congress to attract the labour, the peasants and the youths. They were sufferings from day to day from many grievances. It is these elements that they will have to gather in the Congress. If these elements had not been coordinated, there would not have been Trade Union Congress, the Kisan Sabhas and Youth Leagues. He believed that it would be possible for the Congress to attract them. No doubt that some of their older people were afraid of the youths. Some of them did not understand the difficulties of the Kisans and the oppressed labourers. They will have to take some risk. Perhaps their bringing in might mean a new order of things, a change in the rank of the leaders. The leaders did not fall from the heavens. If the country wanted a new set of leaders let them have them. He thus believed that the ultimate solution of the country's problem depended on the youths. Just as the Non-Cooperation Programme gave a new orientation to the Congress programme, similarly the programme of the youths, workers and peasants would give a new orientation. Therefore, they should look ahead and think out a programme for the future and create a new band of workers. They could only do it if they create a new mentality. What a change they now saw in the country since 1920. If the present programme failed, another wave was bound to come and then there would be a new set of workers and set of leaders.

'They who formed the left wing of the National Congress wanted to declare that Congress was their national organisation, and they stood by it loyally. But they must tell them what was the programme that the country should follow. The new mentality that they wanted to create was the mentality which will hanker after Independence for its own sake. In organising the workers and peasants, it was the duty of the educated youths to take the lead. Just as in Russia and Turkey the youths took a leading part in the freedom battle, similarly Indian youths will have to take the leading part.

'I believe in encouraging and serving the youngmen. If they have any virtues, we must encourage their virtues. I do not believe in surrendering our judgments to older politicians. We have the greatest respect for our elders. Just as the non-cooperators did not surrender their judgments and yet joined in the struggle, similarly they have also joined in the struggle for independence. Our differences are : We want a more fighting Programme. We are going to prepare the country for a far-reaching programme. Are the Kisan Sabhas represented in the Congress now ? Do you give any representation to the youths and the workers ? You have to organise them on the basis of their economic grievances. The country demands a straight answer to a straight question. I believe that a no-tax campaign will be started in some parts of the country. But will that bring them nearer the goal ? If yes, well and good, if not, are you not going to organise the band of youths and going forward with a new programme. I would only say this that the self-immolation of the youngman has raised the country in the estimation of the world. It was wrong on the part of the All-India Congress Committee to condemn the hunger-strikers. Has not the sacrifice of one Jatin Das raised the prestige of the country to a considerable degree ? The leaders have spoilt the atmosphere of the country by condemning the hunger-strikers. Their programme was, therefore, to think progressively and freely.'[74]

There was a conference, on 1st January, of members of the provincial councils and assembly members, present at Lahore, at the residence of Raja Narendra Nath to consider the situation created by the Congress resolution urging council boycott.[75] Amongst those present were Pandit Madan Mohan Malaviya, N.C. Kelkar, M.S. Aney, Dr. B.S. Moonje of the Assembly Nalionalist Party, Satyendra Chandra Mitra, Nilkantadas, and Jamnadas Mehta of the Assembly Congress Party; Sarvottam Rao, Independent, Raja Narendra Nath, Dr. Gokul Chand Narang and Mukand Lal Puri and Sewak Ram of the Punjab Council, Ram Saran Das of the Council of State, Babu Jagatnarain Lal of Bihar and Orissa Council.[76] Consensus of opinion was that the rejection of the Round Table Conference offer by the Congress was premature and the resolution on council boycott ill-timed, and that in view of the stand taken by the Congress there was need for consultation, and coordination between all members of different legislatures as to the action to be taken by them.[77] It was pointed out that the Congressmen whether returned on Congress ticket or not can resign and seek re-election afresh and also can remain in the legislatures at least for the next session.[78]

The statement issued by Pandit Malaviya, Kelkar, Aney, Satyendra Chandra Mitra and Dr. Moonje was as follows :

'We make the public appeal to the Congressmen who are members of the central legislature to suspend their action with reference to the resolution of the Congress about the boycott of the legislatures and not to resign their seats till the 18th. January when it is proposed to hold a meeting of the members of the Congress and nationalist parties in the Assembly at 3 p.m. in the Western Hostel for considering the whole situation.'[79]

Before leaving Lahore on 2 January 1930, Srinivasa Iyengar and Satyamurthi commented on the Congress session as follows. The former said that 'the independence resolution adopted by the Congress has already given fresh life and momentum to national struggle and has toned us all up. Those Dominionwallas who stoutly opposed the change of creed are all now in the Working Committee pledged to independence and I trust they will make good their promise.

'The Congress Democratic Party was forced upon us by the group which had been controlling the Congress for sometime. I am sure this party will live up to its name and will prevent the Congress from lowering the flag.'[80]

Satyamurthi said that the Lahore Congress has not placed any immediate programme before the country. It has merely asked the boycott of legislatures by Congressmen. I have never believed in it. I consider it as much a mistake today as it was in 1920'.[81] He was glad that the Congress Democratic Party had been formed and he invited the Congressmen of the country to join it.[82]

The following statement was issued by Jawaharlal Nehru in connection with the walk-out by some members of the AICC.[83] 'A representative of the press has shown me a statement which has been issued by Mr. Srinivasa Iyengar, Mr. Subhas Bose and some others regarding their walk-out from the All-India Congress Committee meeting last evening and has asked me if I wish to say anything. I don't desire to enter into any controversy in regerd to this matter. I would like to correct certain statement which have been made.

'It is not correct that the names proposed by Mahatma Gandhi for the membership of the Working Committee represented the decision of the last Working Committee. The list was prepared by me in consultation with Gandhiji and several other members of the old Working Committee who were good enough to come to my assistance. Names were put forward by Mahatma Gandhi before the AICC at my request. Some other names were also proposed for the Working Committee. Mr. Jamnalal Bajaj there-upon suggested that a certain procedure should be adopted, and that the House should be asked to decide as to whether they wanted the list proposed by Gandhiji at my request as a whole or whether they wanted separate voting on each individual name.

'Objection was taken to this suggested procedure by Mr. Satyamurti. I pointed out to the House that, in my opinion there was nothing undemocratic in Jamnalal Bajaj's suggestion and that for some years past a convention had gradually grown up for the president to suggest the names of the Working Committee. But I said that before deciding on procedure I would take the sense of the House on it. There was no question at that stage of my taking votes for or against the list. My desire was to see what the general sense of the house was and then to announce procedure which I thought should be adopted. On votes being taken, 21 votes were for the procedure suggested by Mr. Jamnalal and 62 were against it. I informed the House of the figures of the count and was proceeding to give my decision regarding the procedure to be followed; when Mr. Satyamurti hestily and discourteously intervened and without allowing me to finish what I had to say announced his intention to walk out. A member of the House drew Mr. Satyamurti's attention to the fact that I had not given my decision about the procedure yet. I also made this clear but without waiting for my decision, Mr. Satyamurti and a number of others walked out. In view of the voting and the fact that majority in favour of Mr. Jamnalal's motion was not very great, it was my intention not to adopt the procedure suggested by him but to have ballot. I had no opportunity of announcing this before the walk-out, I did so as the members were going out. Subsequently, election by ballot took place. Whilst this election was proceeding, I was informed by a member who had gone out and returned that the protestants who had gone out were prepared to return if I expressed my regret for the procedure I had adopted. I informed him that in my opinion, I had done nothing wrong and I failed to see entirely why I should express regret for anything. Voting by ballot proceeded and 104 members participated besides two or three who were present and did not vote. On the previous motion on procedure 140 members had voted.

'It will thus be observed that Mr. Satyamurti and his group submitted first of all to voting. Then on hearing the result of the court and without waiting for my decision they walked out.

'I regret that some members should have felt aggrieved at what I did and should have deemed it necessary to walk out. Those of my colleagues and myself who recommended the list of ten names did so with no intention of keeping out anybody but because we felt that the best way to give effect to the Congress programme, as laid down at this session was to have a homogeneous body of those who believed in that programme. I understand that the members walking out have made a public statement to the effect that the programme adopted by Congress was neither sufficiently effective. Further it has been stated that while accepting the principles laid down by the Congress they would frame their own programme of action. Another member, who has walked out stated in the AICC as well as to ourselves and the Working Committee to have them on the new Executive when they did not themselves believe in the programme laid down by the Congress.

'I understand Congress Democtatic Party has been started by the Protestants who walked out. Every Congressman is at perfect liberty to start separate groups, but it seems to me amazing that the very day the Congress ended after passing the momentous resolution, some Congressmen should have introduced spirit of faction and should have tried to belittle the efforts of the Congress. This action was reprehensible enough, but the manner of doing, it was even more extraordinary. The extreme haste which was shown almost indicated than an opportunity was sought after to form a separate group so that excess may be found for not acting upto the Congress direction. I regret this greatly. I hope that the country will realise that we have a grim struggle ahead, and will not allow this spirit of faction to increase.'

References

1. Frans Moraes, *Jawaharlal Nehru : A Bibliography,* New York, 1956, p. 153.
2. *The Tribune*, 5 October, 1929.
3. For a full text of his speech see *The Tribune*, 26 December, 1929.
4. *The Tribune*, 29 December, 1929.
5. *Ibid.*
6. *Ibid.*
7. *Ibid.*
8. *Ibid.*
9. *Ibid.*
10. *Ibid.*
11. *Ibid.*
12. *Ibid.*
13. *Ibid.*
14. *Ibid.*
15. *Ibid.*
16. *Ibid.*
17. *Ibid.*
18. *Ibid.*
19. *Ibid.*
20. *Ibid.*
21. *Ibid.*
22. *Ibid.*
23. *The Tribune*, 3 January, 1930.
24. *Ibid.*
25. *Ibid.*
26. *Ibid.*
27. *Ibid.*
28. *Ibid.*
29. *Ibid.*
30. *Ibid.*
31. *Ibid*
32. *Ibid.*

33. *Ibid.*
34. *Ibid.*
35. *Ibid.*
36. *Ibid.*
37. *Ibid.*
38. *Ibid.*
39. *Ibid.*
40. *Ibid.*
41. *Ibid.*
42. *Ibid.*
43. *Ibid.*, The Congress Democratic Party also enunciated its brief programme.
44. *Ibid.*
45. *Ibid.*
46. *Ibid.*
47. *Ibid.*
48. *Ibid.*
49. *Ibid.*
50. *Ibid.*
51. *Ibid.*
52. *Ibid.*
53. *Ibid.*
54. *Ibid.*
55. *Ibid.*
56. *Ibid.*
57. *Ibid.*
58. *Ibid.*
59. *Ibid.*
60. *Ibid.*
61. *Ibid.*
62. *The Tribune*, 4 January, 1930.
63. *Ibid.*
64. *Ibid.*
65. *Ibid.*
66. *Ibid.*
67. *Ibid.*
68. *Ibid.*
69. *Ibid.*
70. *Ibid.*
71. *Ibid.*
72. *Ibid.*, A number of ladies also attended this public meeting.
73. *Ibid.*
74. *Ibid.*, Dr. Muhammad Alam who joined late in the meeting, explained the speech of Subhas Bose in Urdu. Besides Maulana Abdul Bari delivered a short speech and stressed the necessity of the organisation of the workers and peasants by the Congress.

75. *The Tribune*, 3 January, 1930.
76. *Ibid.*
77. *Ibid.*
78. *Ibid.*
79. *Ibid.*
80. *The Tribune*, 4 January, 1930.
81. *Ibid.*
82. *Ibid.*
83. *Ibid.*

7

Civil Disobedience Movement

In its headlines, *The Tribune* dated 3 January 1930 stated, 'Congress Session concluded; President Appeals for Discipline and Determination; Congress Will Meet in February or March; Dr. Kitchlew's advice to Youngmen; Mrs. Naidu's Plea For Unity.'[1] The forty-fourth session of the Indian National Congress came to a close on 1st January 1930 at about 5.40 p.m. amidst scenes of enthusiasm. It was indeed an historic and most momentous session of the India's greatest political organisation, because it was at this session that the Congress, speaking on behalf of the Indian nation, decided that the attainment of complete national independence would be its immediate objective.

It was in fact on the motion of Gandhi, supported by Motilal Nehru that this fateful decision was taken, and the resolution would have gone much further, if they had not exercised a restraining influence on their associates and followers. Besides, Gandhi warned the Congress leaders not to move too fast but to make sure of every step they took. It was his note of caution which he suggested, should be observed in future by one and all.

Besides the proceedings of the Subjects Committee as well as of the Congress clearly showed that Gandhi, Motilal Nehru and other sponsors of the Independence resolution had given their most careful and anxious consideration to the implications of the momentous step which the Congress had taken, and when the delegates dispersed for their states, they were conscious of the fact that they were on the eve of another campaign of non-cooperation against the *Raj*—a campaign which would be more determined, wide-spread and well-organised at all-India level than the first Non-Cooperation Movement 1920-22, because both the leaders and the people had the experience of the previous campaign to guide them.

The Congress, therefore, concluded in a tense atmosphere, which was surcharged with a grim determination on the part of the delegates to win *Swaraj* at all costs and at the earliest possible moment. The concluding speeches of the prominent leaders were pitched in a strong key; and Jawaharlal Nehru, Mrs. Sarojini Naidu and Saifud Din Kitchlew emphasised the need for rigid discipline and firm determination to make the coming struggle successful in every respect.

In his concluding remarks at the Lahore Congress, the president remarked that India's cry for complete independence had already resounded through all parts of the world and had enabled Indians abroad to raise their heads high. He would welcome the purging of the Congress of such men as were content with mere feform of the present order. He clarified a pertinent point that the history of the world taught us that it was not a crowd of sheep that won freedom, but bands of disciplined, well-organised, honest and determined men with unquestionable patriotic fervour and spirit moving in their veins. He, thus, appealed to the country men to prepare itself for the coming struggle.

The other prominent leader who gave vent to her feelings was Mrs. Sarojini Naidu. She indeed spoke with her usual eloquence, congratulated the Congress on the change of creed agreed upon during the session, and appealed to one and all to develop a sense of discipline and honesty of purpose if they wished to achieve their supreme objective—the attainment of complete independence for the country.

Saifud Din Kitchlew acknowledged the debt of Mahatma Gandhi for his message of strict discipline and non-violence during the forthcoming struggle for independence. He expressed the view that if the campaign of non-violent non-cooperation failed to achieve the desired result, it would be open to those who believed that independence could not be obtained without violence to go their own way. 'In the meantime, we take a solemn vow that we shall be strictly non-violent in our speech also, even though we may not be able completely to have control our thoughts and ideas. We solemnly promise to implicitly obey the orders of the Congress.'[2]

The Tribune commented thus : 'There may be a difference of opinion as to the wisdom or otherwise of the fateful decision which the Congress has taken, but there can be no manner of doubt that the national struggle for freedom has received a new orientation at Lahore and has entered upon its decisive and final stage.'[3]

The new Congress Working Committee held its first meeting on 2nd January 1930 to enable the members to exchange their views on the steps to be taken to give effect to the programme chalked out for the year. Mahatma Gandhi made it clear in the Congress that even after deep thinking he had not been able yet to arrive at any formula with regard to the nature or place of the launching of civil disobedience.

Under the caption 'Cult of Bomb' Gandhi wrote in *Young India* in condemnation of violence erupted at various quarters in India. He appealed to the people to launch the movement for independence in a non-violent way. 'There is so much violence in the atmosphere immediately surrounding us that a bomb thrown here or there causes little perturbation. Probably there is even joy in the hearts of some . . . I would despair of India getting freedom by non-violence. Happily I have certain belief that the vast masses who have become conscious of the fact that they must have freedom are untouched by the spirit of violence.

'Let me think what would have happened if the Viceroy had been seriously injured or killed. There certainly would have been no meeting with the Viceroy on 23rd, and, therefore, no certainty as to the course to be adopted by the Congress. That would have been undesirable result.'

Continuing, Mahatma Gandhi took again the net result of political violence practised in the country. 'Every time violence occurred, we lost heavily, that is, military expenditure had risen from violence done to the foreign rules. Violence to our own people whom we may consider to be obstructing the country's progress is an easy natural step.

'We are now entering upon a new era. Our immediate objective, not a distant goal, is complete independence. We can establish independence only by adjusting our differences through an appeal to head and heart. It is not by terrorising or killing those, who, we fancy, may impede our march. Let those who are not past all reason cease to endorse activities such as the latest bomb outrage. Let them openly and heartily condemn these outrages so that the deluded patriots may realise the futility of violence and the great harm the violent activity has every time done.'

The Congress Working Committee fixed 26th January 1930 as Independence Day to be observed through the country.[4]

'It has been suggested that public meetings would be held all over India and a programme explaining the duty of Congressmen, particularly in regard to the resolution adopted by the Congress will be placed before the public at these meetings. All Congress organisations will be asked to hoist independence flags and preach the Congress programme and the position of those who have adopted the responsibility in the matter of Independence, will be made. Gandhiji will prepare the draft of the statement and the members of Working Committee have been requested to supply Mahatmaji with all materials they may supply for this statement.

'The Committee trusts that all the members of the Central

Legislature and the Provincial Legislatures will forthwith resign their seats and devote their attention to the prosecution of the independence programme and convince registered voters to compel the resignation of those who may not respond to the Congress appeal for resignation and appeal to the voters to refrain from participating in elections to the Legislatures.

'The Committee notes with satisfaction the work of the Foreign Cloth Boycott Prohibition and Anti-untouchability Committee, and authorises and requests them to continue the work.

'The Committee calls upon the Provincial Congress Committees to vigorously enrol Congress members and volunteers in their respective areas, and report their numbers to the AICC Office by February 10th for submission to the Working Committee meeting on February 14.'[5]

The Independence Day pledge was a follows. 'We believe that it is the inalienable right of the Indian people, as of any other people, to have freedom and to enjoy the fruits of their toil and have the necessities of life, so that they may have full opportunities of growth. We believe also that if any government deprives a people of these sights and oppresses them, the people have a further right to alter it or to abolish it.'

Pandit Motilal Nehru in a statement to the Associated Press declared that in obedience to the resolution passed by the Indian National Congress, he called upon all members of the Congress Party in the Legislative Assembly and the Council of State to send their formal resignations to the Governor-General forthwith and to let him know as soon as they had done so.[6]

The Congress session being over, the president was asked to address a mammoth meeting of the citizens of Lahore held outside Mochi Gate. Maulana Habibur Rahman presided. The other prominent speakers were Maulana Attaullah Shah Bukhari, Mani Lal Kothari, Baba Gurdit Singh, Pandit Gauri Shankar and Shrimati Shanno Devi.[7]

Maulana Attaullah Shah Bukhari was the first speaker. He said that it was a matter of great pride that after 200 years the flag of complete independence had been hoisted on the banks of *Ravi*. The Punjab was the last province whose conquest completed the subjection of India, and it was a matter of congratulation that in every province a flag of independence has first of all been hoisted. For keeping that flying they looked to their youngmen, and it was their duty to see that it was never lowered. Therefore, the youth of the country should come forward not only to protect the Independence Flag, but to realise the great objective that Mahatma Gandhi had placed before them. For that purpose let them be prepared to have their breasts perforated by bullets. It was a time of making sacrifices and those who were prepared to die could not be conquered. But let them remember that they were to fight this battle of freedom by the weapon of complete non-violence.

The Maulana then referred to the martyrdom of Jatin Das. What a glorious death he died, asked he. The spirit of Das, he believed, would liberate the country. Let the youngmen also learn to die in a noble cause—the cause of the country.[8]

'The speaker advised the young members of the Naujawan Bharat Sabha to rally under the banner of the Congress and carry on a raging and tearing campaign for freedom in every nook and corner of India, especially when the objective of both the organisations was one and the same. Let them all fill the jails if necessary, and be prepared for every sacrifice for the cause of the country. If they could do that, success was certain'.[9]

Appealing to Muslims to take part in large numbers in the battle of freedom, the Maulana declared, 'My religion, my faith is the freedom of my motherland'. Like the Prophet who died for the sake of liberating the Holy Mecca, let the Muslims, he said, also shed their blood for the emancipation of their country.'[10]

Concluding Maulana Bukhari asked the people to follow the lead of Mahatma Gandhi and free their country from foreign yoke. He regretted the audience were clad in foreign cloth. Let them take a vow that in future they would not spend a *pice* on purchasing foreign cloth.[11]

Manilal Kothari next addressed the audience. He said the Punjab was a place of pilgrimage for him.[12] The massacre of the Jallianwala Bagh had created a deep impression on his mind and ever since that day he had felt convinced of the necessity of a change in the government.[13] Formerly Mahatma Gandhi had said the goal of India was *Swaraj* within the Empire if possible, and without it if necessary.[14] Now Gandhi declared in favour of *Swaraj* without the Empire. That declaration had also been made in the Punjab.[15]

Kothari declared, 'We in distant Gujarat look to the Punjab for progress on peaceful lines. By merely holding big meetings we cannot get independence. We will have to work hard. The fight for winning freedom is not a small thing. We will have to make sacrifices. This is what history teaches us. But who are to make sacrifices. The youth and that respectable class of people who hold no property. We in Gujarat hear much about the Punjab youth. During the last four days, I have myself noticed that there is a great enthusiasm in them. As a soldier in the battle of freedom, I will request them to create the power of work in them. Let them become disciplined, devoted and determined soldiers of the motherland'.[16]

Kothari also narrated his past experiences especially the *satyagraha* at Bardoli launched under the leadership of Sardar Vallabhbhai Patel. There the people were so much disciplined and organised that they refused to give anything to government officials without the permission of the Sardar. There was no crime, no lawlessness there. But in the Punjab, he had heard that for every five Punjabis, there was one CID man. This was really unfortunate. He said if they were to fight the battle of freedom by peaceful and non-violent means, they would have to be prepared for many Bardolis. But for that purpose discipline was necessary.[17]

Kothari also observed that if the people of India wanted freedom, they should boycott *en masse* all foreign goods, especially foreign cloth, have their cases decided not by law courts but by *panchayats* and put in their sincerest efforts for the maintenance of Hindu-Muslim Unity.[18]

Baba Gurdit Singh made a short speech emphasising the need of unity to make a common front to their opponent. He made it clear that the decree for independence had been granted by the Congress, and it was then for the people to execute it.[19]

Pandit Gauri Shankar Misra of Ajmer congratulated the country on the declaration of complete independence. Freedom, he said, could not be attained by mere tall talk, but by real and substantial work. Freedom in other countries had been won by youngmen, and, therefore, the adoption of the Independence resolution had laid a great responsibility on the shoulders of youngmen of India. But the great work before them could not be done without discipline.[20]

Shanno Devi who returned a week earlier from Africa after fulfilling her vow of collecting one *lakh* of rupees for the Kanya Mahavidyalaya, gave a message of Indians residing in Africa to the people of India. She said there was no Hindu-Muslim or Sikh question in Africa. Continuing she said let them regard themselves as Hindustani. She regretted that they could not make even the ordinary sacrifice of discarding foreign cloth. She appealed to the audience to part with their turbans and caps. Thereupon a large number of *pagris* and caps were thrown on the platform.[21]

While asking Jawaharlal Nehru to address the audience, the president of the meeting, Maulana Habibur Rahman paid a glowing tribute to his spirit of sacrifice. The very sight of Pandit Nehru, he said, reminded him of the great sacrifice he had made in the cause of the country. He said Pandit Nehru was their real king and people should no longer call him their uncrowned king. He told Jawaharlal, 'The Punjab is a material province. Come here and organise it. I put my services at your disposal. Take any work you like out of me.'[22]

Pandit Nehru was greeted with shouts of *Inqilab Zindabad* when he rose to speak. He said he had come there not to deliver any speech, but to discharge a duty that he could not perform a day earlier in the Congress *pandal*.[23] That duty was to heartily thank the people of Lahore for the grand reception they had accorded to him a few days ago.[24] He said that the country called upon him to occupy that exalted position which he at first hesitated to accept because he realised his incapacity to shoulder such a heavy responsibility.[25] But by the force of circumstances, he was compelled to accept their high position. He admitted that he could not adequately express his thanks for the great honour they had done him on the day of his arrival at Lahore. That honour in fact had been done to the representative of the Congress.[26]

'I find people thirsting for freedom. If any one does some little thing for them, they love him, and in fact overwhelm him with love. . . .I congratulate you on the success of the Congress at Lahore. I also congratulate you for having proclaimed complete independence on 1st January 1930. That day would really be a memorable day in the history of India. The flag of Independence was hoisted at 12 midday, and we felt happy. What we have really done is to place the true objective before us and to express our determination to obtain it as early as possible.

'But you should remember that mere hoisting of the flag does not bring independence. The real battle is still to be fought. It will be mere deception on our part to say that we have got independence.

'You are to prepare yourself for the immediate step the Congress has taken. There is great enthusiasm for freedom. But it is not organised and disciplined and, therefore, it cannot be utilized for any useful purpose. Like a true soldier, discipline yourself. The time is fast approaching when you will be called upon to work as soldiers in the battle of freedom.'

For that purpose they should, said he, strengthen Congress Committees and the volunteer corps. The Congress Working Committee had decided to call upon the country to celebrate the 26th of January as independence Day.[27] He further advised the people that every step they might take forward should be done with care so that they might not have to retreat.[28] 'I have great hopes in your province, and I believe those hopes will be realised the time comes.'[29]

The President issued the following appeal to Congressmen [30] 'The Congress has laid down full independence as its immediate goal In the programme that it has been chalked out, an essential part is boycott of the Councils and committees appointed by Government. I trust that all Congress members of the Assembly, the Council of State, the Provincial Councils and all committees appointed by the Government immediately send in their resignations from these leaders to the Government. An intimation that the resignation has been sent to the Government should be sent to the office of the All India Congress Committee in Allahabad. I trust that members of these bodies who have not gone on the Congress ticket but who agree with the Congress programme, will do likewise. To all Provincial Congress Committees and District and local Committees, I would appeal to give widest publicity to the Congress resolutions and to explain their full implications. The Working Committee will soon issue directions about future work. Meanwhile, the Congress organisations are requested to take immediate steps to put their issues in order and to prepare themselves for the struggle ahead.'[31]

The Civil Disobedience Movement gave Rafi Ahmad an opportunity to do something substantial at the national level. Earlier the Bardoli Satyagraha greatly agitated his mind and developed much sympathy for Sardar Vallabhbhai Patel who achieved marvellous success against Governor Wilson in getting him agreed to grant several concessions to the peasantry of Bardoli and its several villages. Rafi Ahmad indeed did not with to lag behind in the national work—indeed a call from Mahatma Gandhi and Motilal Nehru. Gandhi asked the Congressmen to resign their seats in the legislatures. Rafi Ahmad atonce responded and resigned his seat in the Assembly along with other members of the Swaraj Party. He atonce left for Rae Breli to participate in the Salt Satyagrah—a call given by Mahatma Gandhi in March—April 1930 after the Dandi March came to an end on 5 April 1930. In the 'War Council', Rafi Ahmad was appointed the 'Dictator' and his function was to mobilise the people of the province. Now he moved from place to place, addressed several meetings, met thousands of satyagrahis and apprised them of the Gandhian ideology for achieving Swaraj for India. Everywhere he said, 'organise yourself in a disciplined and non-violent way; fight for the Swaraj.' His advice indeed very effective among the illiterate masses of our country. They took the message of Mahatma Gandhi in a serious way and came out with full real and patriotic fervour. This, in fact, was a great achievement of young Rafi Ahmad Kidwai.

Pledge Taken on Independence day

January 26*th*, 1930

We believe that it is the inalienable right of the Indian people, as of any other people, to have freedom and to enjoy the fruits of their toil and have the necessities of life, so that they may have full opportunities of growth. We believe also that if any government deprives a people of these rights and oppresses them, the people have a further right to alter it or to abolish it. The British Government in India has not only deprived the Indian people of their freedom but has based itself on the exploitation of the masses, and has ruined India economically, politically, culturally, and spiritually. We believe, therefore, that India must sever the British connection and attain Purna Swaraj or complete independence.

India has been ruined economically. The revenue derived from our people is out of all proportion to our income. Our average income is seven pice (less than two pence) per day, and of the heavy taxes we pay, 20 per cent are raised from the land revenue derived from the peasantry and 3 per cent from the salt tax, which falls most heavily on the poor.

Village industries, such as hand-spinning, have been destroyed, leaving the peasantry idle for at least four months in the year, and dulling their intellect for want of handicrafts, and nothing has been substituted, as in other countries, for the craft thus destroyed.

Customs and currency have been so manipulated as to heap further burdens on the peasantry. British manufactured goods constitute the bulk of our imports. Customs duties betray clear partiality for British manufacturers, and revenue from them is used not to lessen the burden on the masses but for sustaining a highly extravagant administration. Still more arbitrary has been the manipulation of the exchange ratio which has resulted in millions being drained away from the country.

Politically, India's status has never been so reduced as reduced as under the British regime. No reforms have given real political power to the people. The tallest of us have to bend before foreign authority. The rights of free expression of opinion and free association have been denied to us, and many of our countrymen are compelled to live in exile abroad and cannot return to their homes. All administrative talent is killed, and the masses have to be satisfied with petty village offices and clerkships.

Culturally, the system of education has torn us from our moorings, and our training has made us hug the very chains that bind us.

Spiritually, compulsory disarament has made us unmanly and the presence of an alien army of occupation, employed with deadly effect to crush in us the spirit of resistance, has made us think that we cannot look after ourselves or put up a defence against foreign aggression, or even defend our homes and families from the attacks of thieves, robbers, and miscreants.

We hold it to be a crime against man and God to submit any longer to a rule that has caused this fourfold disaster to our contry. We recognise, however, that the most effective way of gaining our freedom is not through violence. We will therefore prepare ourselves by withdrawing, so far as we can, all voluntary association from the British Government, and will prepare for civil disobedience, including non-payment of taxes. We are convinced that if we can but withdraw our voluntary help and stop payment of taxes without doing violence, even under provocation, the end of this inhuman rule is assured. We therefore hereby solemnly resolve to carry out the Congress instructions issued from time to time for the purpose of establishing Purna Swaraj.

Letter dated August 15th, 1930, sent by Congress leaders in Yeravda Prison to Sir Tej Bahadur Sapru and Mr. M.R. Jayakar containing suggested conditions for peace.

Yeravda Central Prison,
15th August, 1930.

Dear Friends,

We are deeply grateful to you for having undertaken the duty of trying to effect a peaceful settlement between the British Government and the Congress. After having perused the correspondence between yourselves and His Excellency the Viceroy, and having had the benefit of protracted talks with you, and having discussed among ourselves, we have come to the conclusion that the time is not yet ripe for securing a settlement honourable for our country. Marvellous as has been the mass awakening during the past five months, and great as has been the suffering of the people among all grades and classes representing the different creeds, we feel that the sufferings have been neither sustained enough nor large enough for the immediate attainment of the end. Needless to mention, we do not in any way share your view or the

Viceroy's that civil disobedience has harmed the country or that it is ill-timed or unconstitutional. English history teems with instances of bloody revolts whose praises Englishmen have sung unstintingly and taught us to do likewise. It therefore ill becomes the Viceroy or any intelligent Englishman to condemn a revolt that is in intention, and that has overwhelmingly remained in execution, peaceful, but we have no desire to quarrel with condemnation, whether official or unofficial, of the present civil disobedience campaign. The wonderful mass response to the movement is, we hold, its sufficient justification. What is, however, the point here is the fact that we gladly make common cause with in vishing, if it is at all possible, to stop or suspend civil disobedience. It can be no pleasure to us needlessly to expose the men, women and children of our country to imprisonment, lathi charges and worse. You . . . therefore, believe us when we assure you, and through you the Viceroy, that we could leave no stone unturned to explore any and every channel for honourable peace, but we are free to confess as yet we see no such sign on the horizon. We notice no symptom of conversion of the English official world to the view that it is India's men and women who must decide what is best for India. We distrust the pious declarations of the good intentions, often well meant, of officials. The age-long exploitation by the English of the people of this ancient land has rendered them almost incapable of seeing the ruin moral, economic and political, of our country which this exploitation has brought about. They cannot persuade themselves to see that the one thing needful for them to do is get off our backs and do some reparation for the past wrongs by helping us to grow out of the dwarfing process that has gone on for a century of British domination.

But we know that you and some of our learned countrymen think differently. You believe a conversion has taken place, at any rate, sufficient to warrant participation in the proposed Conference. In spite, therefore, of the limitation we are labouring under, we would gladly co-operate with you to the extent of our ability.

The following is the utmost response it is possible for us, circumstanced as we are, to make to your friendly endeavour :

(1) We feel the language used by the Viceroy in the reply given to your letter about the proposed conference is too vague to enable us to assess its value in terms of the National Demand framed last year in Lahore, nor are we in a position to say anything authoritative without reference to a properly constituted meeting of the Working Committee of the Congress and, if necessary, to the All-India Congress Committee; but we can say that for us individually no solution will be satisfactory unless

(a) it recognises, in as many words, the right of India to secede at will from the British Empire,

(b) it gives to India complete national government responsible to her people, including the control of defence forces and economic control, and covers all the eleven points raised in Gandhiji's letter to the Viceroy, and

(c) it gives to India the right to refer, if necessary, to an independent tribunal such British claims, concessions and the like, including the so-called public debt of India, as may seem to the National Government to be unjust or not in the interest of the people of India.

Note.—Such adjustments as may be necessitated in the interests of India during the transference of power to be determined by India's chosen representatives.

(2) If the foregoing appears to be feasible to the British Government and a satisfactory declaration is made to that effect, we should recommend to the Working Committee the advisability of calling off civil disobedience, that is to say, disobedience of certain laws for the sake of disobedience.

(3) The question of the composition of the proposed Conference and of the Congress being represented at it, can only be decided after the foregoing preliminaries are satisfactorily settled.

Yours sincerely,
Motilal Nehru
M.K. Gandhi
Sarojini Naidu
Vallabhbhai Patel
Jairamas Doulatram
Syed Mahmud
Jawaharlal Nehru

Resolution of Remembrance

January 26th, 1931

We, the citizens of . . . record hur proud and grateful appreciation of the sons and daughters of India who have taken part in the great struggle for independence and have suffered and sacrificed so that the motherland may be free; of our great and beloved leader, Mahatma Gandhi, who has been a constant inspiration for us, ever pointing to the path of high purpose and noble endeavour; of the hundreds of our brave youths who have laid down their lives at the altar of freedom; of the martyrs of Peshawar and the whole Frontier Province, Sholapur, Midnapur District, and Bombay; of the scores of thousands who have faced and suffered barbarious lathi attacks from the forces of the enemy; of the men of the Garhwali Regiment, and all other Indians in the military and the police ranks of the Government, who have refused, at the peril of their own lives, to fire or take other action against their own countrymen; of the indomitable peasantry of Gujrat, which has faced without flinching and turning back all manner of acts of terrorism, and the brave and long-suffering peasantry of the other parts of India, which has taken full part in the struggle despite every effort to suppress it; of the merchants and the other members of the commercial community, who have helped, at great loss to themselves, in the national struggle and especially in the boycotts of foreign cloth and British goods; of the one hundred thousand men and women who have gone to the prisons and suffered all manner of privation and sometimes assaults and beatings even inside the gaol walls; and especially of the ordinary volunteer who, like a true soldier of India, without care of fame or reward, thinking only of the great cause he served, has laboured unceasingly and peacefully through suffering and hardship.

And we record our homage and deep admiration for the womanhood of India, who, in the hour of peril for the motherland forsook the shelter of their homes and, with unfailing courage and endurance, stood shoulder to shoulder with their menfolk in the front line of India's national army, to share with them the sacrifices and triumphs of the struggle; and our pride at the youth of the country and the Vanar Sena, whom even their tender are could not prevent from participating in the struggle and offering martyrs for the cause.

And, further, we record our grateful appreciation of the fact that all the major and minor communities and classes in India have joined together in the great struggle and given of their best to the cause; of, particularly, the minority communities—the Muslims, Sikhs, Parsis, Christians and others who, by their valour and loyal devotion to the cause of the common motherland, have helped in building up a united and indissoluble nation, certain of victory, and resolved to achieve and maintain the independence of India, and to use this new freedom to raise the shackles from, and to remove the inequalities among, all classes of the people of India, and thus also to serve the larger cause of humanity. And with this splendid and inspiring example of sacrifice and suffering in India's cause before us, we repeat our Pledge of Independence, and resolve to carry on the fight till India is completely free.

References

1. *The Tribune*, 3 January, 1930.
2. *Ibid.*
3. *Ibid.*

4. *Ibid.*
5. *Ibid.*
6. See his appeal on the first page of *The Tribune*, dated 3 January, 1930. T. Prakasam informed Motilal Nehru that he had already sent in his resignation.
7. *The Tribune*, 4 January, 1930.
8. *Ibid.*
9. *Ibid.*
10. *Ibid.*
11. *Ibid.*
12. *Ibid.*
13. *Ibid.*
14. *Ibid.*
15. *Ibid.*
16. *Ibid.*
17. *Ibid.*
18. *Ibid.*
19. *Ibid.*
20. *Ibid.*
21. *Ibid.*
22. *Ibid.*
23. *Ibid.*
24. *Ibid.*
25. *Ibid.*
26. *Ibid.*
27. *Ibid.*
28. *Ibid.*
29. *Ibid.*
30. *Ibid.*
31. *Ibid.*

8

No-Tax Campaign

The government of the province felt alarmed at the political activities of Rafi Ahmad. Besides salt satyagraha, his no-rent campaign was an eye-sore for the Raj in his own province. In spite of warning by the government, he did not restrain his activities, rather he accelerated them to the channels thus annoying the functioning of the government. He did not fear arrest or connection or any kind of treatment in the jail. At last he was arrested in June 1930 and put behind the bars for six months. The *Young India* of June 1930 greatly enlogised his services in this satyagraha and called him the 'Hero of Rae Bareli.' He was fined fifty rupees, but he refused to pay this amount. He, in default, was given six months more. In jail, he suffered on account of lack of basic amenities. But he never grumbled as he knew that under the Raj, he could never expect a better treatment.

At the end of 1930, the political atmosphere slightly changed on account of the Labour Party which had come into power in England. At this point of time, the first Round Table Conference was convened in which the leadership of the Congress was absent as all its leaders were in jail. Through the good offices of Tej Bahadur Sapru, V.S. Sastri and M.R. Jayakar, the basis for Gandhi-Irwin meeting was sorted out. It was signed on 5 March 1931. As a result of it, the movement was suspended and the several political leaders and satyagrahis were released from jails.

After release from jail, Rafi Ahmad was elected General, Secretary of the Provincial Congress Committee. He got him engaged in the election of delegates to the forthcoming session of the Indian National Congress to be held at Karachi in March 1931 under the presidentship of Sardar Vallabhbhai Patel. He performed this function in a meticulous way. Soon other, there were communal riots at Kanpur where Ganesh Shankar Vidyarthi, President of the United Provinces Congress Committee, was murdered. This indeed was a shocking news for Rafi Ahmad and he felt very unhappy at the death of a beloved and respectable friend and colleague, Jawaharlal greatly enlogised his services to the people of our sub-continent and called him a brave and far-sighted comrade who always worked in a desciplined way. Rafi Ahmed got raised a Vidyarthi Memorial School at Maharajganj in Gorakhpur. This is how he cherished the memory of his dear colleague and friend.

The no-tax campaign formed the worst shape in Rae Bareli. The tenants' economic condition became from bad to worse on account of the policy of ejectment followed by the government. The attachments and sale of cattle and personal property continued. The main problem was that of the great number of ejected tenants. As this point of time, Rafi Ahmad Kidwai who was the General Secretary of the U.P. Provincial Congress Committee, pressed the government to help them to get back their holdings which in the majority of cases were lying vacant. Besides there arose another problem. The remissions so far granted were for the past season only and nothing had yet been decided about the present and future.

Both Pandit Nehru and Pandit Pant had several interviews with the high officials of the U.P. government on the sad economic plight of the peasantry. As a result of their talks, the government appointed a small committee consisting of their own officials and Zamindars to reduce their rents. In fact Pant was asked . . . . the government to join in the work of the Committee on behalf of the Congress, but he did not think it worth at that stage when many important decisions had already been taken. As a result of the Committee's recommendations, the remissions announced by the Government did not give any relief to the tenant.

Indeed Mahatma Gandhi to showed deep interest in the agrarian crisis of U.P. In this regard he wrote to the officials of the government of India and the U.P. government. He even came to Naini Tal to meet the U.P. Governor Malcolm Haily in this connection.

Gandhi suggested a workable formula which was unacceptable to the Governor. Had the proposed scheme been worked out and remissions to the extent of eight annas and four annas been made in the case of statutory and occupancy tenants respectively, the situation might have been somewhat eased.

The Pant Committee Report which was signed by Govind Ballabh Pant, Rafi Ahmad Kidwai and Venkatesh Narayan Tewary was published in September 1931. It is a comprehensive document of the agrarian sytem and its working in U.P. It gave startling figures on agrarian distress and an analysis of the havac caused by the agricultural slump. The Committee showed that there was an increase of 63% in rent between 1893-94 and 1929-30 while the low level of prices was not touched during the last thirty years. Besides it made a through enquiry into the village economy. It also showed by facts and figures how ridiculously low and arbitrary was the relief sanctioned by the government.

The findings of the Pant Committee Report were discussed at Anand Bhawan, Allahabad. The meeting was attended by Jawaharlal Nehru, Sherwani, P.D. Tandon, Rafi Ahmad Kidwai and Damodar Swarup Seth. It approved all the findings of the Pant Committee and recorded its labour and gigantic work it undertook for the welfare of the peasantry in U.P. A copy of the Report was sent to Mahatma Gandhi.

"The Indian peasant has an amazing capacity to bear misfortune and he has always had more than his share of it—

famine, flood, disease and continuous grinding poverty—and when he could endure it no longer, he would quietly and almost uncomplainingly lie down in his thousands or millions and die. That was his way of escape".[1]

The peasantry was subject to the revages of scarcity years, without adequate reliefs, and when his zamindar or creditor to oblige him, what did a cultivator do for grain? He could rob a store or he could riot. Riots were frequent in the "distressed districts" of the Doab during the grain crisis of 1877 and were tackled with vigorous police measures. He could also emigrate, this, in fact, was a common line of action which the farmers undertook in the Lower Doab and Bundelkhand; they made their way to Malwa when they were badly threatened by scarcity.[2]

In their social origin the taluqdars were a mixed lot, being remnants of old Rajput lineages, some court favourites and administrators. They were wholly rent-receivers and did not themselves participate in the cultivation of land. They gained much importance as a result of their revenue functions in the 18th and early 19th centuries.[3]

P.J. Musgrave has given a comprehensive analysis of the status of landlords and the modes of management of their estates[4] "Many of the landlords never or very rarely saw their estates—some of them reven boasted of it; even for the big landlords who spent part of their time on their estates it was clearly impossible to function without some kind of bureaucracy, a bureaucracy which is traditionally called the estate management".

During this period, all the agricultural classes landlords, peasant proprietors and tenants—became victims of the money-lender who played a significant role in the subsistence village economy. As there were very few legal checks on him, he exploited the poverty of the villagers very much to his own advantage and thus gradually the land passed to him, in numerous cases from many of the smaller landlords and the peasant proprietors. The agricultural debt increased to a record figure and the economic situation began to display danger-signals.

In the United Provinces the agricultural slump of 1929 and onwards had come as a climax to a steadily worsening situation by 1931. Evictions of cultivators by landlords in this region had multiplied in number and the zamindars' oppression increased.[5] This kind of oppressive behaviour of the zamindar had deep linkage with the rise of world agricultural prices, affecting Indian agriculture in adverse proportions. Besides, the disproportion in the rapid development of industry and agriculture in other areas of the world had pushed up agricultural prices. This upward tendency, by which Government revenue and the landlord's rent went up, hardly profited the actual cultivator.

Rent went up much faster than revenue in the United Provinces, and it so happened that the proportion of the relative increase of these two during the first three decades of the twentieth century was nearly five to one. The results were disastrous for the tenant who remained, as ever, at starvation level. But the Government's income from land increased substantially and the landlord's income increased far more under these circumstances. Despite revenue remissions of Rs. 10.9 million and rent remissions of Rs. 41.4 million in 1930-31, the general economic condition of the rural regions deteriorated and economic distress stalked the helpless peasantry.[6] Between the Viceroyalty of Lord Curzon and Lord Irwin, rents had increased by Rs. 66,900,000 whereas land revenue had increased by only Rs. 75,00,000. It is indeed amazing to learn that between the Government and the cultivators, there was an intermediate class of about 160,000 landlords, but the fragmentation of land was such that the vast majority of these landholders paid less than Rs. 100 a year in land revenue.[7]

A few months prior to the historic Lahore Congress in 1929, Jawaharlal Nehru, who happened to visit a few areas of the Panjab, apprised the *Kisans* of their plight, particularly their exploitation by Government agencies and the big zamindars at whose hands they were experiencing all sorts of indignities. He said "the big landlords owned enormous wealth and property and spent their time more or less in idleness, while the poor peasants suffered untold miseries. He asked the peasants to read and write and keep themselves informed of what was happening in India and how crores of rupees out of the taxes paid by them were wasted on new and costly buildings in New Delhi and the exhorbitant salaries of officers . . . He asked the peasants to assert their rights. The exploitation of India would not cease unless the peasants and workers organised themselves. If they could put a fight on their grievances like the peasants of Barodli, they were bound to improve their conditions of life and save themselves from ruin and starvation....Peasants should take to the *charkha* and wear *khaddar*. The spinning wheel would solve the economic problem of this country to a very great extent".[8]

In a major portion of Awadh, zamindars had been taking to *begar* (forced labour), resorting to forcible realisation of rent and numerous illegal exactions. In many villages there was concealment of rents, i.e., the rent was not properly recorded in the official records maintained by the *patwari*, a revenue official at the lowest rung, but something substantially less. In these villages, no receipts were given to the tenants. On the other hand, the unscrupulous zamindars of these villages were more active against the Congress and the *kisans*, and it was in these areas that the condition of the tenants was more deplorable. The zamindars, having realised *kharif* rent from them without giving any receipts, were threatening them that they should pay the full rent (i.e. including the concealed portion), oherwise "they will wholly deny the payment made by tenants for *kharif* and in this manner get more rent out of them than they should pay legally".

The President of the District Congress Committee, Bara Banki, gave a dismal picture of landlord-tenant relationship leading to numerous illegal and coercive evictions and various kinds of exactions.[9] In fact, there had been an awakening among the tenants since the Congress propaganda in 1930 began, and the Congress work in this district chiefly depended upon the support of the ural population. But in areas where the tenants were most oppressed they dared not join the movement in the beginning for fear of severe oppression by their landlords. Indeed, the confidence of the rural masses in the Congress had increased after the truce in March 1931, and there was a much wider awakening. Besides, on account of partial faiture of crops and low prices, there was a big agitation among the tenants for remission of rent, this district being very thickly populated and the most rack-rented.[10]

This situation led to the convening of a few Congress meetings, mostly at the invitation of the local *kisans* themselves, and these meetings were more numerous in the Sadar Tehsil Nawabganj, as was quite natural. It was obvious that the zamindars disliked this kind of awakening, leading to serious economic consequences for them, and they tried their best to keep away the tenants from joining the Indian National Congress and seeking its direct support and sympathy. They even did not desist from doing propaganda among the officials by impressing on them that there was a danger of trouble from the tenants, while they themselves had been terrorising and beating the tenants to realise rents as speedily as they could. The local officials had anti-Congress and anti-*kisan* feelings, because the latter had now allied themselves with the Congress. "From the actions which they—officials—have been taking, it appears that they are in the hands of the zamindars. The zamindars, who have been treating the tenants almost like slaves for a long time, think that they will be nowhere if the tenants are able to assert themselves".[11]

Statement showing ejectments, etc., in the United Provinces:

	Revenue year 1929-30	Revenue year 1930-31
1. Number of arrears of rent suits	340,249	288,465
2. Number of ejectments ordered for arrears	53,421	64,076
3. Area from which ejectments actually took place (in acres)	149,071.254	189,362.960
4. Number of cases in which property was actually sold after distraint	10,897	13,337
5. Number of cases under Section 447, Indian Penal Code, against ejected tenants and number of convictions		
a. Cases	982	1,054
b. Convictions	267	345

The eight days' interlude in the month of October 1930, during the first phase of the Civil Disobedience Movement, did not abate Nehru's activities in any sense. He made himself busy in meeting kisans of his province and apprised them of the tactics they were to use in the no-rent campaign. Besides giving a brief message to his countrymen, he levelled severe criticism against the functioning of the British Government in India. "The success of our movement can well be gauged by the number and variety of ordinances which are produced with regularity in the factories of Simla . . . . Indeed the time has come when, from the point of view of the British Government, every one of us should be a rebel . . . . To-day every man has to choose between the two flags, the flag of Indian freedom and the flag of foreign domination".[12] To achieve this aim, he optimistically remarked: "I am very much alive and kicking. I hope to do my little bit to hasten the dissolution of the British Empire and take part in its final obsequies".[13]

In Rae Bareli, which was one of the prominent centres of the Civil Disobedience Movement during 1930, a large number of peasants flocked to the meetings convened by the Congress. Congress Panchayats sprang up in many villages and preformed the functions of the police and magistrates. National flags were hoisted in many villages.

After a few weeks of the Gandhi-Irwin Pact, a shift in government machinery at the higher level occurred when Willingdon replaced Irwin as the Viceroy in April 1931. An official with less flexibility of mind and attitude and with a long experience of Indian administration, he and his colleagues wished "to work the settlement only on condition that they should not again subject the services and their allies to the strain of renewed civil disobedience countered only with the limited weapons used in 1930 . . . A tough line if conflict erupted again was therefore an essential *quid pro quo* for the settlement . . . ".[14]

The U.P. Government realized the gravity of the situation when prices of cereals and cotton continued to fall, "reaching a nadir in the second quarter of 1931". The Government, therefore, sanctioned remissions of about 18.2% or Rs. 68 lakh in the *rabi* revenue demand and corresponding rent remission of about Rs. 2 crores. The Congress leaders were unhappy about it and Gandhi asked Hailey to institute an enquiry in which Congressmen could participate. This kind of demand was unacceptable to Hailey who opined that the delay in payment involved in an enquiry would endanger the finances of the landlords and the Government.[15]

In May 1931, Gandhi met Emerson and Hailey and discussed with them the problems of the peasantry in U.P. However, he was not prepared to accept the plea of Hailey that the Congress had no right to intervene between the Government and the tax-payers and pressed upon its role as the "poor man's friend" in advising the tenant on rent matters.[16]

Nehru's contention was that rents should correspond with prices, viz, that rent should be reduced to a figure which prevailed in the past. Approximately, this was so about three decades earlier. i.e., in 1901. The other point he made in this regard was that the capacity of the tenant to pay should be assessed after making allowances for the cost of production and a living wage.

In June 1931, Nehru found the situation much worse for the peasants who were being terrorised by the police with the connivance of the *talukdars*. At numerous places, Congress volunteers were being beaten up for peaceful picketing, which was permitted by the settlement. He had no intention of submitting meekly to all this and accompanied Gandhi to Simla to meet the Viceroy. They suggested to the Viceroy that the district authorities should fix the amount of revenue and rent to be collected after consultation with Congress workers, but if this were not acceptable to the Government, at least a detailed enquiry should be ordered to enable temporary adjustments.

The U.P. Government set up a committee to consider future agrarian policy and invited Govind Ballabh Pant to serve as a member. This committee recommended a complicated system of reduction of rents on the basis of the fall in prices but never more than 50%.[17] Thus there could be a reduction of Rs. 4.1 crore out of a total rent of Rs. 18 crore. But the process was cumbersome because numerous formalities were to be observed at the level of revenue officials and zamindars. Even at this point of time, evictions and convictions continued, and by August 1931, there were about 5,000 evictions in Allahabad District and 2,000 in Mathura.

Govind Ballabh Pant apprised the Chief Secretary of the provincial government of the depressing conditions under which the tenants were living and asked for some remedial measures in this regard. He complained thus :[18] " . . . There is a marked tendency to condone, if not to countenance or encourage, coercive and forceful methods in the matter of collection of rents by Zamindars. Tenants' complaints are, as a rule, disregarded and it is a hard fact some of the cultivators who complained against their landlord's excesses and sought protection against them were themselves actually bound down for keeping the peace. I doubt if any formal or legal action has been taken against any Zamindar anywhere in the province . . . Proceedings under Section 107 against Congressmen, peasants and their sympathisers and others under Section 144 seem to be the order of the day and many public workers are naturally agitated and disressed on this account . . . I do not forget that a Zamindar was killed at Bara Banki and I deeply deplore the crime; but I am assured that part of the district where this sad incident happened is outside the zone of the Congress influence and there is not a single Congressman in any of the villages in that zamindari and in its neighbourhood. Molestation of Congressmen in other parts can be no remedy for excess by non-Congressmen in that locality, nor can the atmosphere be clarified by overlooking provocative causes . . . I have received similar reports about repression on the part of local officers and coercion on the part of zamindars from other places also, but, for the present, I am forwarding with this only those relating to Sultanpur and Balrampur in the Gonda district, which is under the Court of Wards . . . I hope that you will appreciate the urgency and importance of the subject matter, and will be pleased to take necessary action."[19]

On 29 June 1931, about 500 Congress volunteers picketed the house of the Raja of Sheogarh because his manner had instituted attachment-proceedings against the defaulting tenants. The Government took action against the leaders of the agrarian movement who, in the eyes of the Government, were guilty of exciting the tenants to refuse payment of rent.[20]

Jawaharlal Nehru informed the Chief Secretary on 15 October 1931, and gave him the reason for the commencement of the no-rent campaign.[21] "I regret greatly that such a step should be contemplated by them, specially at a time when Gandhiji is attending the Ronnd Table Conference. But the question of payment or non-payment is an urgent issue and cannot await the deliberations of the Round Table Conference, or the return of Gandhiji. We have tried to avoid raising any issue which might lead to friction and we shall continue to do so. But fate seems to be against this". He even went to the extent of saying : "It is war : war now and ever till the end of our lives."[22]

However, the Congress propaganda against the British revenue policy remained unabated. In the month of October 1931, Sunderlal circulated a scheme for a parallel government to be brought into force in the Bara Banki district by November 15. He asked the peasants to turn their women into leaders so that when men were arrested, they could lead the *kisan* movement.[23]

While Gandhi was busy in the Second Round Table Conference, the Congress leadership in U.P., wished to avoid any kind of conflict with the Government in his absence. But when his return was delayed and the agrarian situation began to develop rapidly, Nehru sent him a cable informing him of the latest developments. "Agrarian situation becoming critical. Coercive processes, attachments, forcible collection rent continued right through without interval . . . Condition kisans deplorable. Thoroughly exhausted after past six months' continuous harassment forcible measures. Vital urgent problem for kisans admitting no delay"[24] Gandhi expressed his helplessness in the matter but advised him to go ahead according to his lights.

On the same day, Nehru informed the Viceroy that ever since the Delhi settlement, the tenants in the United Provinces had to face a most difficult situation. They had been treated to every kind of indignity and harassment and every device was employed to make them pay the rent which in their state of economic disaster, they had been unable to pay at the harvest time. They were threatened with dispossession of their crops and in many cases they were actually dispossessed. He pointed out that the new scale of remissions for the current agriculture year was inadequate in principle and in its application. Even the nominal remissions were threatened to be cancelled if the tenants failed to pay up their rent in full within a month. Therefore in their sorry plight they were left with no other option but to think of withholding payment of rent.[25]

When the negotiation and the correspondence between the Government and the Congress leaders were going on, the collections for the current season were to commence on 15 November 1931. At this point of time, the U.P. Congress Committee, on the advice of Sardar Patel, directed the *kisans* of Allahabad district to withhold payment of rent and revenue.[26]

This kind of direction to the *kisans* by the Congress leadership was seriously noted by the Government of India which directed Hailey to strike hard. "With the conservatives back to power in Britain and the Second Round Table Conference a failure, the Government of India had clearly decided to turn their backs on Irwin's settlement; and the harsh Bengal Ordinance and the drastic policy favoured in the U.P. were both parts of a general return to a policy of repression. Willingdon and Emerson went to Lucknow to speed up matters, but Hailey refused to be hustled . . . So in the U.P., at any rate, there continued what Jawaharlal described as an impossible situation."[27]

At this point of time, Nehru, who convened a conference of *kisans* at Allahabad on 25 November stated emphatically : "If we are to die, we shall die after a fight. I do not want a half-way settlement or a half-way fight".[28] He had the feeling that the Government would not delay his arrest. The *Pioneer*, a pro-government newspaper, even hinted at his deportation.[29]

But this kind of action was not possible, as Willingdon confessed in a communication to Samuel Hoare, the Secretary of State, on 13 December 1931 :

> "One thing I do regret very much in all this business and, that is, we have no power of deportation out of India. It would be an enormous advantage if we can get hold of 15 or 20 of these leaders, send them right away to the West Indies or somewhere, instead of having to keep them under surveillance in some province or other."[30]

In December the Provincial Congress Committee directed the members of the District Congress Committees to commence the no-rent campaign in Allahabad, Rae Bareli, Etawah, Kanpur and Unnao.[31] As a result of this action, the payment of rent in these districts came almost to a standstill.[32] Landlords were practically unable to collect any rent in the districts of Rae Bareli, Barabanki, Lucknow, Pratapgarh, Allahabad, Agra and Meerut. The Government ordered the Commissioners to provide police assistance to landlords so that they could carry on the processes of eviction and distraint.[33] This was considered the convenient way to smash the Congress support and sympathy for the peasantry and also to gain the loyalty and cooperation of the zamindars.

The Government of U.P. was slightly fearful of the fact that Nehru might precipitate the issue on the arrival of Gandhi. It, therefore, wished to grant some concessions to the tenants in order to strengthen its case. It lowered the water rates, introduced a bill to save tenants from eviction if they paid two-thirds of the arrears due for the previous four years, and also offered early measures to protect tenants against debts.

At the same time, the Government had made up its mind to take action against Nehru and other Congressmen. The New Ordinance had given such powers to the Government, which was now quite sure that the Congress leadership had exploited the economic crisis to its advantage to seek the following and support of the kisans, thus violating the spirit of the truce. It also declared that Nehru had preached class warfare. On his return to Allahabad from Bombay, the Government lost no time in serving Nehru with a notice not to leave the city without official permission and, at the same time, the U.P. Provincial Conference scheduled to be held on 26 December was banned. Nehru was arrested on 26 December for violating the order restricting him to Allahabad. On 26 December 1931, the Viceroy wrote to the Secretary of State: "The Delhi Pact at all events is dead and gone, murdered by Jawaharlal Nehru and Abdul Ghaffar."[34]

Soon the repressive measures were applied all over India. Gandhi, Sardar Patel, numerous other Congress leaders and satyagrahis were in jail. H.G. Haig, the Home Member, opined : "Jawaharlal is a fanatic. There are threatenings of on attempt to revive a no-rent campaign in the U.P. Jawaharlal Nehru is the author of that policy and his release would obviously give it a definite stimulus".[35]

Jawaharlal Nehru, however, explained the action of the Government thus : "The machinery of coercion, legal as well as illegal, began to move. Ejectment suits brought against thousands, attachments of cows, bullocks, personal property, beatings of agents of landlords . . . . They came to us in large numbers, complaining bitterly, telling us that they had followed our advice and paid what they could and this was the consequence . . . The District Congress Committee (Allahabad) office was surrounded all day by a distraught crowd. My own house was equally besieged and often I felt like running away and hiding myself somewhere, anywhere, to escape this dreadful predicament".[36]

Thus the agrarian question in the United Provinces was much more an economic issue than a political one. In this context, Nehru was of the opinion that while Gandhi had assured the Viceroy that even if he did not attend the Second Round Table Conference, he would not resume Civil Disobedience so long as the ference was in session. But Gandhi had made it clear that this kind of assurance would not apply to any local economic struggle that might be forced on the Congress.[37]

The no-tax campaign had one significant result in the province. It shifted the centre of gravity of the political struggle launched soon after the historic Dandi March of Gandhi and his 78 associates from its urban base to the rural base and "it thereby revitalised the movement."

There were practical difficulties for the Congress to make this campaign broad-based and spread its objective in a major part of the province. For this Nehru had a sense of confession. "Our chief difficulty in those days was one of communication, of getting people to know what we were doing or what we wanted them to do. Newspapers would not publish our news for fear of being penalised and suppressed by Government, printing presses would not print our leaflets and notices; letters and telegrams were censored and often stopped. The only reliable method of communication open to us was to send couriers with despatches, and even so our messengers were sometimes arrested. . . . It was organised with some success and the provincial centres were in constant touch with headquarters as well as with their principal district centres".[38]

The Congress, however, was cautious to see that the Civil Disobedience Movement did not develop as an anti-landlord campaign. By devising such a measure, it was conscious of the fact that numerous rich peasants participated in the movement and some big landlords had a sympathetic attitude towards the Congress leadership as well as its movements.

Thus the appeal of the Congress leadership had been addressed to both zamindars and tenants not to pay land revenue. But this appeal was not very effective, for the zamindars and Nehru regretted that most of them did pay their revenue, even some of those who sympathised with the national struggle. It was apparent that the pressure on them was great and they had more to lose by not paying. The movement soon spread to some other districts of the United Provinces. But in many districts it was not "formally adopted or declared, but in effect tenants withheld their rents or, in many cases, were wholly unable to pay them owing to the fall in prices. As it happened, neither the Government nor the big zamindars took any widespread action to terrorise the recalcitrant tenantry for several months. They were not sure of their ground, as they had the political struggle with civil disobedience on the one side, and the economic slump, resulting in agricultural distress, on the other. The two merged into each other, and the Government was always afraid of an agrarian upheaval. With the Round Table Conference in session in London, they were not keen on adding to their troubles in India or on giving a still more striking demonstration of 'strong' government".

During this period, the Provincial Government resorted to a novel step which produced much commotion in the rural areas. The district authorities issued remission slips in the names of the tenants, stating clearly how much remission had been allowed and containing a threat that unless the amount then due was paid up within a month (sometime the period mentioned was shorter), the remission could be cancelled and the full sum realised by legal process which meant ejectment, attachment of property, etc. Nehru called it ". . . . a very foolish threat on the part of the Government or their local officials and it was not, we were told later, meant seriously. But it lessened the chances of a peaceful settlement very greatly and led inevitably, step by step, to conflict".

In the United Provinces, this struggle was centred in the rural areas. The remissions offered to the tenants were not considered adequate by the Congress leadership. The Government was anxious that the Congress should not get the credit for these remissions, but at the same time it wanted to give to the peasants as many remissions as possible to keep them quiet. These remissions, considerable as they were, did not solve the agrarian problem, but they did ease the situation. This struggle brought suffering to thousands of peasants in the province and numerous people were "completely ruined" by it. But the pressure of the struggle brought millions of peasants almost the highest possible remissions under the existing system, though the petty seasonal gains did not amount to much.

References

1. Nehru, Jawaharlal : *An Autobiography* (New Delhi) 1962, p. 306.
2. Whitcombe, Elizabeth: *Agrarian Conditions in Northern India* (New Delhi) 1971, p. 197.
3. Siddiqi, Asiya : *Agrarian Change in a Northern Indian State, 1819-1833* (Oxford) 1973, p. 44.
4. See his article on 'Landlords and Lords of the Land Estate Management and Social Control in Uttar Pradesh, 1860-1920' in *Modern Asian Studies*, 1972, pp. 257ff.
5. Home Pol. File 33/XVI, K.W., 1931.
6. Neale, Walter C: *Economic Change in Rural India: Land, Tenure and Reform in Uttar Pradesh, 1800-1955*, (Yale University Press) 1962, pp. 114-15.
7. Gopal, S : *Jawaharlal Nehru, A Biography, Vol. I. 1889-1947*, (Delhi) 1976, p. 154.
8. *The Tribune*, 12 March 1929.
9. *Agrarian Distress in the United Provinces*, pp. 88-112.
10. *Ibid.*
11. *Ibid.*
12. See Gopal, S : *Selected Works of Jawaharlal Nehru*, Vol. IV (New Delhi) 1973, pp. 391-92.
13. *Ibid.*
14. Brown, Judith M. : *Gandhi and Civil Disobedience, The Mahatma in Indian Politics, 1928-34* (London) 1977, pp. 215-16.
15. Home Poll. File 33/XI, 1931.
16. Home Poll. File 33/IX, 1931.
17. *The Leader*, 12 October 1931.
18. *Agrarian Distress in the United Provinces*, pp. 238-41.
19. *Ibid.*
20. Home Poll. File 33/XVI, K.W., 1931.
21. *A.I.C.C. Papers*. File 54, Part III, 1931.
22. *The Tribune*, 25 October 1931.
23. Home Poll. File 33/37, 1931.
24. *A.I.C.C. Papers* : File G-140, pt. III, 1931.
25. Home Poll. File 33/36, 1931.
26. *The Leader*, 18 November 1931.
27. Gopal, *op. cit.*, pp. 167-68.
28. *The Leader*, 27 November 1931.
29. *The Pioneer*, 27 November 1931.
30. *Templewood Papers*; Willingdon to Samuel Hoare, 13 December 1931.

31. *The Bombay Chronicle*. 7 Dec. 1931.
32. Home Poll. File 18/12, 1931.
33. Home Poll. File 33/XI, 1931.
34. *Halifax Papers* : Viceroy to Secretary of State, 26 December 1931.
35. Home Poll. File 31/97, 1932.
36. Nehru, *op. cit.*, pp. 304-5.
37. *Ibid.*, p. 299.
38. *Ibid.*, p. 236.

9

The Assessment

Rafi Ahmad Kidwai's role in the freedom movement of our sub-continent is most significant. Born in a middle class family, he joined the Gandhian movement while he was a college student. As soon as he came into contact with the Nehru family, he began to show more enthusiasm and patriotic fervour for Indian nationalism. He always aspired for Hindu-Muslim unity and maintained his secular identity throughout his long political career. His participation in Non-Cooperation Movement, Civil Disobedience Movement and the Quit India Movement was unique in the annals of our history. He suffered in jail and took pride in this suffering.

As a Congress leader in U.P. and Minister in the central cabinet, he was approachable by high as well as low in our society. He possessed no assets and his pay and perks would flush out for the poor and the needy. Gandhi and Nehru respected him as a nice human being and a dynamic political leader. He met an untimely death on 24 October 1954 and was accorded rich tributes by one and all.

MR. R. A. KIDWAI DIED

Speech Cut Short At Delhi Meeting

Death on Arrival at Residence

Great Loss to Congress and Government

State Funeral to be Accorded

New Delhi, Sunday,—Mr. Rafi Ahmed Kidwai, who won India's Food Battle, Died Suddenly this evening after Addressing a Puplic Meeting. He was 60.

It was during the meeting itself that he complained of a choking feeling. Unable to complete his speech, he Asked to be Driven Home.

He was almost dead when the car reached his official residence about 8 p. m. Among the first to be informed was the Prime Minister, now in Mukden.

Mr. Kidwai will be accorded a State funeral. In deference to the wishes of his family he will be buried on Tuesday in his home village of Masauli, near Bara Banki.

Within half an hour of his death, a crowd of mourners, including his colleagues in the Cabinet and members of Parliament, arrived to pay an affectionate homage to their departed friend. The crowd grew as the night passed. There were many tearful eyes.

Today was not the first time that Mr. Kidwai had complained of heart attack. The ailment, in a mild form, frequently recurred. That is why he sometimes suddenly withdrew from official duties going into the countryside in search of rest and recuperation.

It was in defiance of doctors' advice that he want to Kanpur from where he returned only this morning. His friends also advised him rest. His unvarying reply was : "Work has to be done".

Mr. Kidwai will be missed in a dual capacity—as one of the leading Congressmen and as a successful administrator.

His association with the Congress started as early as 1921. In the days of the non-co-operation movement, he was in the vanguard of the fight. He first went to jail in 1922.

After that he was in every defiance movement, repeatedly courting arrest. He probably spent over 10 years in jail, a record not excelled by many.

Organizing Ability

In Uttar Pradesh, he gradually began to wield an unrivalled political power, gained mainly by his unique organizing ability.

It was never put to better use than in the 1936 election when he was President of the State Congress Parliamentary Board. The great success which the Congress won was freely attributed in his masterly strategy.

When later he became Revenue Minister in Pandit Pant's pre-war Cabinet, he initiated far-reaching tenancy reforms in the State, conferring security on the tenants. He was the precursor of zamindari abolition, for which he had agitated for years in the Uttar Pradesh countryside.

When Mr. Nehru formed his first Cabinet in 1947, inclusion of Mr. Kidwai in the Government caused no surprise.

At The Centre

In the Central sphere, first as Minister of Communications and later, after the last general election, as Food and Agriculture Minister, he proved an extremely successful administrator whom his departmental secretaries respected spontaneously.

One of them once said to me :

"This man is a terror. We produce a scheme, argue in its support as best as we can and he upsets it all by his unconventional suggestions".

Unconventionality was his outstanding trait. As Communications Minister he was the author of "buy your own telephone" as well the night air mall. Both schemes, to conservative minds, appeared of questionable utility. He made them a success.

As Food Minister he pinned his faith, much against the Planning Commission's advice, on gradual decontrol.

Body to Lie in State

Mr. Kidwai will be given a State funeral.

The burial will take place at Masauli near Bara Banki in Uttar Predesh, which is Mr. Kidwai's home village.

The body will lie in state at his residence from 9 a.m. to 3 p. m. today to afford an opportunity to the public to pay homage. It will be carried to the ceremonial platform at the New Delhi railway station via York Place, Queensway and Connaught Place in the afternoon. The special train will leave New Delhi at 7 p. m. for Lucknow where it will stop for two hours before proceeding to Masauli.

Flags will fly at half mast over all public buildings in Delhi and the State capitals today. All Government offices will remain closed for the day.

Mr. Brahm Prakash, Chief Minister of Delhi, has appealed to the business community to keep their establishments closed today.—PTI.

Endless Queues

First among the mourners to call at Mr. Kidwai's house was the President, Dr. Rajendra Prasad. He had tears in his eyes as he laid a wreath on the body. He stood in silent prayer for two minutes while *maulvis* chanted verses from the Koran.

The President than met Begum Kidwai and spoke words of solace to her. Then he spent about 15 minutes in Mr. Kidwai's bedroom which also served as his study—his favourite corner in the house where he breathed his last. An odd assortment of medicine bottles, a radio-set and two silver-framed pictures, one of Dr. Rajendra Prasad and the other of Mr. Sri Prakasa, were found in the room. There was the usual disorder everywhere which Mr. Kidwai loved so much. His forage cap lay on a tiny table near the bedstead along with his spectacles case.

Moved to Tears

Others who called at the house included Maulana Azad, Mr. Lal Bahadur Shastri, Mr. A. P. Jain and other Central Ministers, M.P.s and members of various political parties. Many were moved to tears. Several Congress M.P.s were seen sobbing.

Wreaths were laid on the body on behalf of the Vice-President, the Prime Minister and the Home Minister. A wreath was also placed on behalf of the diplomatic corps and another on behalf of the Food Ministry. Several diplomats came to pay homage to the dead and placed wreaths on the body.

Before the procession started, a special *namaz-e-janaza* was offered at 1 p.m. Maulana Azad led the prayer which was held in the garden of Mr. Kidwai's house.

Receptions Cancelled

The usual Monday ceremonial parade at Rashtrapati Bhavan was abandoned. The President has also postponed the presentation of gallantry awards which was to be held at Rashtrapati Bhavan tomorrow evening. The reception which was to have followed the ceremony has been cancelled. The Diwali reception has also been cancelled.

Pathetic scenes were witnessed as the body left Mr. Kidwai's house. Several women swooned. especially among them an aged family maid of the Kidwai family.

MAN OF GREAT ORGANIZING CAPACITY

—Dr. Prasad

The President immediately on hearing Mr. Kidwai's death sent the following message of condolence to Mr. Nehru :

"Deeply distressed to inform you of the sudden death of Rafi Ahmed Kidwai this evening. The country has lost in him an able and resourceful a ministrator and a man of great organizing capacity whose services both during the period of struggle and since independence had been most invaluable."

All India Radio cut short all its music programmes in its home services from 9.45 p. m. onwards.

Mr. Lal Bahadur Shastri, Union Minister for Railways and Transport said in a broadcast : "We have lost one of our most valued colleagues and the country a senior and sound statesman who dedicated all his own for his country".

Mr. Jagjivan Ram. Union Communications Minister, said in Vijayawada : "I am stunned. The loss is irreparable."

Mr. G. V. Mavalankar, Speaker of the Lok Sabha, said in Ahmedabad that the death of Mr. Kidwai was an "incalculable loss to the nation at this stage." He was a brilliant administrator, man of drive, quick decision and firm action, he added.

Mr. Brahm Prakash, Chief Minister of Delhi, said "A stateman of a high order. a great selfiess patriot, and a man with an intensely human heart has passed away, leaving a gap in the country's life which can never be filled. His death is an irreparable loss to the whole country".

Mr. Mauli Chandra Sharma, President of the Jana Sangh, said in Delhi "Mr. Kidwai was one of the most efficient administrators of our time, and the country and the Cabinet will both be the poorer for his sudden passing away".

Mr. C. Rajagopalachari, said in Madras that in the death of Mr. Kidwai "India has lost one of her most dynamic figures and her Government has lost one of its ablest and most devoted members".

Mr. Morarji Desai, Chief Minister of Bombay, said : "Mr. Kidwai was a very able administrator and the recent example of it was his successful handling of the food policy. His death is an irreparable loss at this juncture to our country".

Pandit Pant, Chief Minister of U. P., said in Lucknow : "His services to the country will be ever remembered. His was dedicated life. He worked with indomitable courage, resourcefulness, energy and devotion for the liberation and betterment of the entire people in a matchless way."

Mr. J. N. Vyas, Chief Minister of Rajasthan, said in Jaipur : "I have no words now to express my feelings and it is difficult to bear the shock. He was a great friend of mine and more than a brother to me."

Mr. Purushottamdas Tandon, former. Congress President, said in Allahabad : "He was one of the builders of the Congress in U.P. He was an extraordinary person in several ways and had a lovable individuality. Above everything else, he had a divine gift of a heart which felt for others and was generous without any calculations. His departure will cause a big gap in the Congress politics".

Early Education

Born in 1894, Mr. Kidwai was educated at the MAO College, Aligarh. After his graduation from Allahabad University he began studying law but gave it up to join the non-cooperation movement in 1921. Since then he was closely associated with the Congress. He was Secretary and President of U.P. Congress Committee during 1922—26 and was sentenced to one year's imprisonment in 1922.

In 1924 he was elected a member of the U.P. Legislative Council on the Swaraj Party ticket. He was again imprisoned during the civil disobedience movements of 1930-32.

In 1936 he became President of the U.P. Congress Committee and played a leading role in organizing the election campaign that swept the Congress into power.

In 1937 he was elected to the U. P. Legislative Assembly and became Minister for Revenue and Jails. He resigned in November 1939 when the Congress went out of office at the outbreak of World War II.

1940-41 Satyagraha

Mr. Kidwai was arrested during the individual satyagraha movement in 1940-41 and again in May 1942, three months before the launching of the "quit India" movement, when he was detailed in the Bareilly central prison.

In 1946 he was re-elected to the U.P. Legislative Assembly and became Minister for Revenue Home and Jails. In July, 1946, he was nominated a member of the Congress Working Committee and the same year was elected to the Constituent Assembly of India which had been converted into Parliament of the Republic of India from January 26, 1950.

On August 15, 1947, Mr. Kidwai became Minister for Communications in the Central Cabinet. He resigned from the Congress and also the Union Cabinet in 1951 to join the Kisan Mazdoor Praja Party organized by Acharya Kripalani. He rejoined the Congress the same year and was elected to Parliament as a Congress nominee in the general elections. With effect from May 13, 1952, he held the Portfolio of Food and Agriculture in the new Cabinet.

Address at Delhi Meeting

At a public meeting in Delhi on Sunday in support of Congress municipal candidates Mr. Kidwai was obviously feeling unwell and he spoke with great effort. At one time his voice was choked and he asked for a glass of water. Five minutes before he ended his speech he set down and asked the audience to excuse him.

He spoke for nearly 20 minutes. At the end of his speech he was unable to complete his sentence and was taken away in a car.

This was the first Congress public meeting Mr. Kidwai had addressed in Delhi.

Before Mr. Kidwai addressed the meeting, Mr. Kidwai's achievement in solving India's food problem was praised by

Mr. C. Krishnan Nair, President of the Delhi Pradesh Congress Committee. Mr. Kidwai was described as an able administrator and one of the best politicians of the country. Poems were recited praising Mr. Kidwai's services on behalf of his country.

PROFOUND GRIEF ALL OVER INDIA

Offices Closed, Markets Observe Hartal

India heard the news of Mr. Kidwai's death with profound grief. Flags flew at half mast on all public buildings and Congress offices in the States. Government offices were closed.

Hartal was observed in Lucknow, Allahabad and Kanpur where all shops were closed. In Bombay, all markets closed, and in Calcutta and Ahmedabad the principal markets suspended business.

More leaders joined in paying tribute to the late Food Minister. These included two Cabinet colleagues in New Delhi, Mr. K. C. Reddy and Mr. M. V. Krishnappa, Mrs. Pandit and Mr. C. D. Deshmukh both of whom are now in Tokyo, Mr. K. M. Munshi, Governor of U. P., Chief Ministers of various States and PCC chiefs.

Mrs. Pandit, "In Rafi's death we lost a great man whose place will not be easily filled. To me his death is a personal loss".

Mr. C. D. Deshmukh, "Mr. Kidwai's death is a very great national loss and very severe personal bereavement to me". He added that the satisfactory food situation in India was largely due to Mr. Kidwai's bold and sagacious policy. "Mr. Kidwai is sure to go down in history as one of the ablest of administrators and one of the noblest men. His place both in the Government and Congress organization would be difficult to fill for a long time".

Sardar Swaran Singh, "India has lost a great and noble

patriot who lived a life of long suffering and sacrifice. His approach to many difficult and intricate problems was bold, imaginative and unorthodox. His door was open to all who approached him for help and he would utgrudgingly extend his help to those in need of it".

Mr. Arun Chandra Guha, Union Deputy Finance Minister, said : "He was not only great in ability, but also truly good in heart and genial in nature. He has left no children, but quite a number of men will feel themselves orphaned at his death—so great was his affection for colleagues and people in distress".

Mr. Bhimsen Sachar, said in the death of Mr. Kidwai the country had lost "a great patriot, a great administrator, a great organizer and above all, a great friend". It would be difficult to fill the void, he added.

Mr. Sri Prakasa, Madras Governor, said : "For over 35 years now we have worked shoulder to shoulder in the public field of U.P. in the utmost amity and goodwill and today like hundreds of others who were in intimate contact with him I feel widowed".

Mr. Triloki Singh, PSP leader, said : "A fighter all his life, Mr. Kidwai was above all human, and a person more compassionate will not be seen for generations to come. He was an institution in himself and his presence inspired confidence in an hour of crisis".

Mr. B. Ramakrishna Rao, Hyderabad Chief Minister, said : "The Prime Minister has lost a loyal and able colleague and the country a tried patriot and able administrator. He took bold decisions in spite of opposition and carried them out successfully".

Mr. Jairamdas Daulatram, Assam Governor, said : Mr. Kidwai's life was one of storm and controversy and yet of substantial achievements".

Mr. S. K. D. Paliwal, Vice-President of the All-India

Krishikar Lok Party, said : "The death of Mr. Kidwai is a great blow to the nation. His marvellous work as Food Minister has drawn the applause of the whole nation".

Dr. Sampurnanand Home Minister of U.P., said : "We have lost one of the biggest figures in Indian politics".

Mr. Kala Venkat Rao, former General Secretary of the Congress, said : "The death of Mr. Kidwai removes from our midst a great and colorful personality. India has lost a great man. Mr. Nehru a trusted friend, and the Congress an eminent worker".

Mr. K. Santhanam. Lt. Governor of Vindhya Pradesh. said Mr. Kidwai displayed a remarkable capacity for initiative and rapid evolution of far-reaching policies.

Mr. G. M. Sadiq, President of the Kashmir Constituent Assembly, said he was "stunned" on hearing of Mr. Kidwai's death. "He was one of those on whom the country had great hope and confidence and his loss is irreparable".

Mr. G. S. Bajpai, Governor of Bombay, said : "In Mr. Kidwai the Centre loses one of its best Ministers, the country a stout-hearted patriot and his friends the most generous and affectionate comrade".

Mr. Balwantrai Mehta, General Secretary of the Congress, said in Bombay that India "mourns the loss of one of its best patriots. He was a sound fighter for freedom and one of the greatest Nationalist Muslims who had not the slightest tinge of communalism in him".

Col. Raghbir Singh, Chief Minister of PEPSU. said : "The untimely death of Mr. Kidwai is an irreparable loss to the country. His bold and wise food policy saved the country from a crisis".

Pandit Shukla. Chief Minister of Madhya Pradesh, said : "Quietly and unostent tiously he helped hundreds of people as best as he could. He could be relied on to successfully do things in the most difficult and trying circumstances".

Acharya Kripalani, MP, Chairman of the Praja-Socialist Party, said Mr. Kidwai was "one of our formost fighters for freedom. He was man of the masses and mixed with them on equal terms. His generosity knew no bounds. It was not confined to his friends but extended to all who approached him for help. He was a man of exceptional administrative ability which was illustrated in the bold and unorthodox way in which he recently tackled the difficult food problem against all odds. In him the country has lost a great nationalist and patriot".

Mrs. Sucheta Kripalani, MP, said : "His shrewd common sense and his practical handling of problems weie a great asset to the Central Cabinet".

Mr. K. M. Munshi, Governor of U.P., said : "Mr. Kidwai was a tower of strength both in the Congress Working Committee and the Central Government. The able manner in which he brought about the decontrol of food in this country will always be remembered as a stroke of masterly statesmanship. In the Government he stood very close to the Prime Minister, whose very heavy task will now be heavier still".

Mr. S. N. Agarwal, General Secretary of the Congress, said : "Mr. Kidwai was a pillar of strength not only to the Union Government but to the Congress organization as well. The ingenious and courageous manner in which he solved the very difficult problem of food production in the country will always be remembered by the nation with gratitude".

Sardar Gurmukh Singh Musafir, President of the Punjab Pradesh Congress, said : "Mr. Kidwai's loss at this time is shocking more especially when Mr. Nehru recently expressed a desire to be relieved of the strenuous duties that he has to look after. He showed tremendous organizational capacity as Food Minister."

Mr. S. D. Sharma, Chief Minister of Bhopal, described Mr.

Kidwai as "an outstanding statesman, administrator and politician who enjoyed the confidence of all sections of the people".

Mr. C. P. N. Singh, Governor of Punjab, said: "Mr. Kidwai was a pillar of strength to us and to our country. He hated communalism and was a leader of most progressive views".

Dr. Y. S. Parmar, Chief Minister of Himachal Pradesh, said: "In Mr. Kidwai the country has lost not only a senior stateman but a most dynamic personality who inspired faith and confidence".

Dr. P. Sitaramayya, Governor of Madhya Pradesh, said: "Rafi was not a Minister wedded to any one portfolio. Communications. Food or Kashmir, he had clear-cut views on each subject and he could easily carry conviction to others. He was the 'personal assistant, to the Prime Minister in the Cabinet and personal representative outside it".

Dr. Sushila Nayar, Health Minister, Delhi State: "A man of indomitable will and great courage, a loyal friend, he endeared himself to all who came in contact with him".

Mr. Gopinath Aman, Delhi's Minister for Law and Revenue said: "A rare combination of wisdom and action. He died in harness".

Mr. C. M. Trivedi, Governor of Andhra, expressing his profound regret said: "It is to him that we owe decontrol of food".

The Maharaja of Jaipur, Rajpramukh of Rajasthan, in a message to Dr. Katju, said: "We all in Rajasthan mourn and share in the country's sorrow at the passing away of one of its great sons and statesmen". In another message to Mrs. Kidwai, the Rajpramukh said: "We send you all our heartfelt sympathy in the grievous loss that you have suffered".

Mr. Shambhunath Shukla, Chief Minister of Vindhya Pradesh : "His sudden death is a great loss to the country and the Government. I ofier condolence on behalf of myself and the Vindhya Pradesh Government."

Mr. Basheer Ahmed Sayeed, Judge of the Madras High Court, said: "Mr. Kidwai was a great personality, who always worked for cementing the relationships between the various sections of the community. As a Minister, his reputation was the highest and he brought to bear the highest standard of efficiency in the departments which he held under his portfolio."

Mr. Takhatmal Jain, President of the Madyhabharat Pradesh Congress, said : "I am greatly shocked to hear the sad news of the sudden death of Mr. Kidwai. He was a very capable Congress leader and a great administrator, and it is difficult to fill the void created by his death."

Mr. Radhanath Rath, Orissa's Finance Minister, said Mr. Kidwai was an able administrator and an astute politician, whom the country could ill-afford to lose at the present juncture. He would be long remembered for having safely seen the country through a food crisis, which needed quick and correct decisions. It would, indeed, be very difficult to fill the void.

Mr. Sadasiv Tripathi, Revenue and Supply Minister, Orissa, said Mr. Kidwai was a strong man with kindness Many were the occassions when he handled delicate situations with firmness. If the country was today free from the food anxiety, it was wholly due to Mr. Kidwai's courageous handling of the situation.

Dr. Harekrushna Mahtab, Secretary-General of the Congress Parliamentary Party, was completely overwelmed at the suddenness of the news.

Mr. Girja Shankar Bajpai, Governor of Bombay, said : "I am deeply shocked to hear the sad news of Mr. Kidwai's death. I had known him since he was the whip—and a most successful one—of the old Swaraj Party under the late Pandit Motilal Nehru's leadership. His vigour and organizing capacity were conspicuously manifest then. Real scope for these came after the Congress assumed office. As Minister both in U.P., and more recently in the Centre, he left the impress of his personality on whatever he touched. His handling of the food policy of the Government of India was among the more outstanding of his successes."

Mr. P.N. Rajbhoj, M.P. and General Secretary of the All-India Scheduled Castes Federation, said : "The country losses one of the most successful Central Ministers, Mr. Kidwai's vigorous handling of various problems, coupled with his keen intelligence, made him successful in everything he undertook. He was one of the Central Ministers commanding respect from all sections of Parliament.

"The people in India have lost one of their best friends in the death of Mr. Kidwai".

Mr. S.R. Vasavda, President of the Indian National Trade Union Congress, said : "It is indeed a pity that a cruel fate has robbed Mr. Nehru of a valuable colleague."

Mr. M.D. Tumpalliwar, President of the Nagpur Pradesh Congress Committee, said Mr. Kidwai was Hindu-Muslim unity incarnate.

Mr. Haribhau Upadhya, Chief Minister of Ajmer, said it was the saddest, news in recent times and the most shocking. Mr. Nehru will feel the loss most.

Mr. Y.B. Chavan, Bombay Food Minister, in a message of condolence on Mr. Kidwai's death said : "Bombay has lost a very good friend, who was continually helpful in the matter of food policy in the State. He was a great administrator and patriot."

Mr. N.V. Gadgil, M.P., said: "Mr. Kidwai was not merely my colleague in the Cabinet and a co-worker outside, but a close and personal friend. His unorthodox ways of dealing with awkward situations and knotty problems always created a host of critics and a host of admirers. He file of the party. His generosity towards all, and particularly his sympathy and consideration for the workers of the Party, are well known."

Mr. Asoka Mehta, Socialist leader and M.P., said : "I am shocked to hear the news of Mr. Kidwai's sudden demise. He was always so full of life, and though he was a controversial figure, everyone, irrespective of party affiliations, was in him a friend and a colleague. He was one of our ablest administrators and one of the few men in this country who were bold and imaginative. His death is a national loss."

Mr. P. C. Sen, West Bengal's Food Minister, said: "Shocked to hear of the sudden demise of our friend, Mr. Kidwai, who in a short space of time solved the food problem of India. He was a tower of strength to both the Congress organization and the administration."

Mr. Kesava Menon, former Indian High Commissioner in Ceylon, said: "I am shocked to hear of the sudden and premature death of Mr. Kidwai. He was an efficient Food Minister and a great Congressman. His loss at a time like this will be deeply felf throughout the country."

Mr. N. Sanjiva Reddi, Deputy Chief Minister of Andhra, said though Mr. Kidwai completed the job allotted to him, he was young enough to undertake greater and more difficult jobs.

Mr. Kala Venkata Rao, former General Secretary of the Congress, said: "The death of Mr. Kidwai removes from our midst a great and colourful personality. We will miss him greatly at this moment when we have launched a stupendous programme for India's economic development. India has lost a great man, Mr Nehru a trusted friend, and the Congress an eminent worker."

Mr. T. Viswanatham, Andhra Law and Finance Minister, said: "It is a shocking news to his close associates like me.

But for his courage, there would not have been the present freedom in the food movement and availability in the country. His death is a very great loss to the country."

Mrs. Renuka Ray, Relief and Rehabilitation Minister, West Bengal Government, said Mr. Kidwai was one of Mahatma Gandhi's staunchest lieutenants.

Mr. B. Ramakrishna Rao, Hyderabad's Chief Minister, said: "The Prime Minister has lost a loyal and able colleague and the country a tried patriot and able administrator. He took bold decisions in spite of opposition and carried them out successfully."

Mr. Ravi Shanker Shukla, Chief Minister of Madhya Pradesh, said: "The news of Mr. Rafi Ahmed Kidwai's death this evening at Delhi has come to me as a great shock. The whole country will mourn his death. To me it is a personal loss of a great friend. Quietly and unostentatiously he helped hundreds of people as best as he could. He could be relied on to successfully do things in the most difficult and trying circumstances. The Congress has lost in him a shrewd politician and the country an able administrator. On my behalf and on behalf of the people of this State. I extend my most heartfelt condolences to the bereaved family."

Mr. Krishna Ballabh Sahay, Revenue Minister of Bihar, said: "Bihar will remember him in particular with all gratefulness for his ready help in her many difficult hours."

Mr. Shyamanandan Sahaya, Vice-Chancellor of Bihar University, said: "The sad and sudden disappearance of Mr. Kidwai from the scene of action of a country where leaders like him are hard to find is, indeed, a blow which even Providence should have thought twice before inflicting on a country like ours. The Prime Minister would be hard put to it to find someone to take his place."

Seth Govind Das, President of the Mahakoshal P.C.C., said: "The death of Mr. Kidwai was a tremendous loss to the nation. Mr. Kidwai, who was known to me since 1921, bore no communal touch. He succeeded in resolving the most complex food problems in the country. The nation has lost a great patriot and a great administrator."

Mrs. Lilavati Munshi, Vice-President of the All-India Women's Food Council, has asked all Annapoornas in the country to suspend their business for Monday.

Kunwar Guru Narain, leader of the Opposition in the U.P. Legislative Council, said even the worst critic of Mr. Kidwai was the greatest admirer of his qualities of head and heart.

Mr. Mohanlal Gautam, Minister for Local Self-Government, U.P., said Mr. Kidwai dedicated his life for his country before and after independence.

Dr. Y. S. Parmar, Chief Minister of Himachal Pradesh, said in a message: "The death of Mr. Rafi Ahmed Kidwai is bound to shock the whole country. In him the country has lost not only a senior statesman but the most dynamic personality, which inspired faith and confidence.

"A man of few words but of action as he was, he steered the country clear of the food shortage at a time when the future seemed very dark. He was also a very great organizer. It will not be possible to fill the void which has been created. The condolences of the whole nation go to the family of the deceased."

Mr. Nabakrushna Chaudhuri, Chief Minister of Orissa, said: "To hundreds of persnos like me, in all ranks of life, to whom Mr. Rafi Ahmed Kidwai was more than a friend, it is an irreparable loss. India has lost in him a trusted and tested servant, who was in the forefront not only in the struggle against imperialism but also in our present struggle against hunger and poverty. Millions will cherish his memory with love and reverence."

Sri Mukut Beharilal Bhargava, M.P. and the Ajmer Congress chief, has wired to Mrs. Kidwai offering his condolences in her bereavement.

Mr. Ramesh Chandra Bhargava, Speaker of the State Assembly, said that India had lost a great politician.

Mr. C. P. N. Singh, Governor of Punjab, said: Mr. Rafi Ahmed Kidwai was one of the most valiant fighters for freedom. He never wavered or hesitated in doing what was in the interest of the country. He hated communalism and was a leader of most progressive views. Whatever problem he touched, he was able to solve it with courage, imagination and firmness. He was one of the most successful administrators in the country and the departments over which he presided will bear the mark of his ability and genius for a long time. Few people know how much he contributed in the battle for freedom which the Nepalese fought a few years back. He was a source of strength to everyone of us and we greatly mourn his sudden death at an important time in our history, when his ability and experience were proving a great asset. He was a great friend of Punjab, and the loss to us is irreparable."

Bakshi Ghulam Mohammed, the Kashmir Premier, accompanied by his Cabinet colleagues, Mr. Gulam Mohammed Sadiq and Mr. Girdharilal Dogra, who arrived in New Delhi from Srinagar, went to Mr. Kidwai's residence in the afternoon to pay their homage.

Bakshi Ghulam Mohammed said at the Srinagar airport before starting: "Mr. Kidwai was a man of few words, but great decision and action. He was the friend of all those who suffered with him in the freedom movement."

Mr. V. V. Giri, former Union Minister for Labour, said: "It is a terrible shock to the country and to those who had the privilege of working with him as his colleague. He was a comrade who stood by his friends and colleagues under all circumstances. He was an administrator of the highest order and he accomplished wonders on the food front. His loss is irreparable at the present juncture in India's history."

Mr. S. N. Agarwal, General Secretary of the Indian National Congress, said: "Mr. Kidwai was a pillar of strength not only to the Union Government but to the Congress organization as well. The ingenious and courageous manner in which he solved the very difficult problem of food production in the country will always be remembered by the nation with gratitute."

Sardar Gurmukh Singh Musafir, President of the Punjab Pradesh Congress, said: "Mr. Kidwai's loss at this time is shocking, more especially because Mr. Nehru recently expressed a desire to be relieved of the strenuous duties that he has to look after. He showed tremendous organizational capacity as Food Minister."

Bawa Daswandha Singh, President of the Punjab State Nationalist Sikh Party, said in Mr. Kidwai's death, the Sikh community had lost one of its well-wishers.

Mr. Ramdas Gandhi, son of Mahatma Gandhi, said Mr. Kidwai had ably tackled the food problem, "We lost one of us," he said.

A Comrade's Loss

Mr. Jain, recalling his 30-year-old association with Mr. Kidwai, said Mr. Kidwai was one of those who had nothing to do with caste, religion or community. He was a brave soldier who loved his country more than the Congress. Mr. Kidwai remained unbaffled and unaffected even on the death of his brother at the hands of communalists during the communal disturbances and restored communal harmony in the country through his relentless campaign for Hindu-Muslim unity. His house, Mr. Jain added, was like a rest house where unbounded hospitality was extended to all. Citing an example, Mr. Jain said once a person came to his house as a stranger and stayed with him for two and a half years.

Mr. Brahm Perkash said when the mortal remains of Mr. Kidwai were laid to rest in his family graveyard in the village of Masauli, a mass of humanity, irrespective of religious and political considerations, stood stunned in solemn silence and in utter distress and bereavement for their beloved leader who had been a living example to them of a high and magnanimous personality ever willing to extend his helping hand to all. Mr. Perkash said Mr. Kidwai was always guided in his actions and thoughts by humanitarian considerations which was the pivot of his policies and decisions.

Mr. Mauli Chand Sharma said Mr. Kidwai died in harness while on duty like a soldier in the battlefield. He called him a *faqir* in the true sense of the term. In tackling the Kashmir issue, Mr. Sharma added, Mr. Kidwai's role could be characterized as an outstanding one and only history would bear testimony to it.

Goswami Ganesh Datt said Mr. Kidwai was a *karam yogi* and his association with Mahatma Gandhi and the Congress for the last 40 years inspired him to serve the country.

Mir Mushtaq Ahmed, representing the Praja Socialist Party, said Mr. Kidwai's life was a challenge to the reactionary forces which were out to disrupt the peace and harmony of the country. Mr. Kidwai worked as a cementing force.

Mr. Sham Nath said the services rendered by Mr. Kidwai to the cause of the country would be written in golden letters in the history of India. The ideals that he placed before himself and worked for it during the last 40 years were worthy of emulation and that would be the fittest homage which the people of the country could pay him.

GLOOM ALL OVER THE COUNTRY

Offices & Markets Close, Flags fly at Half Mast

Flags flew at half mast over Rashtrapati Bhavan, Central Secretariat, Parliament House, and Government offices in New Delhi as also on all public buildings and Congress offices in different States on Monday as mark of respect to the memory of the late Mr. Rafi Ahmed Kidwai.

Government offices remained closed in many places, including Bombay, Saurashtra, Ajmer, Bhopal, Andhra and U.P. Hartal was observed in Lucknow, Allahabad and Kanpur, where all shops were closed. In Bombay, all markets were closed, and in Calcutta and Ahmedabad the principal markets suspended business.

Kanpur: Local markets, banks, and the Government Treasury remained closed. Bi-weekly markets in the rural areas also remained closed. Special Roadways buses are being run from Kanpur to Masauli, the home town of Mr. Kidwai, to enable people to be present at the burial time.

Allahabad: A meeting of citizens expressed its heart-felt grief and sorrow at the sad and sudden demise of Mr. Kidwai. The meeting, organized by the Allahabad Congress Committee, said in a resolution that the people of India would do well if they followed the noble example set forth by Mr. Kidwai. "In his death not only the Congress has lost a pillar of strength but the country has also missed an able administrator". The Government Treasury and all local banks were closed.

Banaras: Government offices and a number of shops remained closed in Banaras. Many public institutions held meetings to pay their homage to Mr. Kidwai.

Meerut: All Government offices remained closed. A procession was taken out and a public meeting was held here to mourn the death of Mr. Kidwai.

Aligarh: The Goverment of India Press, the University, post offices, courts and banks here remained closed. The university staff and students and members of the Executive Council held a meeting to mourn Mr. Kidwai's death. A public meeting was also held in the evening and glowing tributes were paid to him.

Chandigarh: Flags flew at half mast over all Government buildings.

Srinagar: All Government offices remained closed in Kashmir and flags flew at half mast over all State buildings. Srinagar markets remained closed.

Ajmer: Government offices, courts and educational institutions remained closed and flags at all State and public buildings flew at half mast.

Jubbulpore: A complete hartal was observed here. Flags on Government buildings flew at half mast. A condolence meeting was organized by the Town Congress Committee.

Amritsar: Almost all offices, schools, colleges and business establishments remained closed.

Patiala: The P.E P.S.U. Cabinet at a special meeting adopted a resolution expressing deep grief at Mr. Kidwai's death.

Bhopal: All Government offices in the State remained closed.

Karachi: Offices of the Indian High Commission in Karachi, Dacca and Lahore were closed. Flags flew at half mast on the High Commission buildings and offices. Illuminations planned in connection with the Diwali festival by the High Commission staff have been cancelled.

Dr. Mohan Sinha Mehta, Indian High Commissioner, addressed a condolence meeting attended by the entire staff of the Mission in Karachi.

Kurnool: All Government offices here and at district headquarters were closed and flags flew at half mast on State buildings.

Bombay: All Bombay markets remained closed. Mr. Purshottamdas Thakurdas, Former President of the East India Cotton Association, said the cotton traders of Bombay were shocked by the distressing news. All Central and State Government offices here remained closed and a number of meetings were arranged to pay homage to the departed leader.

Rajkot: A Government notification issued today expressed "deep regret" on the sad demise of Mr. Kidwai and directed that flags on Government buildings be flown at half mast as a mark of respect to him. All Government offices here remained closed.

Agra: Shocked by the stunning news of Mr. Kidwai's death people were seen here weeping. All markets were closed. A condolence meeting was held, where many speakers praised his services to the nation.

Jammu: A public meeting was held here in the evening under the presidentship of Mr. Budh Singh, M.P.

Broadcasts by Munshi and Sampurnanand

Lucknow. Oct 26.—Mr. K.M. Munshi, Governor of U.P., in a broadcast last night from the Lucknow Station of All India Radio, described the late Mr. Kidwai as a tower of strength both to the Congress and the Cabinet".

A very able administrator and resourcefull diplomat, he achieved great distinction when within a few weeks of taking over as Food Minister in 1952 he succeeded in launching the policy of decontrol, he said. This measure, already overdue, could never have been achieved but for the initiative and influence Mr. Kidwai possessed, he added.

In a touching reference to the close relations that existed between Mr. Nehru and Mr. Kidwai the Governor said: "Panditji, already bearing a heavy and auxious burden, will now be without the skill which Rafi Saheb brought to bear on the affairs of the Congress and Government."

Dr. Sampurnanand, the State's Home Minister, in his broadcast said that Mr. Kidwai possessed some of those great qualities which men coming after him might well seek to emulate.

NUMEROUS CONDOLENCE MEETINGS HELD

High Praise for Kidwai's Services to Nation

Hundreds of organizations and individuals on Monday paid glowing tributes to Mr. Kidwai as a patriot, administrator and planner. Dr. Sushila Nayar said : "Rafi Saheb carried to completion the battle for decontrol which Mahatma Gandhi had launched towards the end of his life."

Mr. S. N. Agarwal, General Secretary of the Congress said : "Mr. Kidwai was a pillar of strength not only to the Union Government but to the Congress organization as well."

The Diwali week holiday atmosphere which prevailed in Delhi on Sunday disappeared on Monday as the news of Mr. Kidwai's death became known to the public through the radio and the Press. A hushed silence prevailed instead indicating the grief of the people who remember the departed leader with gratitude as the man who solved their food problem.

While flags were flying at half-mast on Government officers, embassies and public buildings, banks and business houses remained closed. Responding to the call of the Chief Minister, Mr. Brahm Perkash, city traders closed their shops for the day. Post and telegraph offices were also closed.

All public functions and meetings scheduled for Monday were cancelled. Firms which opened in the morning closed after passing resolutions of condolence. Banks were closed by a special order of the authorities. The Imperial Bank of India said they received instructions from the Reserve Bank which also remained closed.

Cancelled Engagements

Electioneering for the Delhi municipal elections, for which Mr. Kidwai appears to have laid down his life, stood suspended. Even rival candidates belonging to parties other than the Congress suspended their activity for the day.

Among public engagements cancelled were : the International Philatelic and Postal Exhibition and the centenary theatre dance recital by Mrs. Indrani Rehman, the Diwali-eve celebration at Chelmsford Club and the Radio Sangeet Sammelan. The Sammelan programme included award of music competition prizes by the President. The function will now be held on Thursday.

Bold and Competent

Dr. Sushila Nayar said : "In Rafi Saheb's death the country has lost a stalwart, statesman and a veteran fighter who was in the vanguard of our freedom struggle under the banner of Mahatma Gandhi. A man of indomitable will and great courage, a loyal friend, he endeared himself to all who came in contact with him. A great organizer and an administrative genius, Rafi Saheb carried to completion the battle for decontrol which Mahatma Gandhi had launched towards the end of his life. The Congress and the country will find it difficult to fill the void left by his passing away. To many like myself the personal loss is irreparable. When he made an appointment with me for 9 a.m. on Monday little did I know that it was to place a wreath at his feet."

Mr. Agarwal said : "In Mr. Kidwai we have lost a great statesman, an able administrator and a valiant fighter for freedom and democracy. Mr. Kidwai was a pillar of strength not only to the Union Government but to the Congress organization as well. The ingenious and courageous manner in which he solved the difficult food problem will always be remembered by the nation with gratitude. The A.I.C.C. offers heartfelt condolences to the bereaved family."

Mr. Mustaq Ahmed, Secretary, Delhi State branch of P.S.P., said the country had lose a "valiant fighter for the freedom of the country and one who contributed his all in the reconstruction of the motherland."

Mr. Daljit Singh, Chief Whip, Delhi State Congress Legislature Party, said : "His night air mail service, 'own your telephone scheme' and solution of the food problem will pass into history."

The All-India Fine Arts and Crafts Society said : "In him we have lost a most sincere worker for the reconstruction of our country." The Federation of Posts and Telegraph Unions recording its grief said that "the country has lost one of the noblest sons and greatest statesman."

Shri Sanatan Dharam Sabhas of Punjab and New Delhi and the Lakshmi Narain Temple Trust held a condolence meeting at Gita Bhawan on Monday morning and offered prayers for the departed leader.

Mr. Govind Sahai, M.L.C. (U.P.), said : "The nation has lost Mr. Kidwai, a great symbol of national unity."

India's Loss

Delegates participating in the symposium on solar energy and wind power, being held at New Delhi, passed a condolence resolution, which said : "The gathering deeply mourns the great and tragic loss to India by the death of Mr. Kidwai and conveys to the President, the Prime Minister, the people of India and the family of Mr. Kidwai its heart felt sympathy and condolence. India has lost one of her greatest sons, a great patriot and a dynamic personality."

Officers and staff of the Communications Ministry condoled the death of Mr. Kidwai, at a meeting.

Communications Staff Condolence

The officers and staff of the Ministry of Communicating met to condole the death of Mr. Kidwai, Mr. Raj Bahadur, Deputy Minister for Communications, who presided, said Mr. Kidwai had left his mark on the political life of India as well as on the various Government Departments which he guided as Minister.

Post & Telegraph Offices Closed

All P & T offices were closed on Monday as a mark of respect to the memory of the late Mr. Kidwai.

Tuesday, will also be treated as a P & T holiday on account of Diwali instead of Wednesday. October 27, as scheduled earlier.

High Commission Offices Closed

Karachi, Oct 25—Offices of the Indian High Commission in Karachi, Dacca and Lahore were closed today as a mark of respect to the memory of Mr. Kidwai.

Flags flew at half-mast on High Commission buildings. Illuminations planned in connexion with Diwali by the High Commission staff have been cancelled.

Dr. M.S. Mehta, the High Commissioner addressed a condolence meeting attended by the entire staff of the Mission in Karachi.—PTI.

Philatelic Exhibition Programme

As a mark of respect to the memory of the late Mr. Kidwai, who was formerly Minister for Communications, the International Philatelic and Postal Exhibition as well as the Centenary Theatre were closed on Monday Consequently, the programme of Indian dances of Indrani Rehman will now be held on Wednesday, October 27, at 6-30 p.m. and the Mushaira at 9-15 p.m.

Food Ministry Staff Condoles Death

A condolence meeting of the officers and staff of the Ministry of Food and Agriculture was held on Monday morning at Jaisalmer House. Mr. M. V. Krishnappa, Deputy Minister, presiding.

Mr. Krishnappa said that almost the last words of Mr. Kidwai related to the improvement in the country's food situation, a cause very dear to him.

Speaking on behalf of the Ministry, Mr. H. M. Patel,

Secretary, said they had been fortunate in working with Mr. Kidwai who was a unique personality in many ways.

After the meeting, the staff and officers went to the residence of the late Mr. Kidwai to pay their last respects to his memory. Floral wreaths were laid by Mr. Krishnappa and Mr. Patel. An official of the Ministry laid wreaths on behalf of Dr. P. S. Deshmukh, Minister for Agriculture, who is now in Japan.

Dr. Deshmukh is returning immediately to New Delhi.

Loss of a Great Patriot

Twenty-five countries, participating in the symposium on Solar Energy and Wind Power in New Delhi passed a resolution stating that in Mr. Kidwai "India has lost one of her greatest sons, a great patriot and a dynamic personality."

Investiture Ceremony Postponed

The President has postponed till October 27 the investiture ceremony which was to be held at Rastrapati Bhavan today to present gallantry awards. The reception which was to be held after the ceremony has also been postponed.—PTI.

Ghazanfar Ali's Message

Mr. Ghazanfar Ali Khan, Pakistan's High Commissioner in India, in a message from Jhelum, Punjab (P), released in New Delhi on Monday said : "The news of the sudden and tragic death of my dear and esteemed friend, Rafi Ahmed Kidwai, has come to me as a stunning blow. An outstanding administrator and statesman, he lived and died in the service of his country."

My Ismail Kamel, Egyptian Ambassador in India, said : "On this very sad day of the passing away of the great patriot and leader, Shri Rafi Ahmed Kidwai. I express to the Indian Government and the people of India on my behalf and on behalf of my colleagues our most heartfelt condolences."

Nepal Premier's Praise

Calcutta, Oct. 25—The Prime Minister of Nepal, Mr. M.P. Koirala, condoling the death of Mr. Kidwai said in a statement here : "The sudden demise of Mr. R.A. Kidwai has come to me as a shock. He had many friends in Nepal and I believe all of them will feel the same way as I do. His contribution to the cause of democracy in Nepal will ever be cherished by those who know how much he had done for it."

Mr. B. P. Koirala, President of the Nepali Congress and General Suvarna said : "In his death Nepal has lost a great well-wisher and a valuable friend."

The Samaj, the only Nepali daily in Kathmandu, published the news with black borders.—PTI.

MR. NEHRU EXPRESS DISTRESS

Condolence Messages from China

New Delhi, Monday. Mr Nehru has expressed deep distress at the death of Mr. Rafi Ahmad Kidwai, one of his "dearest and ablest colleagues" in his messages from Dairen (Manchuria) to Dr. Rajendra Prasad, Begum Kidwai and others.

"The passing away of old comrades always brings a wrench and a sense of loneliness. Shri Kidwai's death is even a deeper blow," says the Prime Minister in a message to the nation through the Press.

Earlier, today a brief message was received from the Prime Minister, who perhaps know of the death over the radio, before official information reached him, advising the Home Ministry to arrange a funeral with full honours.

Brave and devoted

The following is Mr. Nehru's telegram to Dr. Rajendra Prasad : "Your telegram about Shri Rafi Ahmad Kidwai's death just received here. I am deeply distressed at the passing away of one of my dearest and ablest colleagues. There was none braver than him and none more devoted to the cause of the country. Both Government and India have suffered a very great loss. For me, both as an old colleague and as Prime Minister, the loss is even greater, and I have a sense of loneliness."

In a condolence message to Begum Kidwai, Mr. Nehru says : "I cannot tell you how deeply pained I am to learn of Rafi Ahmed's death. His personal qualities brought him a host of friends all over India.

Krishna Menon's Tribute

U.N. H.Q., Oct. 27.—Members of the Indian delegation to the U.N. on Monday condoled the death of Mr. Kidwai.

Mr. V. K. Krishna Menon, leader of the delegation, referred to the great part played by Mr. Kidwai in the freedom movement, in building up the Congress and after independence as an administrator.

Mr. Menon described Mr. Kidwai as a "man of the people, worker among workers and in special circumstances of our country a great harmonizing factor. He detested communal or other antagonisms. The country has lost a great public servant."

Mr. Justice P. N. Sapru, a personal friend of Mr. Kidwai, was sobbing when he declared Mr. Kidwai was "one of our greatest institutions.

The other members of the delegation, Mr. D. K. Barooah, Mr. Purushottam Tricumdas and Mr. Thirumal Rao paid tributes to Mr. Kidwai as an administrator, organizer and a loyal friend.

Teheran : Members of the Indian Embassy staff here mourned the death of Mr. Kidwai by holding a meeting in the Chancery. Addressing the staff, the Indian Ambassador, Dr. Tara Chand, feelingly referred to the sacrifices and sufferings of Mr. Kidwai in the service of India. Describing him as a man of courage, imagination and independence of mind, the Ambassador recalled his achievements in the Ministries of Communications and Food and Agriculture.

Kathmandu : The offices of the Indian Embassy and the Indian Military Mission were closed for the day. A meeting of Indian citizens held in the Embassy paid homage to Mr. Kidwai. The Indian Ambassador, Mr. Gokhale, said : "Rafi Sahib lived and died in the service of the country."

FRIEND

Great Servant of Nation

Maulana Azad's Tribute

Maulana Azad, said on Monday night that the late Mr. Rafi Ahmed Kidwai would always be remembered for the selfless way he served the nation.

"It is a strange thing" he said in a broadcast from the Delhi station of A.I.R., "that a man's real worth is only fully appreciated when the merciless hand of death snatches him away from our midst. We have felt this within a few hours of the passing away of Mr. Kidwai. It is now widely known how deeply has this separation been felt by millions of people."

Maulana Azad said Mr. Kidwai was one of those who got an opportunity to serve the country both during the struggle for freedom and later after the attainment of independence. When the country needed sacrifice of every comfort from our countrymen, Mr. Kidwai was in the forefront and bore smilingly the brunt of every suffering. And when the National Government was formed and the best talent was needed, Mr. Kidwai ably fulfilled that role also. "Mr. Kidwai's life represents a model of perfect synthesis of sacrifice and ability, he said."

Praising Mr. Kidwai's services to the nation, Maulana

Azad said that Mr. Kidwai played a notable part all through in all, Congress movements, especially in U.P., where he became a Minister in the first Congress Government in 1938. When the Congress formed the Central Government, Mr. Kidwai was brought from U.P. to the Central Cabinet. Mr. Kidwai acquitted himself brilliantly in whatever job he was assigned.

"Mr. Kidwai's solving of the country's food problem is a glorious part of his life which without doubt the country will always remember," said Maulana Azad.

Maulana Azad said that when the country's history was written, Mr. Kidwai's name would surely appear in letters of gold among those who sacrificed their all for the country's good at the time of struggle and who helped in consolidating that freedom.

At Barabanki Station

The five-mile route from the Barabanki railway station to Masauli was divided into three sectors, each under the charge of senior officials. The provincial armed constabulary lined part of the route.

The villagers, including women and children, had gathered on the roadside to pay homage to the departed leader whose name was a household word in the State.

Masauli, a village with a population of over 4,000, wore a gloomy appearance and the fields were deserted all over.

As the procession following the gun-carriage wended its way through the dusty village roads, lanes and by-lanes, the inmates of the hamlets on the route stood in silence.

At the residence of Mr. Kidwai, a large crowd of relatives, including his three brothers, had collected to perform the last rites.

Pandit Pant, who had followed the procession, was already at the residence to receive the body.

It took the procession about two hours to reach Mr. Kidwai's residence.

The gun-carriage reached the residence at 12 o'clock and immediately the bier was carried inside the house by his relatives.

Mourning Villagers

A vast crowd of mourners lined both sides of the main entrance. The inmates of the house then performed the rites and the bier was taken out in a procession and carried to the family burial ground.

The grave had already been dug to consign the body of Mr. Kidwai by the side of his father.

The spacious family graveyard surrounded by trees and sugarcane and corn fields had been limemarked for the passage of the funeral procession.

A small canopy had been spread over the grave to protect the mourners from the autumn sun.

Amid recitations from the Quran, the mortal remains of Mr. Kidwai were lowered into the grave by his relatives. An old man, described as a village school-teacher, broke down as the body was being lowered.

KIDWAI BURIED IN FAMILY GARVEYARD

Thousands at Funeral

Lucknow, Oct 26.—Amidst recitations from the Qoran and cries of "Allah-c-Akbar" from 30,000 people. Mr. Kidwai was laid to rest beside the grave of his father in the village of Masauli in Bara Banki district shortly after noon today.

His brothers, close relatives, political associates and their wives stood weeping at the graveside as the body was gently lowered into the freshly dug grave. Pandit Pant was seen wiping his eyes as the last board was put in place.

Mr. Lal Bahadur Shastri laid wreaths on behalf of Dr. Rajendra Prasad, Mr. Nehru and the Government of India. The Chief Minister of Bihar, who was unable to come, sent his private secretary with floral offerings.

The village of Masauli, 11 miles from Bara Banki, was filled with a seething mass of humanity as the gun carriage brought Mr. Kidwai's body to his doorsteps. A great wail rose from the house as the women of the family received the body which was kept in the house for 30 minutes.

Mr. Kidwai's three brothers and four nephews carried the body on their shoulders to the inner parts of the house, while Cabinet Ministers and other mourners waited outside along with a vast concourse of humanity. Among them were village folks, some of whom had travelled as many as 60 miles to pay their homage. Long before the zamindari abolition, Mr. Kidwai had distributed his entire landed property among the cultivators of this village.

After religious ceremonies at his ancestral home, the body was brought out and taken in procession to the burial ground. A military band with dressed drums provided the music and 500 men drawn from the armed forces lined the route to an open field surrounded by a coming sugarcane crop.

The body was then placed on earth for Janaza Namaz, facing the minarets of the village mosque 200 yards away. A select assemblage lined up behind it. Short prayers were offered and then the body was lifted up again and taken to the graveyard.

As the time for the final rites approached, a hush fell upon the assembled crowd broken occasionally by a sob or a muffled cry. Slowly and steadily, step by step, the body was brought along the graveside. As it was prepared for its final resting place, women cast their precious belongings, scent bottles and small metal boxes into the grave for interment with him.

Wrapped only in a sheet, the body was then lowered into the grave while Muslim divines as his friends and relatives recited the Kalma. Pandit Pant was praying silently.

Three volleys from an army firing party announced that Mr. Kidwai had returned to the earth. As his closest relatives were casting the first sods and the grave was being filled in, an army bugler sounded the Last Post.

At Bara Banki

When the funeral train arrived at Bara Banki at 10-15 a.m. pall-bearers gently lifted the body to the gun carriage. As this was being done a firing party furnished by the army presented arms. Army officers headed by Brig Jayal, the Sub-Area Commander. Lucknow, saluted and the firing party reversed arms.

Sorrowing townsmen watched and prayed as the army band with muffled drums began playing the Dead March and the gun carriage started moving slowly in procession through the packed streets.

The procession was headed by motor cyclista after which came the escort party, the firing party, the band with drummers and the bearer party. Then came the gun carriage and the pall-bearers followed by the chief mourners. Ministers political leaders and prominent citizens of Lucknow and Bara Banki.

The rear escort detachment completed the formal procession but thousands followed the body and bade Mr. Kidwai farewell on the outskirts of the town.

From there the mourners got into vehicles and Mr. Kidwai's last journey to his home village of Masauli began.

Earlier a vast grief-filled crowd paid its homage in flowers and tears as the special train carrying Mr. Kidwai's body steamed into the Charbagh Railway Station at 7 a.m.

The rays of the morning sun were streaking on the platform as the compartment in which lay Mr. Kidwai in a mass of flowers came to a halt amidst shouts of "Kidwai ki jai".

The 3rd Battalion of the Provincial Armed Constabulary mounted a guard of honour after which the mourners led by Pandit Pant, the Chief Minister, began to file past slowly.

Mr. Kidwai's body was received at the station by his younger brother Mr. Mahfooz Ahmed, and his other close relatives who entered the compartment where his face could hardly be seen amidst flowers.

Draped in the national flag Mr. Kidwai's face bore the signs of utmost contentment and peace, as indeed was his chief characteristic even during the worst crisis.

There was also a faint smile, familiar to many who knew him as friend, benefactor and national leader.

Within half an hour of the train's arrival the crowd on the platform and around the railway station had increased. No fewer than 50,0C0, including many women and children, had collected at Charbagh.

Mr. Kidwai's body was accompanied among others by Mr. L B. Shastri, the Railway Minister, and Mr. A.P. Jain, Minister for Relief and Rehabilitation. Three U.P. Ministers also travelled in the train.

As a result of last-minute consultations it was decided not to bring out Mr. Kidwai's body on to the platform. It was allowed to stay in the incense-filled compartment and a heart-rending wail rose from the multitude as the train slowly steamed out of the railway station and Lucknow of which Mr. Kidwai was the truest citizen and whose every place was familiar to him.

Wreaths Laid at Intermediate Stations

Bareilly, Oct. 26.—The special train carrying the body of Mr. Kidwai passed through Bareilly at 1-45 this morning.

Over 3,000 people filed past the compartment in which the body was kept.

At Bareilly wreaths were laid on behalf of the district authorities and other organizations.

Government officials, prominent citizens and leading Congress workers, MLA's and MLCs, women and students were among the large gathering present at the station.

Earlier, when the train reached Moradabad at 10-20 p.m. there was a gathering of over 10,000 on the platform.

The Provincial Armed Constabulary presented a guard of honour.

Similarly large crowds turned up at Rampur and Hapur where wreaths were laid.—PTI

MR. KIDWAI'S SERVICES PRAISED

Condolence Meeting in Delhi

Thousands of people, Hindus, Muslims and Sikhs, representing different political parties attended a meeting held in Gandhi Grounds on Wednesday to condole the death of Mr. Rafi Ahmad Kidwai.

Three days ago Mr. Kidwai addressed his first and last meeting from the same platform under the auspices of the Delhi Pradesh Congress Committee.

The speakers at the meeting were Mr. A.P. Jain, Union Minister for Rehabilitation and a close associate of Mr. Kidwai, Mr. Mauli Chandra Sharma. President of the Delhi State Jana Sangh, Mr. C. Krishnan Nair, President of the Delhi Pradesh Congress Committee, Chaudhry Brahm Prakash, Miss Sarala Sharma and Mir Mushtaq Ahmed of the Communist and Praja Socialist Party respectively.

The speakers described Mr. Kidwai as a "valiant soldier" and an "architect of new India".

"Fearless and Tactful"

Mr. Jain said Mr. Kidwai was fearless and tactful. He loved his country more than the Congress. He was charitable and helped the poor and the needy. Mr. Kidwai's house was open to all—even to his adversaries. Mr Jain asked the people not to forget the last words Mr. Kidwai uttrred before his death—the Congress alone was in a position to take the country towards progress.

Mir Mushtaq Ahmed said that Mr. Kidwai worked for his country till his last breath. He was a man of action and whatever responsibility he undertook he fulfilled it. His life was an open chapter and it was for people to emulate his example.

Mr. Mauli Chandra Sharma said Mr. Kidwai had a big hand in shaping the present Kashmir policy.

Mr. C. Krishnan Nair said that Mr. Kidwai served his country faithfully both as a Congressman and a Minister of the Central Government. He was a friend of all and was always ready to sacrifice for his friends. Mr. Nair described Mr. Kidwai's house as a "dharamshala" where everybody could have food and shelter. As Food-Minister his work was magnificent. He gave the country freedom from controls which was the cherished desire of Mahatma Gandhi.

Maulana Hifz-ur-Rehman, MP, said that Mr. Kidwai was not dead: he still lived in their hearts Those who died for others were always remembered.

Chaudhry Brahm Prakash said that Mr. Kidwai was a friend of all and he served the country faithfully.

Dr. Sushila Nayar described Mr. Kidwai as a "shining star".

HUNDREDS ATTEND SOYUM CEREMONY OF MR. KIDWAI

From Our Special Representative

Lucknow, Oct. 28.—Hundreds of Mr. Kidwai's friends and relatives as well as representatives of the various political parties this morning assembled at the village of Masauli, 30 miles from here, to pray for the soul of the departed leader and to participate in the soyum ceremonies.

Some had come from Bombay, Delhi, Punjab and West Bengal to condole with Mr. Kidwai's family and to join in this act of prayer and homage which is held on the third day of the funeral.

There was mass recitation from the Koran from 7 a.m. and fatihas and prayers for Mr. Kidwai were offered at his house, in the village mosque and at the graveside. Among the visitors were a large number of women friends and relatives of the Kidwai family who had been unable to come on the day of the funeral.

Recitations from the Koran, known as Qul, were led by Maulana Jamaluddin Abdul Wahab of Firangi Mahal who had also officiated at the funeral. Many broke down during the prayers at Mr. Kidwai's graveside.

The soyum ceremonies lasted for four hours.

Glossary

Ahimsa	non-violence
Aman	peace
Bunia	member of the business community
Bapu	name often given to Mahatma Gandhi
Bharat	India
Chamar	untouchable caste, a leather worker
Charkha	spinning wheel
Dal	association
Desh	country
Dharna	a sit-down strike
Fakir	a Muslim ascetic
Ghat	bank of a river
Guru	teacher
Harijan	name which Gandhi gave to an untouchable
Hartal	stoppage of work and business
Himsa	violence
Inquilab	revolution
Istri	a woman
Jai	victory
Jalsa	a public meeting
Khadi	hand-spun and-woven cloth
Khilafat	the line of succession to the Prophet Muhammad
Kisan	a peasant
Lakh	1,00,000
Lathi	stick
Mahila	a woman
Mahatma	a high-souled person
Murdabad	down with

Nari	a woman
Prabhat Pheri	an early morning procession
Purna	full
Raj	commonly used for British rule in India
Ryot	peasant
Sabha	meeting
Sainik	sepoy
Samadhi	grave
Samiti	an association
Sangh	an association
Satya	truth
Satyagraha	non-violent resistance
Seva	service
Swaraj	self-government
Swadeshi	principle of using only articles of indigenous make
Thana	police station
Vakil	a lawyer
Vidyapith	national institute
Zamindar	landlord
Zindabad	a word used for victory

Bibliography

Primary Sources

A.I.C.C. Papers.

Speeches and Writings of Rafi Ahmad Kidwai.

Contemporary newspapers.

The Collected Works of Mahatma Gandhi Selected Works of Jawaharlal Nehru, edt. by S. Gopal.

Secondary Works

Andrews, C.F., *The Indian Problem*, Madras, 1921.

Bakshi, S.R., *Simon Commission and Indian Nationalism*, New Delhi, 1977.

Banerjea, S.N., *A Nation in the Making*, London, 1929.

Bipan Chandra, *Communalism in Modern India*, Delhi, 1984.

Bose, S.C., *The Indian Struggle*, New York, 1964.

Chintamani, C,Y., *Indian Politics Since the Mutiny*, Allahabad, 1947.

Chopra, P.N., *Rafi Ahmad Kidwai.*

Das, C.R., *India for Indians*, Madras, 1921.

Fischer, Louis, *The Life of Mahatma Gandhi*, London, 1962.

Gopal, S., *The Vicevoyalty of Lord Irwin*, 1926-31, Oxford, 1957.

Hasan Mushirul, *Nationalism and Communal Politics in India*, 1916-28, Delhi, 1974.

Irwin, Lord, *Indian Problems*, London, 1932.

Kripalani, J.B., *Gandhi : His Life and Thought*, Delhi, 1970.

Mitra, S.M., *Indian Problems*, London, 1908.
Nehru, Jawaharlal, An Autobio.
Pal, B.C., *Swadeshi and Swaraj*, Calcutta, 1954.
Rai, Lajpat, *The Political Future of India*, New York, 1919.
Rajendra Prasad, *An Autobiography*, Bombay, 1957.
Setalvad, C.H., *Recollection and Reflections*, Bombay, 1946.
Templewood, Edward, *Nine Troubled Years*, London, 1964.

Index